WHAT'S BIG AND PURPLE AND LIVES IN THE OCEAN?

THE MOBY GRAPE STORY

A JAWBONE BOOK
FIRST EDITION 2018
PUBLISHED IN THE UK AND THE USA BY JAWBONE PRESS
3.1D UNION COURT,
20–22 UNION ROAD,
LONDON SW4 6JP,
ENGLAND
WWW.JAWBONEPRESS.COM

ISBN 978-1-911036-31-9

EDITOR TOM SEABROOK
JACKET DESIGN MARK CASE

PRINTED BY REGENT PUBLISHING SERVICES LIMITED, CHINA

1 2 3 4 5 22 21 20 19 18

CONTENTS

PREFACE

They were a phenomenon. Record companies flocked to see them, and excited executives elbowed each other out of the way to sign them up as the Summer of Love fast approached. It became an all-out bidding war. In the years that followed, their music influenced such giants as Led Zeppelin, R.E.M., Bruce Springsteen, and so many others. Their debut LP is regarded as a classic of 60s pop and is often cited as the best album to spin out of San Francisco. Much more than a pop album, it's a unique work of musical alchemy and sheer exuberance. It stands at #124 on *Rolling Stone*'s '500 Greatest Albums Of All Time,' by the way.*

* To put this into perspective, Janis Joplin's *Pearl* stands at #125, Jefferson Airplane's *Surrealistic Pillow* #146, and Santana's debut stands at #149. Further down the list, T.Rex's *Electric Warrior* is #160, Lou Reed's *Transformer* #194, Pink Floyd's *Wish You Were Here* #211, and Queen's iconic *Night At The Opera* #231. The Grateful Dead's popular *American Beauty* holds down #261 while *Workingman's Dead* stands at #264. So, to reach #124 is quite a feat—but let's face it, just to make this illustrious list is an achievement. The *Rolling Stone 500 Greatest Albums Of All Time* was initially released in magazine form as a special issue on December 11, 2003. Two years later, it was re-released as a book. A revised, updated version of the list was published in 2012. The panel gathered for this project numbered over 250 and included such folks as Lou Adler, Beck, Hal Blaine, Jon Caramanica, Robert Christgau, Cameron Crowe, Clive Davis, Dr. John, Antoine 'Fats' Domino, The Edge, Flea, Ben Fong-Torres, David Fricke, Art Garfunkel, David Geffen, Chris Hillman, Lenny Kaye, Moby, Yoko Ono, Robbie Robertson, Chris Robinson, Rick Rubin, Fred Schneider, Bud Scoppa, John Sebastian, and Steven van Zandt.

The band played a killer set at the historic Monterey International Pop Music Festival in June '67, and they spearheaded a form of three-way guitar interplay that critics soon dubbed *crosstalk*. They were respected by peers and revered by some of the biggest names in rock criticism. Yet something's wrong with this picture. If this was such a great band, why don't more people know who they are? The answer to this question can only be found in a story—the story of one of the most underappreciated bands in rock history. One of rock's best kept secrets.

•

Moby Grape's debut album is something I unearthed. I imagine it was the same for many of the happy few who already know of the band. It wasn't a matter of just buying another album. It was greater than that—a feeling of discovery. Listening to that album for the first time was like being let in on a wonderful secret.

Everyone who knows and cherishes Moby Grape—and who did *not* grow up in the 60s—has a story about their entry into the band's world. Often, it was through word-of-mouth; kinship was likely involved. Perhaps it was an old hippie uncle, or a family friend who was a teenager in the late 60s, or maybe it was someone from California, even the Bay Area. It might've been that music buff you once knew, the one with bookshelves filled with magazines with such exotic names as *Shindig!*, *Mojo*, *Goldmine*, *Record Collector*, *Relix*, and *Ugly Things*.

If Moby Grape were recommended to you, it was probably something like being invited into Freemasonry. You were picked out. Somehow, someone who had listened to Moby Grape's music—and had set foot inside that aural lodge—decided you were a candidate to become a fan of the band. As a candidate, you were invited to step into in a world that is unique, one that isn't known to the masses. *Moby Grape* is a soundscape of musical chemistry, and it's a tale of epic proportions. It's a whole mythology with its own heroes and villains.

•

When I was in my early twenties, I worked for a set designer who went to Berkeley in the late 60s. Harley saw the Grape perform with his own eyes, back when they were on the top of their game. When he told stories, I listened intently. Knowing this set designer was like knowing someone from Biblical times, or someone who'd walked through the world of Achilles and Odysseus. For me, the 60s has always been a bit of a dream.

Born in 1972, the year of *The Godfather* and *Ziggy Stardust*, I grew up on a diet of listening to mostly pop but also some rock and disco when I was young. My parents' album collection included such acts as The Beatles, Elvis, Nilsson, ABBA, Gordon Lightfoot, and The Guess Who. While I cherished their music, I hadn't discovered these artists for myself. I didn't choose them. I cherished them, but they were chosen for me. Over time, these artists became the foundation of my love and appreciation of music. Yet as I got older, I began to expand my circle of songs, albums, and artists.

Somewhere around 1982, I happened upon the hit parade. Every Thursday evening, I'd listen to the CHUM countdown on the radio, handwriting the week's latest chart. When it came out the following day, in the *Toronto Star*, I'd cut it out and keep it in my *CHUM chart* folder. As music videos because a dominant form of art, I was swept away by artists like Dexys Midnight Runners, The Stray Cats, Duran Duran, Culture Club, Tracy Ullman, and of course David Bowie.

Thinking about this period of my life, I recall a morning when one of my friends arrived at school with breathtaking news. A small crowd of people listened quietly as he told us about 'Blue Jean,' a new Bowie video. Somehow, my friend's dad had seen the video *before* its North American release. I can still hear some of the words used to describe that video: 'He's all silver—it's like something out of *Star Trek*.'

As I got older, I learned how to play the guitar and got my own record player. I was discovering new music as well—both to listen to, and to play. At the time, records cost three or four dollars at one of the many used record shops around the city. In the late 80s, record shops were all over. With thirty dollars, you could buy up to eight or nine albums. That's Led Zeppelin's entire output. At that time, I had various jobs, working as a janitor, cycling deliveries for a drug store, and so on, and I used a hefty portion of my money to buy albums. First, there was the solo output of The Beatles. Then there was The Who, The Rolling Stones, The Kinks, The Beach Boys, Pink Floyd, Led Zeppelin, The Yardbirds, and on and on. After a while, I moved into progressive rock, with bands like Yes and Jethro Tull. But there came a point when I wanted more. There *had* to be more.

Around that time, I'd sometimes take the subway downtown with a friend or two, get off at a station, and just walk. Usually we'd start off at Yonge and Bloor, then stroll south on Yonge, making our way all the way down to Queen. Then we'd turn west and meander over to Spadina, or even Bathurst. Along the way was an endless array of record shops. On Yonge, there was Sunrise Records, Records On Wheels, the Record Peddler, Rotate This, Play De Record, Sam The Record Man, A&A, and, later, HMV. On Queen, there was more: Kops Kollectibles, Driftwood, Penguin Music. Some of the folks who worked in these shops were like museum docents, or even sages. Some had *lived* through the 60s and *been* to events like Woodstock. Conversation in these shops wasn't idle chitchat, it was dialogue—imagine Plato's dialogues, where *every* conversation is about music. That's what it was like.

The Incredible Record Store was unforgettable. Located on the west side of Yonge, it was just south of Bloor. To get to the shop you had to climb a narrow, fluorescent-lit staircase with walls plastered in 60s artwork and posters. It was as though you were ascending a steep, cavernous passageway to a rock temple. Run by Jonathan Lipson, the shop wasn't just a place to browse and buy things—it was a gathering place, an art gallery, and a museum. On its walls and tables and behind the glass cases at the checkout counter were various treasures: original concert posters from classic artists, sketches by Jim Morrison, a handwritten note by Leonard Cohen ('This is the best record store in the country'), unused tickets from Woodstock, Randy Bachman's old guitar, and more. There were also photos of musicians who had popped into the shop and even helped behind the counter, like Carlos Santana. Stapled to one wall near the store's entrance was a battered copy of The Beatles' notorious 'butcher' album. I once asked Jonathan how much it was. 'That isn't for sale,' he solemnly replied.

This was a much different world than the world of buying songs on the internet. You could walk into any one of those shops with no idea of what you'd find, or what you'd discover, or what you'd learn.

In the late 80s, I got my hands on a book that changed my life as a fan of music, a musician, and a person. While I was on one of my journeys along the circuits of used bookshops that ran on Queen Street, I found a dog-eared copy of the 1983 edition of the *Rolling Stone Album Guide*. Although this book was years old, it had much to offer. It was as though this battered old guide was an ancient text or a map from long ago, made by cartographers who lived in a different world. I used the guide to navigate the terrain of rock, pop, country, punk, and so on from the 80s, to the 70s, to the 60s, and beyond. With this book, I entered unchartered waters. On the advice of the reviewers, I learned about a whole slew of artists and albums that were completely new to me: the prolific and weirdly poppy Frank Zappa & The Mothers Of Invention; the raspy howl of Captain Beefheart & His Magic Band; that wacky group from Scotland, The Incredible String Band; and Moby Grape, a mysterious group from San Francisco.

During my teenage years, I'd often flip through my *Rolling Stone Album Guide*. Each band's entry was like a narrative, a little story—a snapshot of sorts. Some of these stories were longer and some were shorter. It depended on how commercially and critically successful the artist was perceived to be. It also depended on the length of the artist's career. The album ratings were, of course, arbitrary, yet they were intriguing nevertheless. I didn't always agree with the ratings afforded to different albums, and I also didn't always agree with the explanations put forward to rationalize the ratings. Yet I was drawn to this book.

The *Rolling Stone Album Guide* was like a massive report card for every rock star going, big and small. I was especially curious about that elusive inner circle of five-star albums that were sparingly sprinkled throughout the 600-plus-page tome. It was an honor roll of sorts. And it had nothing to do with commercial success. According to the guide, a five-star album is 'Indispensable: a record that must be included in any comprehensive collection.' I liked to peruse the many entries in the tome, scouring the book for new artists, new albums to explore. Secretly, I wanted to buy every one of those five-star albums—or at least listen to them.

Flipping through the pages, then, I was intrigued by the entry on Moby Grape. In it, Billy Altman gushes:

> Moby Grape made only one good album, but what an album it is. That its debut LP is as fresh and exhilarating today as it was when it exploded out of San Francisco during 1967's Summer of Love is testament to the band's visionary concept of eclectic American music. Swirling within Moby Grape are elements of jazz, country, blues, and plain old raveup rock & roll. Yet all of it is so well integrated into the group's execution (five members who all sing, write and play brilliantly) that it's impossible to pigeonhole any of the album's thirteen songs. Lead guitarist Jerry Miller and bassist Bob Mosley propelled the band instrumentally but the two rhythm guitarists, Skip Spence and Peter Lewis, and drummer Don Stevenson also contributed heavily.

Now, *this* was an album worth seeking out. Naturally, I was interested in finding the band's debut, which sounded like it was some sort of holy relic from the Summer of Love—which, for me, meant the days of yore. As I pored over Altman's words, I couldn't wait to find and listen to this album. Honestly, I wondered to myself, after reading what Billy had written, who *wouldn't* be interested in finding this mythical album?

Yet there is more to the entry on the Grape. If the first paragraph of his sketch is inviting, the second is ominous, and positively intriguing. Continuing his review of the band, Billy states, 'The Grape's rapid downhill slide remains one of the mysterious tragedies of the late 60s. *Wow* was a complete failure, a double album that included a "bonus" jam LP that made absolutely no sense in terms of the group's strongest point: tight song construction. A half-dozen albums are no longer available; they vary from solid country- and blues-influenced rock to sheer musical confusion.'

While Moby Grape's debut receives a perfect rating, their only other studio album to be rated in the guide does not fare so well. Awarded a paltry one star, the band's sophomore effort, entitled *Wow*, was tossed into an undesirable pile of albums rated as 'Poor: records in which even technical competence is at question, or which are remarkably ill-conceived.'

This was a mystery to me. I couldn't understand how a band could descend from seeming perfection to such a low, a virtual musical rubbish heap, in the matter of one year. Whether this compressed story of the band was true or not, it was fascinating. I was captivated.

One day, at Kops Kollectibles, I overheard two people talking about the 1984 Edsel edition of *Moby Grape*. At one point, one of the two said, 'I found *Truly Fine Citizen* in New York last year.' After pausing, he blurted out, 'I paid way too much for that album.' I remembered the name, and was reminded that this was one of those bands I wanted to investigate.

Heading back to Yonge, I soon found myself in Sam The Record Man.* After striding to the 'M' area of the rock/pop CDs, I found three CDs in the 'Moby Grape' section: *Moby Grape*, *20 Granite Creek*, and *Live Grape*. All three were priced between $25 and $30, the most expensive being the band's debut. It was pricy—most CDs at the time were between $10 and $15. I had about $40 with me, which was enough to buy one CD. It had to be the debut.

After returning home, I was excited to listen to the album—and the band—for the first time. I didn't realize it at the time, but in terms of the band's story, the Grape's debut is the high-water mark of act one. And *20 Granite Creek* marks the highlight of the second act of their story.

F. Scott Fitzgerald famously said that there are 'no second acts in

* Located at 347 Yonge Street, and the flagship of a vast fleet of record shops, Sam's was an old building with numerous hallways, oddly shaped rooms, unexpected floors, and endless nooks and crannies. It opened in 1961, when the record store empire was twenty-four years old—and in 2007 it finally closed its doors forever. Sam Sniderman opened his original shop in 1937. When I was a teenager, in the late 1980s and early 1990s, Sam The Record Man was still in its heyday. The workers there were knowledgeable, and, in addition to shiny new albums, Sam's featured unexpected dusty treasures—even nuggets that were out of print.

American lives.' He wrote that line shortly before his tragically premature death in 1940. If Fitzgerald had lived a few decades longer, he would've seen a great many second acts. The world of rock'n'roll, after all, is chock full of them. The first part of this book is the second act of Moby Grape's two-act story. The first act, the one about San Francisco, comes later.

•

When I decided to write about Moby Grape, I found as many things as I could about the band and their world: concert handbills, programs, newspaper articles, and so on. I treaded through the beat, hippie, and counterculture movements; San Francisco; the ballrooms; the poster art; and many other things. I spoke with promoters, artists, musicians, roadies, and fans. As I read and conversed about all these things, I began to understand the context within which the band's music was written and recorded. It was as though I had a point of contact—albeit a tenuous one—with the band's landscape, their lived reality.

After a while, I got in touch with some members of the band, and I spent time getting to know them, talking with them about their memories and perspectives. They've been generous with their time and their readiness to talk about Moby Grape. During all this, I even dreamed about the Grape and their music.

All these things are part of the story you hold in your hands.

Let's begin.

PART ONE

GRANITE CREEK

GYPSY WEDDINGS AND ROCK'S FIRST FULL-ON REUNION: THE SECOND RISE AND FALL OF MOBY GRAPE

CHAPTER ONE

SECOND CHANCES IN THE SANTA CRUZ MOUNTAINS

Moby Grape's elusive fifth release is the lost chapter in the band's history. The album is called *20 Granite Creek*, which is the address at which it was recorded. Granite Creek itself is in California, tucked away in the Santa Cruz Mountains. But you'll hear more about that later.

The second rise and fall of Moby Grape is a tale with seven main characters: Bob Mosley, Gordon Stevens, Peter Lewis, Skip Spence, Jerry Miller, Don Stevenson, and David Rubinson. Six of these characters are visible on the cover of the album, in an image that, like the past, is blurry in parts and sharp in others.

The cover of the album is simple. A large white frame surrounds a rectangular photograph of the band. Around the photograph is a thin black line. In the top right-hand corner of the white frame is a red postal stamp comprising a small circle and seven wavy lines. Inside the top of the circle are the words 'Moby Grape,' and at the bottom are the words 'Granite Creek.' A large number '20' stands at its center. With this postal stamp insignia, the album looks as though it has been sent somewhere. To the listener, perhaps.

Shot outside, the photograph mixes sunlight with shade. The members of Moby Grape stand in a forest clearing with branches hanging overhead. The vegetation on the ground has been burned yellow, but the trees all around the six figures are a dark shade of green.

Bob Mosley is to the left of the photograph, looking downward. He's staring at something on the ground. He has dirty blonde hair and broad shoulders. Born in San Diego, he used to surf, and he did a stint in the marines. He sings and writes songs that intermingle blues with soul music. He also plays the bass with power, authority, and when necessary, tremendous speed.

In the foreground, near the center of the photograph, is Gordon Stevens. He's wearing beige pants and a light beige top. He has shoulder-length light brown hair, bangs, and a long beard. He grew up in a musical family, playing a variety of instruments. He works in his family's music shop in San Jose. Over the years, he's played many different types of music.

Standing behind Gordon, slightly to the right, is Peter Lewis. He's tall and thin, with dark brown hair and a beard. He's wearing jeans and a buttoned-up white shirt. He has his arms tucked behind him. He grew up in Hollywood but moved to New York when his parents got divorced. He was somewhat well known before Moby Grape on account of his mother being Loretta Young, the famous actress. He's played in a surf band and a folk-rock band, and worked as a commercial pilot. While he sometimes writes brisk songs, he usually writes songs that are gentle and introspective. Of all the members in Moby Grape, his voice is the softest.

In the foreground, standing to the right of Peter, is Skip Spence. Like Bob, Skip is looking to the side, gazing at something on the ground. He's wearing dark pants and a white T-shirt, and he has a jacket folded in his hands. Born in Windsor, Canada, Skip moved between numerous states with his family before settling in California. He played drums in Jefferson Airplane before co-founding Moby Grape. Like Gordon, he plays a variety of instruments. He has an energetic, unpredictable personality. The three years that preceded this photograph were difficult ones for him.

Behind Skip, standing to the right, is Jerry Miller. He's wearing a buttoned-up shirt and dark pants. He's also wearing a wide-brimmed hat, which is useful, because he's standing in the sun. He has long brown hair and a beard. He plays lead guitar. Stepping out of the fifties music scene, Jerry plays smoothly, with licks that intersect blues with jazz with country. He also sings. When his favorite guitar was stolen in the spring of '67, he went on an adventure to get it back—a road trip that involved bikers and hundred-dollar bills. A half-century later, he's still playing that same guitar.

Off to the right side of the picture is drummer and singer Don Stevenson. He has very long dark hair and a moustache. He's wearing a buttoned-up blue top and jeans. Like Jerry, Don grew up and paid his dues in the Seattle area playing in R&B bands in the northwest coast. He and Jerry knew one another well before Moby Grape formed. As a team, they are the most prolific songwriters in the Grape.

The man who took the photograph is David Rubinson. Born and raised in New York, he spent years working for Columbia Records. While scouting bands in San Francisco in the autumn of 1966, he caught one of Moby Grape's shows at a nightclub called the Ark, a ferryboat dry-docked at Waldo Point Harbor in Sausalito, and was captivated. In addition to producing three Moby Grape albums, Rubinson plays a variety of instruments on the band's recordings.

•

It's early 1971. *Apollo 14* landed on the Moon on February 5. Three days later, the Nasdaq Composite, a new stock market index, made its debut. On February 13, South Vietnam, with US support, invaded Laos. Two days later, the UK and Ireland made the switch to decimal currency. Nearly a month later, John Lennon released his single 'Power To The People,' and just over two weeks after that, on March 28, the final episode of *The Ed Sullivan Show* was broadcast on CBS. The following day, an LA jury recommended the death penalty for Charles Manson, and US Army lieutenant William Calley was found guilty of twenty-two murders at the Mai Lai Massacre.* In April, Sierra Leone became a republic, and

* Although Calley was sentenced to life in prison, he would later be pardoned.

near the end of the month, on April 28, protesters numbering 500,000 in Washington DC and 125,000 in San Francisco marched against the Vietnam War …

At this point, Moby Grape have been apart for nearly two years. The members of the band have scattered and are pursuing their futures on their own. Just a few years earlier, they had all bought homes in Boulder Creek, yet since then the four-piece band has dwindled to a three-piece, and over time some members have sold their places and moved away.

Living near San Jose, Skip Spence is jamming and occasionally performing with various local musicians, including Tom Johnston, John Hartman, and Gordon Stevens. Sometimes they play music from his solo album, *Oar*, in and around Santa Cruz. At one point, he put together the short-lived band called Pachuco.*

Bob Mosley is living in Hawaii and playing at the Red Noodle nightclub with his band Snake Leg, with Woody Berry, Frank Smith, and Alan Wehr. Snake Leg formed and initially performed in California, after Mosley was

* Much has been written about Skip Spence over the years. Perhaps the best place to start is the booklet that accompanies the 1999 Sundazed reissue of his *Oar* album. It opens with a thoughtful piece by longtime Grape fan and *Rolling Stone* scribe David Fricke, entitled 'The Man Who Loved Too Much.' Following this is a reprint of Greil Marcus's positive review of *Oar* for *Rolling Stone*, taken from the magazine's September 20 1969 issue. Next is an astute reflection on Skip's music by Jud Cost, entitled 'Through A Glass Darkly,' and it closes with David Rubinson's original liner notes for the album. One year prior to the Sundazed reissue, Richie Unterberger wrote an interesting piece on Skip for his book *Unknown Legends Of Rock 'n' Roll*. More recently, a lengthy piece on Skip appeared in the book *Lovers, Buggers & Thieves* by Martin Jones, while a noteworthy article by Andrew Lau on Skip's solo album, drawing from an extensive interview with David Rubinson, appeared in the *Crawdaddy* webzine in November 2009.

Few articles describe Skip Spence's activities between *Oar* and *20 Granite Creek*, however, and most speak to his connection to The Doobie Brothers. In a 2014 interview with Mathis Hunter for *Creative Loafing*, Patrick Simmons recalled, 'I ran into him a couple of years later in San Jose just walking around and we reestablished a friendship. Unbeknownst to me, he was friends with Tom Johnston and John Hartman [of The Doobie Brothers]. So he's the one that introduced me to them. He was playing with them in a little combo that they had earlier. Skip had a band called Pachuco and there was a gig that the rest of those guys in that band weren't able to play, and Skip had been jamming around with Tom and John and another bass player at that time. So he cobbled them together and they ended up playing this gig that I was also on the bill, and Skip introduced me to John and Tom and we got to be friends. All of us jammed together from time to time. Skip was just a fountain of energy, basically. An interesting … stylist … an all around good guy.'

discharged from the marines in July 1970. Before joining the marines, Bob went to college and worked as a janitor for a short while.

Jerry Miller is playing with The Rhythm Dukes, a five-piece band that features Fuzzy John Oxendine on drums, John Barrett on bass, Ned Torney on rhythm guitar, and Henry 'Rick' Garcia on tenor sax.* Although they've been playing live for two years and recorded some of their music in Marin County, they have yet to sign with a record label.

Don Stevenson, meanwhile, is still living in Boulder Creek, playing with drummer and singer Larry Biancalana and keyboardist Richard Dean. They play locally as a rotating duet, Don and Larry taking turns playing with Richard. Don was with The Rhythm Dukes, too, for a very short while. 'I was in The Rhythm Dukes for maybe ten or fifteen minutes,' he later tells me. 'I sat in with them and did some singing and I played some cowboy guitar and maybe some percussion. Fuzzy John was their drummer.'†

In California, Peter Lewis has worked as a furniture mover but shied away from performing live. According to Matthew Greenwald at allmusic.com, Lewis attempted to put a solo album together with David Rubinson, but the project was eventually aborted.

David Rubinson, a sort of mentor and anchor for Moby Grape—the man who signed the band to Columbia Records—has since formed Fillmore Incorporated, a production company, with the legendary concert promoter Bill Graham. Like Bill, David has always had a soft spot for Moby Grape, and he still holds their music in high esteem—when, that is, they play to their potential.

Although Moby Grape are finished, they are still held in high regard by rock critics like Lester Bangs, Greil Marcus, Paul Williams, and Robert Christgau. And they still get name-checked in interviews by everyone from the reclusive Phil Spector (who isn't flattering) to the up-and-coming

---

* Ned Tourney formerly played with The Chocolate Watchband. Interestingly, Jerry Miller's distinctive lead guitar can be heard on the Chocolate Watchband track 'Devil's Motorcycle' from the band's final studio album, *One Step Beyond* (Tower, 1969).

† All quotations from Don Stevenson and Jerry Miller (except the dream sequences or other identified sources) are taken from interviews I conducted with them in late 2016 and throughout 2017. While most quotations from Bob Mosely stem from interviews he gave to Ted Burke and Steve Roeser, others draw from my own interview with him in early 2018.

•

For the most part, that drama would unfold in the sunny mountains of northern California.

Running along California's Pacific Coast are numerous mountain ranges that give the effect of the depths of the ocean reaching closer and closer to the sky as the land stretches eastward. This is true of the San Francisco Peninsula, which features both mountains and valleys. At the bottom of the peninsula, beginning in Monterey Bay, the Pajaro River winds thirty miles into California's interior. It marks the southern edge of the Santa Cruz Mountains, which trek northward, through the counties of Santa Cruz, Santa Clara, and San Mateo, forming a long ridge.

Scattered around the Santa Cruz Mountains are many cities and towns. One of these urban hubs is Santa Cruz itself, a tiny dot on the Pacific coastline on the northern edge of Monterey Bay. Santa Cruz has a moderate climate, a moderate-sized population, and to the north, east, and south it is surrounded by the mountains of its namesake, which are dominated by redwood trees—the tallest and largest trees in the world.

Over the past few decades, the likes of Brian Wilson, J.J. Cale, and Quentin Tarantino have referenced Santa Cruz in their songs and films. Unsurprisingly, given its climate and location, the city had become a destination point as a seaside resort community in the late 1800s. A century earlier, Santa Cruz—'Holy Cross'—was established as a Spanish settlement. Long before that, the land upon which the city now stands was the home of the Awaswas, one of the peoples of the Ohlone.

Like a rugged crack on the land, Branciforte Drive juts out from Santa Cruz to the north. Along the road, the east side is marked by the greenery of DeLaveaga Park. Not far from the city, only about a mile or so to the north, Branciforte Drive splits into two separate roads. Moving almost directly northward is Granite Creek Road, and branching off, Branciforte Drive itself continues its circuit to the northeast. Shortly after this fork in the road, a few hundred paces to the north, is a vast parcel of land that runs across the east side of Granite Creek Road.

Covered in trees and bush, the property at 20 Granite Creek Road spreads across nearly four acres. Granite Creek itself flows through the property, running north and south. From Granite Creek Road, the property appears deceptively to be covered almost entirely in bush, apart from a small entrance. Behind the wall of trees and bushes that run along the roadway is an old home that can be reached by taking a long, winding lane that stretches into the property, running over a small bridge, over Granite Creek, and up a gentle hill, upon which stands an old Victorian house and a rundown garage.

The vast wooden home is painted white. The second floor is bigger than the first as part of it stretches over the wooden porch that dominates the home's entranceway. The porch itself is supported by large white pillars that run across its exterior. It is the sort of porch where one can sit in the afternoon, safely sheltered from the rays of the sun or the drops of the rain.

The home exceeds 3,300 square feet and totals ten rooms, including seven bedrooms and two washrooms. Running vertically from the first floor to the second is a large bay window that's split between a ground-level living room and a bedroom on the second floor. When the building was completed in 1898, it would've been heated by its fireplace as well as a woodstove. While the woodstove was no longer in the home by the late 60s, the fireplace remained intact. The house was owned for years by two sisters, both teachers, Vera and Phyllis Thomas, but by 1970 it had been vacant for a while and was beginning to deteriorate.

Tucked away in the Santa Cruz Mountains, 20 Granite Creek is, most simply, an address in California. In 1971, however, it was also the site of the first real reunion in rock'n'roll. For the members of Moby Grape, it was, for a time, a home and a place to create and record music. Nearly half a century later, it's become a distant memory. Yet *20 Granite Creek* is very much alive. It's a puzzle piece in the mythos of Moby Grape—and a remarkable album to boot. But how did it begin?

•

In the early months of 1971, after negotiations with David Rubinson and Bill Graham at Fillmore Incorporated, Clive Davis, who ran Columbia Records, arranged to sell the group's contract to Mo Ostin at Reprise

Records. Rubinson, who had initially signed Moby Grape to Columbia years earlier and produced the band's first three albums in a brisk twenty-month period from March '67 to November '68, now went about recruiting the members of the band, hoping to return Moby Grape to their former glory, like the proverbial phoenix rising from its ashes.

Everyone was apprehensive, some more than others. Although Skip Spence had recorded a solo album—writing, arranging, and playing everything on it in a matter of days, back in December '68—his playing since then had been intermittent. While he was justifiably proud of *Oar*—which remains a unique musical and poetic statement—the album did not sell well, and it soon went out of print. It did, however, attain cult status early on, having received glowing reviews from respected critics including Lester Bangs and Greil Marcus. But a return of Moby Grape, *with* Skip Spence?

It was understandable that anyone in the band might feel reluctant about a reunion. By the early 70s, Moby Grape had already become the stuff of rock legend. As the story goes (and this one's true) they were celebrated—championed, even—within a few months of their first rehearsal. As they moved from the cramped quarters of the Ark to the busier surroundings of the Avalon and Fillmore Ballrooms, record company executives jostled one another as they engaged in a bidding war to sign the band. They were signed at a time of great expectation. Yet over the years, as facts mingled with fictions, the band's story became one of mythical proportions—and myths are hard to live up to.

Rarely in life does anybody get a second chance, but for Moby Grape, this reunion was just that. It meant far more than five musicians getting back together to write and perform and record. The circumstances had changed. This wasn't a repeat of '66. Gone was the sunny exuberance and electrical musical community of the Bay Area. The Ark was no longer a nightclub in Gate 6 of Waldo Point Harbor in Sausalito, and the Avalon Ballroom—a Chet Helms/Family Dog Production—had been closed for years. The Fillmore West was on the verge of closing, too, as a beleaguered Bill Graham readied himself to step away from rock venues and promotion.

The 1971 iteration of the Grape would not set up shop in San Francisco.

Instead, they would find a location near Skip's home in San Jose. For everyone—including new band member Gordon Stevens and returning producer David Rubinson—this reunion represented an emotional journey. And a gamble, too.

If Moby Grape could recapture the magic of their explosive beginnings, or at the very least *some* of that energy, then the reunion was worth a try. Like a yin/yang symbol, along with the excitement and possibility of the positive, there was also the possibility of failure. Moby Grape experienced great loss during their short original tenure—the loss of Skip's mental stability and emotional well-being, failed marriages, artistic frustration, and commercial disappointments, among other things. While a reunion represented a chance for the group to rise once again, it also represented the possibility of disappointment—be it critical, commercial, emotional, or economic.

For each band member, the possibility of a reunion involved a process of weighing the potential highs against the potential lows. It was also a matter of finding the mental and emotional strength—and physical stamina—to revisit the past and pursue an artistic and ambitious dream that seemingly had evaporated just as the 60s reached their endpoint.

While times were changing, renting a house in the country was a decision *of its time*. By 1971, a variety of bands had taken this approach—what Robbie Robertson would call a 'clubhouse' concept.* It's an approach that, at least in part, comes out of two themes of the 60s—the commune and the return to the country. Bob Dylan and The Band tried this out when they wrote and jammed at Big Pink in upstate New York. Extensively bootlegged for years, their recordings from these collaborations during '67 and '68 would later be released as *The Basement Tapes* in 1975. The Band would repeat this approach in the pool house of a home they rented in West Hollywood when recording their sophomore album in late 1968 and early 1969, *The Band*. Fairport Convention wrote and mapped out their fourth album, *Liege & Lief*, while staying at a house in Farley Chamberlayne

* 'It was the clubhouse technique of making music,' Robertson notes in the *Classic Albums* episode about The Band's eponymous second album. 'You could go to a place and you're not on the clock. And you could do whatever you want to do.'

throughout the summer of 1969. During the summer and autumn of 1970, The Rolling Stones recorded much of *Sticky Fingers* at Mick Jagger's Stargroves estate using their own mobile truck. The following summer, they would record the bulk of *Exile On Main St.* at a villa Keith Richards rented in Nellcôte, France. Other albums created under these sorts of circumstances during the same period include Captain Beefheart's *Trout Mask Replica*, Steeleye Span's *Hark! The Village Wait*, and Led Zeppelin's untitled fourth album.

In one sense, then, *20 Granite Creek* fits right into this cluster of 'clubhouse' albums. Yet like so many of these records, *Granite Creek* was a roll of the dice—and for everyone involved, the band's reunion came at a cost to their time, energy, emotion, confidence—and, in a very real sense, their nervous systems.

For Gordon Stevens, new to the group, these complications were just as intense. Although he wasn't in the group during the San Francisco days, he was well aware of the dualities on the horizon, the twin possibilities of success and failure, limitlessness and limitation, excitement and apprehension. With his recent musical and supportive history with Skip, Gordon represented an anchor, or keel, for the mercurial musician.

For David Rubinson, producer and musical director, cheerleader and surrogate parent, the possibilities were immense. When the idea of a reunion began to solidify in early '71, it was only a possibility, and a faint one at that. That spring, Don Stevenson and Gordon Stevens flew from California to Hawaii to try to convince Bob Mosley to re-join Moby Grape for what it was hoped would be the first of many new albums.

WESTBOUND DREAM

The horizon is a perfect line in the distance, marking a point where the dark blue of the ocean meets the clear azure of the nearly cloudless sky. Far below, a blanket of water moves calmly, almost slowly. Although the ocean dominates the view, it's miles away. Heading westward, the plane cuts through the air at nearly 550 miles an hour, gliding at an altitude of over 3,600 feet. It's a smooth flight with minimal turbulence, but also a long one. By the early afternoon, the plane has been in the air for nearly four hours, and it's still over an hour away from its destination. Onward it moves, heading further and further west.

The plane isn't flying at capacity. Its passengers are trekking to the islands for a variety of reasons, including business meetings, holidays, and honeymoons. Seated near the middle of the plane are two young men, one in his early thirties and the other in his late twenties. They both have long hair and are dressed casually, in jeans and buttoned-up shirts.

The older of the two, Gordon Stevens, sits beside the window and looks out at the ocean. His mind wanders as he drifts into sleep. The younger man, Don Stevenson, is excited, expectant, and nervous. The last few weeks have been a whirlwind.

Unlike Gordon, Don knows Bob well—or at least he did. But that was years ago. Going back over his own chronology, Don figures he hasn't seen Bob in two years.

'Can I get you a drink?' a flight attendant asks.

'Do you have Jameson's?'

'Of course. Would you like it neat or on the rocks?' the attendant asks, picking up a small glass from inside the trolley.

'On the rocks,' Don answers.

Filling the cup with three ice cubes, the flight attendant then selects a bottle from the many that fill the trolley's platform.

'So, is this a holiday?' she asks.

'I'm going to see if my friend's going to come back for another album. We were in a band together.'

'What's your band's name?'

'Moby Grape.'

'Why'd you break up?'

From somewhere in the back, a man clears his throat.

'Miss, if you're not too busy, can I get a drink?' asks a middle-aged man with a trim haircut, from a seat a few rows behind Don.

'Of course,' the flight attendant smiles. 'Good luck,' she says to Don, before unlocking the trolley wheels and pushing it down the aisle.

Don thinks about the day Bob tried to teach him how to surf. He laughs to himself, then yawns. Although he's excited and expectant, the long flight has made him weary. He has a lot on his mind, and his mind is back in California. The idea of seeing Bob again, and trying to get him to come back to California, is complicated.

Don considers the last time he saw Bob, in the spring of '69. He thinks about how shocked he was later, when he heard that Bob had joined the marines. He leans his head back and yawns, closes his eyes, and starts to fall asleep.

Moments later, Don is awakened by the sound of a young woman's voice, speaking through the airplane speaker system. He recognizes it as the voice of the flight attendant from before.

'The plane will be landing at Honolulu International Airport in approximately ten minutes,' she says. Reading from a short script, she cheerfully informs passengers of the time of day and temperature in downtown Honolulu, as well as the names of the pilot and co-pilot.

'Welcome to Hawaii, the Aloha State.'

Next to Don, Gordon gazes out the window, lost in thought, wondering how things will unfold over the next few days. Don turns to Gordon and notices that his traveling companion is awake now too.

As the plane draws ever closer to Honolulu, the two musicians consider the task that stands before them. Slowly, surely, the plane begins its descent. The waters below have changed and now appear to be covered with debris, yet it's an illusion. The off-white shapes floating below are not pieces of debris at all. They're not even floating. Rather, they're the crests of waves, big and small, as the waters of the Pacific Ocean come crashing into the beaches and harbor.

With a quick jerk, the plane jolts down, causing the stomachs of its passengers to jump, as though they're speeding down the sharp decline of a tall rollercoaster. The pilot quickly returns the plane to its gentle descent, and there is a collective feeling of relief on the airplane as the craft eases downward, moving ever closer to the asphalt runway that covers a large patch of land that surrounds the terminal. Moments later, the plane lands smoothly on the ground, first accelerating and then slowing slightly as it speeds down the long runway before halting on the burning-hot asphalt that encircles the John Rogers Terminal, a bustling new building not yet ten years old.

Stepping off the plane, Don and Gordon are struck by the colors that surround them. The lush, deep greens are different from the ones in California. It is terribly humid out, and the air hangs heavily in a sort of dampened stillness. Even the air is different in Honolulu. At once, the two young men come to a new appreciation of just how far they've traveled.

They take a taxi and check into their hotel. With their appointment set for the evening, they still have a couple of hours to kill. While Gordon rests upstairs, Don makes his way to the hotel bar. Perched on a stool at the bar, he nurses a glass of Jameson's on the rocks, a glass of water on the side.

For Don, the past few weeks have been a whirlwind. Just a month earlier, he was resting in the Santa Cruz Mountains. At that point, as far as he was concerned, Moby Grape was a path that had reached its end. Two years earlier, he and Jerry had recorded Moby Grape's fourth album in just three days, with Peter Lewis making some reluctant but spirited contributions. And that was it.

When Moby Grape disintegrated and transformed into the Rhythm Dukes, initially to fulfill some of the Grape's performance obligations, Don and Jerry felt as though they had come full circle. After all, they had played together in The Frantics—and, for a short while, Luminous Marsh Gas—before Moby Grape even had their first rehearsal. Yet Don did not play with The Rhythm Dukes for long. He left the band in the summertime, disillusioned with the entire music business.

Then, out of the blue, Don learned that Columbia Records is ready to sell the Grape's recording contract to Mo Ostin at Reprise/Warner Bros. But in order for them to make a new album, the original lineup of the band is needed. And Bob Mosley, living in Hawaii and playing with a new band, is reluctant to reform Moby Grape.

In silence, Don mentally weighs the options and possibilities associated with the whole situation, and the possibility of a reunion. In 1971, though, the notion of reforming a rock band is virtually unheard of. The idea of band reunions has not yet become a part of the music business lexicon. The Yardbirds broke up. Cream ended. The Beatles' dream is over. Even the reunion of the original lineup of The Byrds is still two years away.

Through 1970 and into the spring of 1971, the notion of reforming Moby Grape has been a fantasy—an impossibility. Moby Grape went through so much during their brief tenure, and the very paperwork encircling their identity is unwieldy and unresolved. There isn't a template for a rock reunion. Yet somehow the wheels are in motion.

Sitting in a hotel bar in Honolulu, Don thinks about these things, wondering what will happen next.

CHAPTER TWO

'THEY PACKED EVERYTHING UP, AND THEY GOT OUT OF THERE.'

April 2017. An older man wearing jeans and a leather coat steps into the café. He stands around five-foot-ten and has a full head of salt-and-pepper hair. Removing his sunglasses, he shakes hands with me, then steps up to the counter and orders a cappuccino. When it's ready, he comes over to my table and sits down.

I start by asking him what he recalls of that trip to Hawaii, when he and Gordon went to try to get Bob to come back to the band.

'I met a woman there,' Don Stevenson replies. 'I was introduced to her by Jim, a friend of mine. I stayed with her a short while. You know, the most interesting thing for me was the swim,' he smiles.

> There are all these canals on the islands, going through sugarcane plantations. They flow through the plantations to irrigate the land. And those plantations are huge. She took me swimming through the canals. That was a trip! And it ended up in one of the lagoons where you just think, *this is where they take the pictures for paradise*. Swimming through the canals was just beautiful, with the sugar canes on either side. You get to the very end and there's a waterfall, and then you go underneath and

> swim right under the falls. I have to tell you, *that* is the most vivid memory I have of our trip to Hawaii to get Mos.

'What do you remember about Bob?' I ask.

'I remember playing with him. Me and Gordon went to the Red Noodle and checked him out. And we did jam some, and talk some, and smoked a little bit. Then we all came back and made *20 Granite Creek*.'

Pondering this, I recall that Bob Mosley joined the marines after leaving Moby Grape in '69. I also know that he was apparently kicked out of the marines the following summer, and I suspect he might've taken a lot of convincing to re-join the band.

'It was hard for Bob. It was hard for all of us. For Bob, probably a little more so. I don't remember a hell of a lot about the trip. I do remember going to the Red Noodle and having a bit to eat and then jamming with Bob and his band. And I remember he decided he was going to try it—and come back.'

I ponder the chronology of the reunion for a moment. The earliest mention I have been able to find of it is in the May 8 1971 issue of *Billboard*. In a column on the San Francisco scene, Mary Turner wrote, 'Moby Grape is back together and will appear along with Eric Burdon and War at the On the Cure Arts and Industry show May 13–23.' I ask Don if he remembers the show at all, but he doesn't. For a couple of seconds, I consider what to ask next, and then I think back to *20 Granite Creek*—how the band had signed to Reprise, rented the house, and set up a little recording studio there.

'I think Reprise rented the building, which was really old. It was totally deteriorated. It was set back off the road and you had to drive up through Manzanita trees through the driveway. You had to go quite a way before you got to the house. The house was set aside in a little clearing.'

During their short, blazing life in the late 60s, Moby Grape recorded in Columbia's studios in Los Angeles, New York, and Nashville. Working at Granite Creek, I suggest, must've been a very different experience.

> It was completely different. It was unreal. There was a detached

> garage that was no longer used as a garage. We found an old dump on the property, and my friend Mark Alexander and I dug in and found these old beautiful bottles, like artifacts.
>
> One time Skippy and I went out looking for gold, like gold mines. We had a long pole and we went around the property, it was huge. It was a long, thin pole. What you'd do is stick the pole in the ground and see how soft the ground is. Sometimes you'd find something like the site of an old outhouse and other times you'd find old objects that people used long ago. Like plates. Stuff like that.

The band members lived together at the house for some of the time, too, Don explains.

> I had a bedroom upstairs for a while. It was nice: it had a bay window and the bed was right in the bay window. I was there with a lady—her name was Mary. She had been a Santa Cruz Mountain woman. I always thought she was great.
>
> I lived there *most* of the time. Not always, but most of the time. Other people would stay there, but Skip and I were the only ones in the band really living there. We had two others with us at the time—they were kind of like our roadies. One of them was my friend Mark Alexander.

When Don mentions this, I recall something Mark Alexander himself once told me about Granite Creek:

> I got one of the nicer rooms in this one-hundred-year-old home. It was about a fifteen-by-fifteen-foot sitting room off the upstairs master bedroom. It had a suite door between my room and the master. There was an identical master directly below the upstairs master. These two spacious masters were the nicest rooms in the house. Each had a beautiful Victorian fireplace. These rooms

were originally occupied by the two spinsters who had built the house. One of the spinsters had died in her upstairs bedroom, long before we moved in, and they had boarded up the room after her death. We only found out belatedly that her room had been reopened just prior to our occupancy. More on that subject a little later. The house was built with milled old-growth redwood siding. Milled siding was a rarity for homes of this vintage, and it was painted a pale, faded yellow. The near-original, beige kitchen had a linoleum floor, which was probably put down in the 1950s, by the look of it. There were only two cabinets in the kitchen; one for the sink, and one for dishes above it. Neither even had doors. The sink cabinet had a curtain instead. On the right end of the sink cabinet, you could still see remnants of the old hand-operated water pump that brought water into the kitchen. There was a walk-in pantry off the kitchen, and a small bath. The flush-toilet must have been added after the original build, because you could still find the detritus from an old outhouse just behind the kitchen. It was a beautiful home, right on the creek. Out the back door behind the kitchen was a dilapidated old garage, which had probably once been a small stable. It was overgrown with berry vines. The kitchen windows looked out across the dirt driveway to a beautiful hundred-year-old cedar tree. The property was four or five gorgeous acres. Adjacent to the kitchen was a small den that they used as the makeshift control room for the recording gear. A door opened off the den into what had once been the library and was converted into a primitive studio where the band laid down tracks. When I moved in, they had already started recording.*

* I conversed with Mark Alexander—an informal intern for the band who lived at Granite Creek—multiple times in 2017. All quotations from him in this book draw from our conversations and correspondences. When I asked him about how he got involved in the Granite Creek project, he told me, 'My start in the music/recording biz began as a live-in caretaker/roadie. It was my reward from Don for being one of two people who helped convince him to reunite with the Grape.'

I wonder about their living arrangements during this period. 'Everyone kind of looked after themselves,' Don tells me. 'Some did communal meals, but Mary and I looked after ourselves. We had our stuff in the kitchen—and we labeled our things, like the milk,' he laughs. 'It was like a staffroom kitchen.'

'How was all the equipment set up?' I ask.

> I had a room, and Skip had a room in the house. And Ed Bannon, an engineer, would drive a truck up there with equipment from San Mateo. We set everything up in the main room where we recorded. It wasn't a living room—it was a former library on the first floor. It was quite large. So we had all the wires and mics, and most of the equipment into that room.
>
> I remember when Bob got there. He drove up from San Diego. He's a San Diego surfer god. [*Laughs.*] He drove up and he had his guitar and amp, and all his stuff in the back of his truck. He unloaded everything and he was ready to go. Skippy was already there at that point.

After rehearsing for a time, the band started recording.

> I remember we recorded in two different spots. We recorded up in the peninsula for 'Chinese Song.' For part of it. And we recorded in the house. There weren't many big formal rehearsals. It was a bit like the original album. Somebody would come in with a song and we'd be sitting around the front room and we'd play it. And all the amps and everything were set up in the recording room. It was in the living room where we would go and sit down and whatever and somebody would come in with a song and we'd all start adding to it. Then we'd go and we'd record it.

As well as jamming and recording at the house, the band played some shows locally during those months together in 1971, up in the Santa Cruz Mountains, at a place called the Chateau.

> It was on a road called Old Santa Cruz Highway. It was occupied by bikers, by and large. Some of the guys who helped Jerry get his guitar back when it was stolen in back in '67 were there. Some of the guys were in the Gypsy Jokers, which is a motorcycle club. And we'd go up there and play.
>
> I think we did two or three gigs. It was mostly because they were friends of Jerry's and friends of Skip's. And they paid us. You couldn't tell if they liked you or not—because they'd just be so stoned they wouldn't really react. When we'd finish our shows they'd just look up at us.

Some of the bikers would come down to Granite Creek sometimes as well.

> One day, some of the guys had a table set up by the garage, the one that was by the house. And they had this table set up with aluminum foil and glass containers and burners. They pretty much felt at home because we were all playing up there and we were friends. But Mary, my girlfriend, didn't know that. And it was just fine actually, because the last thing in the world we wanted was somebody cooking up meth out in our garage on 20 Granite Creek—particularly because we were doing an album for Reprise. And there was some hope for the future. I mean, it could've turned bad for us.
>
> So Mary, who didn't know any better, saw what was going on, and she marched out. She's a very beautiful lady with long black hair and olive skin. And she walked right out with her back straight, and she had something like a ladle in her hand. She marched over to the table where those bikers were and she ripped into them: You son of a bitches, you pack this shit up! There's recording going on in there! There's an album being

> done in there! There's careers on the line and you guys are cooking up speed! Pack your shit up and get the hell out of here!

Fortunately, Mary's outburst served to defuse the situation. 'Those guys were like little children who were caught doing something wrong. They packed everything up, and they got out of there.'

Don breaks into laughter, and I join in. Knowing that Bob was the first to leave the band during the *20 Granite Creek* period, though, I wonder if this drama precipitated his departure.

> Bob didn't stay long. He did 'Ode To The Man At The End Of The Bar.' And we didn't play with him on that one. Rubinson played piano and Bob played drums on that one, if I recall. And he played on a few other songs, but I don't think it was all of them. Of course, he played on 'Gypsy Wedding.' He may have played on 'Horse Out In The Rain,' too. I can't remember the specifics. I can't remember how much Skip played on, either. But everyone else played on 'Gypsy Wedding,' and 'I'm The Kind Of Man That Baby You Can Trust.' That's a nice little groove. I had a cymbal thing going on with that one, with the line, 'Baby I'm the kind of man that you can trust.' You've got 1-2-3-4, and you emphasize the two, but I got independence with my hi-hat. It would go on the ending with *chk-chk-chk-chk*, 1-2-3-4 on the offbeat. To me it created a great little groove.
>
> Bob also played on 'Road To The Sun,' of course. That was another of his songs. But … he had an abrupt departure. I can't remember what he played on exactly, but I know that he didn't like what was going on in the house—because of some of the behavior that was going on. He packed up and said, 'I'm getting out of here.' He was pretty disgusted with what was going on.

Skip, meanwhile, played on 'Chinese Song': 'The one he wrote. That's Skippy, me, and Gordon, I think. We did that one mostly at Pacific Studios in San Mateo. He might've played on another one or two as well, but I can't remember for sure.'

I ask Don what a typical day at Granite Creek would have been like, and he describes the mood as 'really casual.'

> We weren't going to meet up at a specific time. David knew how to handle that. And he stayed there sometimes. You know, *20 Granite Creek* was more like our first album. It was live again. I don't think there was a whole lot of overdubbing. There was more writing going on in the house. So we'd get together, with Jerry and me, or Peter would show us a song. It was like how we were at the beginning, when we showed each other our songs at the Ark and at Skippy's apartment back in '66. We'd just come in and see what was going on. Then, we'd say, 'Let's record it.' And we'd record it. So it's fresh, you know.
>
> When Gordon came in, he'd been playing with Skippy long enough that he knew how to move in and out—like Skip. And he's very intuitive. He played on my solo album, *King Of Fools*. He's just phenomenal, especially on the title track. He just does some interesting bass playing on that one. Back when we were doing *20 Granite Creek*, Gordon was always available musically. And he is a very sophisticated man. He can speak to you about the opera, about the theater, about mathematics. He can speak to you about anything. When it came to playing, he brought all that to bear.

The band continued working on the album into the summer, while also fulfilling live commitments. 'We did some live shows in New York,' Don says. 'I know I had my birthday when we were still at 20 Granite Creek, and that was in October, but the album was out by then. I think we had to move out shortly after my birthday.'

•

Listening to Don, my mind wanders back to a conversation I had previously with Mark Alexander. When I asked Mark about their routines at Granite Creek, he told me:

> A typical day would depend on how late the recording sessions went. They often went until 2am, but that could be just the engineer and maybe Rubinson playing around with things. It seemed that the musicians got burned out by and large by, say, one in the morning. Sometimes things would go later. I can remember one time where Mosley was in the back of his pickup truck, trying to sing a vocal overdub. As I recall, the false dawn was coming by the time they gave up on that endeavor. So that was a very late night. I remember going to bed at halfway reasonable hours, staying up to eleven or twelve or something, and hearing music throughout the night, in my sleep—just as somebody was working on something down there.

•

Later that evening, I call Jerry Miller. We've been chatting for months, and it's become a comfortable routine. Although it's 9pm in Toronto, it's just 6pm where he is, in Tacoma, Washington. It's springtime, and both cities are creeping toward the warmth of summer.

I begin by talking about the opening song on *20 Granite Creek*: how the whole album starts off with a bang, with the powerful bass and drums of 'Gypsy Wedding.'

'That was Bob,' Jerry chuckles. 'He didn't want no gypsy wedding.' Jerry breaks into the opening line of the song, as though the mere thought of the song has an infectious hold over him. 'We played that one quite a bit,' he recalls. 'It had to do, I do believe, with Bob himself. He was such a catch in those days, all the girls wanted to get with him. I think he kind of got fed up with it and he didn't want to get into any entanglements at the time.'

When I start to ask about the other songs on the album, Jerry sets down his phone. I can hear him rustling around, looking for the record itself. After a minute or two, he returns.

> 'About Time' is an interesting tune. I don't know a lot about the story behind it. It's just Don's. But that's Andy Narell playing steel drums in the second part of the song. That was beautiful. David Rubinson came up with Andy for that.
>
> 'Goin' On Down To Texas' was a true story of Peter's. He was going down to Texas to see his girlfriend, Charlotte.
>
> I don't know a lot about 'Road To The Sun.' I think basically I just played on that one. That's how it was sometimes. I don't think Bob told me much about the whereabouts of the lyric, or what inspired him on that one.

After a few seconds of silence, Jerry exclaims, 'I love "Apocalypse!" I love that one! I do it myself, you know, at my gigs. Of course, I only get about half of the lyrics right!' he chuckles.

I then ask him about the last song on the album, 'Horse Out In The Rain,' mentioning how I once went through a period of playing that song over and over again, during which time I couldn't stop listening to the words.

'Yeah,' he says. '*Waiting for the summer to come around again.* You can picture it. I mean, it's a picture song. You can just see it. And you can feel sorry for the horse, too.' He pauses. 'I think, basically, we were the horse. Waiting.'

•

Perhaps Moby Grape really *was* the horse waiting in the rain. They were, after all, constantly waiting during that *20 Granite Creek* period. And whenever something they were waiting for arrived, something else—something new they'd need to wait for—would appear in the distance.

The waiting started when everyone had to be gathered for the reunion. It continued after they had their first rehearsal. They were waiting to write new songs, to see if new songs would come to them. All the while, they were waiting see if they could recapture their old magic, as songwriters and performers.

They were still waiting after they'd moved into 20 Granite Creek, waiting to write and record their new material. Then they were waiting to return to the ballrooms in San Francisco and New York—and, all the while, they were waiting to finish recording, mix the songs, and then release the album. In that sense, *20 Granite Creek* is not just the story of the Grape's reunion, it's a story of their perpetual waiting.

•

As I lie in bed later that night, a story Mark Alexander once told me about Granite Creek springs into my mind:

> As I mentioned before, the house had been built by a pair of spinster sisters. After one of them died in the upstairs master bedroom, it was sealed up until we moved in. No one ever mentioned this to me. And my bedroom was the former sitting room to that master. Anyway, I was sitting on my bed one sunny summer morning, writing a humor poem.
>
> As I glanced up from the page toward my windows at the front of the house, I was momentarily startled by the ghost of an old woman staring back at me (this has never happened to me before or since then!). I quickly recovered my composure and said these words to her: 'I'm not scared. What do you want?'
>
> She never responded, but she definitely looked upset! Then she simply vanished. I kept this experience to myself for a few weeks. But then one day I overheard Don's girlfriend, Mary, as she was relating a story to a visiting friend of hers. As Mary told it, a few weeks earlier she was visited by another mother and child; and her son, Justin, and the guest's daughter were playing in an adjacent room. The women were chatting when they heard the little girl exclaim, 'Oh Mama, look at the pretty lady!' Mary and her friend went into the room where the kids

were and asked, 'What lady?' The girl said that there had been a pretty old lady in there, but she disappeared.

It was then that I told Mary of my strange encounter. We later heard the story, from our realtor, of the woman dying in the bedroom upstairs and how the room had been sealed up until our occupancy. If ghosts actually do exist, then I would say that the prim and proper Victorian spinster was trying to express her extreme upset over her home being defiled by sex, drugs, and rock'n'roll.

A few weeks later, an artist friend of Rubinson's and the Grape's came to stay for three weeks. Her name is Helen Hersh, and she does rock posters and album covers, among many other things. I believe she has pieces in the Rock and Roll Hall of Fame. Anyway, Helen stayed in the ghost's room next to mine. Nobody mentioned the ghost to her, which hadn't been seen since my encounter. But sure enough, she was appearing to Helen almost every night. I guess Helen felt understandably intruded upon. Finally, Helen had had enough and told the woman to get the hell out! The ghost obliged, and no one ever saw her again.

I've been an agnostic and a follower of science for many years, so I really don't know about all this ghost stuff. But if string theory is even close to right, there may be as many as ten dimensions in our universe! And even with all our sophisticated measuring devices and particle accelerators, we can currently only measure in four dimensions, including the one of time. We can only account for about 5 percent of the universe, though we know the other 95 percent is there. We just don't know what those other dimensions look like, let alone how many there are and whether ghosts can populate them! Who knows? I'm open to explanations.

CHAPTER THREE

GRANITE CREEK

20 *Granite Creek* starts with a bang—a deep bass kicking things off on the left speaker. For a split second, the bass plays on its own. Very quickly, the drums join in, instantly locking into a steady groove. At a higher register on the right speaker, a lead guitar, played by Jerry Miller, steps in, mirroring the blues riff the bass has repeated over-and-over again.

As this pattern plays a few times, additional guitars chime in, swirling around each other, adding the odd run of notes or percussive supports for the song's basic, thumping rhythm, which moves forward, ever energetically. After the basic pattern repeats five times, Bob Mosley rips into 'Gypsy Wedding,' belting out his lyric:

Bought myself a motorbike
To keep my head on straight.

A motorbike?

There's a whole mythology about Moby Grape—or, more specifically, about Skip Spence and motorcycles. Upon being released from the psychiatric ward of Belleview Hospital, he had bought a motorcycle with the money he received from Columbia Records to record his solo album,

Oar. The story goes that he hopped on his bike and rode it down to Nashville in November '68, right after he exited the hospital. Ironically, this all unfolded a few short months after the counterculture classic *Easy Rider* was filmed. And, as the legend goes, Skip was supposedly wearing his pajamas for the durations of this nine-hundred-mile journey.

That wasn't how it happened, but the myth persists.

Earlier that year, Skip wrote 'Motorcycle Irene,' a sketch of a rough-and-ready female biker whose story ends dramatically—and loudly. Recorded in January '68, this fun song put a humorous spin on an old classic, 'Leader Of The Pack.' 'Motorcycle Irene' appeared on Moby Grape's *Wow* album, which was released in April '68—less than two months before Skip's breakdown.

Years later, in the early 70s, Skip Spence and Moby Grape played the Chateau Liberté, a legendary rock'n'roll bar and biker hangout.* Just a few miles north of the house on Granite Creek, deeper in the Santa Cruz Mountains, the Chateau was originally constructed in 1865 as a log cabin. By the end of the century, it had become a Wells Fargo stagecoach stop; when prohibition rolled around, it transformed into a speakeasy. For a while, the Chateau became a restaurant and inn, even hosting horse rodeos from time to time. Over the years, its name changed from Chateau Boussy, to Redwood Chateau, to Chateau Regis, before its owners finally settled on Chateau Liberté in 1971.

Before long, the Chateau was frequented by the Gypsy Jokers and the Hells Angels. During these heady times, it hosted indoor and outdoor concerts featuring the likes of Jerry Garcia, Hot Tuna, Dan Hicks, and The Doobie Brothers. Even for California, this log cabin bar was a unique setting, like some sort of counterculture retreat. The aging chalet stood by an old pool that was sometimes tidy and other times filled with algae and salamanders. All of this was tucked into a clearing within a vast forest filled with towering redwood trees that provided large canopies on sunny days.

It's unsurprising, then, that a motorcycle appears on the first line of

* Interestingly, a few short years after Moby Grape's motorcycle songs were recorded, Robert M. Pirsig's classic *Zen & The Art Of Motorcycle Maintenance* appeared on bookshelves.

20 Granite Creek—or *any* Moby Grape song or album, for that matter. Motorcycles, after all, are a part of the band's landscape and mystique.

When 'Gypsy Wedding's' lively solo begins, I'm reminded of the Grape's famous guitar *crosstalk*, although this time the talk bounces between Bob Mosley's bass, Jerry Miller's lead guitar, and Peter Lewis's shifting between rhythm and lead.

Absent from 'Gypsy Wedding,' and from much of the album, is Skip Spence. By 1971, Skip had been through a lot. But while he may not have played on much of the album, his contributions would prove invaluable.

As I listen to the song charge forward, I think back to something else Mark Alexander once told me:

> I do recall that they never got a complete single take of 'Gypsy Wedding' that they were satisfied with. What you hear is Rubinson's magic in splicing together two different takes. And I think that there might have been a tiny—but to David noticeable—timing difference between the two. One was the tiniest bit slower than the other, maybe. Somehow, he managed to make it work in the primitive analogue-tape world. The whole album's recording process was varied, and, at times, piecemeal. It could be anything from one-take wonders to endless solo overdub attempts, and anything in between.

After two minutes and twenty-three seconds, 'Gypsy Wedding' ends just as it begins, with a dynamic and abrupt thump. It's followed by a song that transports us back to Moby Grape's earlier forays into country-rock, 'I'm The Kind Of Man That Baby You Can Trust.' It isn't country but it isn't rock, either. Gordon Stevens's electric viola is prominent in the mix, as are Don Stevenson's backing vocals.

When I ask Jerry about the song, he sighs.

> I'm not sure if that's what I had in mind for the title, but that's how it came out on the album. I wrote that one right about

> that time. You can hear Gordon Stevens playing viola on that one. He had Stevens Music in San Jose. He was a real cool guy, a real funny guy. He had a good sense of humor. He was a good friend of Skippy's for a long time, and Tommy Johnson and The Doobie Brothers. I was invited to be in that band. John Hartman called me and asked me if I wanted to come down and get into the band with him and those guys. I was up in Boulder Creek in the mountains in Santa Cruz, and it was about 108 up there. And I said, 'No. I'm not coming down to San Jose now.' So that was another opportunity blown. But a guy like me, a lounge lizard didn't want to go down to San Jose that day.

Jerry laughs cheerfully. 'It sure wouldn't have hurt my pocketbook any!' He pauses, then adds, 'But it left them to do the good things that they did.'

The next song, 'About Time,' gives Don Stevenson a chance to reflect and shine as a songwriter. Split in two, the first half of the song is haunting and the second is downright jaunty. In the opening half of the song, instead of sounding like a fiddle, Gordon's electric viola wavers along, giving the melody an unearthly feel. Don's vocal delivery only reinforces this unearthliness; his words harken back to the Grape's complications with royalties and lawsuits, and their struggle to survive. It could be a song about a relationship gone wrong, with two people parting ways. It could also be a song about a band.

When we chat about the song, Don tells me, 'It's probably the only song that I wrote by myself on our first albums. It's kind of autobiographical. It's about my life. My wife and I were leaving each other around that time.' When I suggest that it could also be about the band, Don laughs heartily. 'It was also about the *band*,' he chuckles. 'I should've just said that.'

At the song's midpoint, as though a switch has been flipped, the melody instantly transforms from dour to carefree while still maintaining its reflective nature. Here, Moby Grape's instrumentation takes an unexpected turn, with Stevens strumming a mandolin. Like so many of the musical risks taken on the album, the band somehow pulls it off. Although the words continue to tell a sad story, the melody and vocals are exuberant, optimistic even.

The narrator of 'About Time' speaks from experience. Prior to joining Moby Grape, Don had many experiences. He played in a variety of local bands on the Northwest Coast, hitchhiked and rode the trains across America and Europe, traveling up and down the West Coast with The Frantics, among other things. Like Don, the narrator has traveled to many places, seen many things, and, ultimately, he's come to terms with his current situation. He may not fully understand *why* he's arrived at this destination point, but he accepts it.

> With that one, David Rubinson asked me if he could put steel drums on it. And I had mixed feelings about it. I liked the very beginning. I played guitar on that one. I had a lot of vibrato on the guitar. It was just supposed to be very delicate. Just the atmosphere of the sound. Then, when the steel drums come in, it's so shocking. But as I look back on it now and listen to it, I think that it's kind of cool. It's kind of interesting. I still have mixed feelings about it. It's different. It's grown on me over time. But I'm still not one hundred percent happy with it.
>
> On 'About Time,' Gordon came up and we had a time, kind of like a twenty-, twenty-five-minute period where we talked about that song. Gordon's an intellectual, so, musically, he's very interested, and very interesting. So, the song had a very unusual format, and we talked about that over a cup of coffee in the kitchen. And he put together his cello part, or rather his viola part, as we spoke—he was planning what he was going to do. And he also was enthusiastic about the steel drums—which I wasn't enthusiastic about. And even now when I look back on it, I kind of wish that the steel drum wasn't on it. But it does kind of take the song from this melancholy piece, you know we put a lot of reverb on the guitar, very melancholy—and then: *bam!* It snaps, and then suddenly you're on the top of a mountain

> looking out and what do you see? As far as getting together at Granite Creek, I certainly remember that time, co-creating with Gordon.

The three remaining songs on the first side of the album span a total of seven minutes. They are short, richly varied, and filled to the brim with images and instruments. First there's 'Goin' Down To Texas,' Peter's bouncy rocker, reminiscent of 'Fall On You,' a powerful song the band played at their first rehearsal in the late summer of '66. 'Goin' Down To Texas' is a song of possibility and hope, representative of the album itself.

After a fleeting minute and fifty-six seconds, Peter's boisterous tune gives way to Bob Mosley's soulful and mellow 'Road To The Sun.' With Bob's ever-powerful vocal supported by pitch-perfect harmonies, the song features a mini-bridge with Don's drums tightly entangled with Bob's bass. It's a song about a relationship, devotion, endings, and an unknown future.

'That's a cool song!' Bob tells me. 'We recorded it at the house. We had a mobile truck outside, and we brought the studio inside the house. I just wrote it and we recorded it. It was that simple. Nothing to it.'

Closing the first side of the album is 'Apocalypse,' Peter Lewis's poem about the end of the world. Throughout the tune, Peter creates evocative images, punctuated every third and fourth line by tightly harmonized backing vocals. The entire melody is supported by ongoing guitar crosstalk braided with Gordon's viola, which is prominently featured in the mix.

If we're to take *20 Granite Creek* as a picture of both hope and apprehension, then 'Apocalypse' represents the latter of the two. In just thirteen lines, Peter draws a series of sharp images. The lyric opens in a pastoral setting, with the narrator's perspective of a tranquil summer day. Yet that tranquility is soon interrupted by the arrival of one of the Four Horsemen of the Apocalypse, who bring a warning to humanity. Moving to the second verse, the narrator relays the specifics of the Horseman's warning. In this description, he spells out a litany of catastrophes from the end of time—a time that is upon us. While these are terrible images, and frightening ones, the narrator accepts his fate. In what seems to be a state of resignation, or perhaps tranquility, Peter calmly, solemnly sings the song's final verse.

It's a song of *eschatology*, or the end of time. It's also a great song, Don tells me.

> It's very scary, you know. Talking about the earth being flushed and pulled aside and a raging sea rolls out from the land: '*Soon the valleys of the earth will be cracked and pulled aside / And the scorching sea will flow out from the land / Rising always higher, till it's finally left facing / Just its own reflection blazing in the sun.*'
>
> That last line, 'Learning how to die.' It's intense. Gordon playing viola on it added something special. Just like 'Horse Out In The Rain.' That extra instrument added a lot. I think Gordon's playing might have come from that feeling he developed playing with Skip. Because there's that sense that—you want to resolve—with a song like 'Apocalypse.' You want it to be threatening and scary and mystical. It's not like G-C-D, it's like chords that have overtones to them, like in Indian music, where there's sympathetic tones. There's a lot of sympathetic tones going on there. But they're scary. It's not a happy thing. But it's interesting, and in a way, I find 'Apocalypse' beautiful.
>
> I think that Gordon manages to have that flair where he plays in and out. That's what Skippy does. What was interesting about Skip—which was the same as Gordon—he didn't play *anything*. He just played *everything*. He could move in and out of what everybody else did. And he did it in such a way! Because if you can imagine, that's eighteen, twenty-two strings in total, with three guitars and a bass—and Skip would weave in and out—and he wouldn't step on anyone. Well, they would never step on each other; Skip never stepped on anyone. He was very sympathetic, and he was understanding, and he was emotional. Emotionally available. And he was spiritual. He was all those things when he was playing.

•

The second half of *20 Granite Creek* begins with a splice, the tape having been cut mid-note. The track quickly finds its footing and a pattern begins, one that is repeated many times with a few swerves along the way. It's filled with the sounds of a koto, electric viola, bass, and drums, an uncommon instrumentation for a rock song. It isn't a rock song at all.

'Chinese Song' is a spiral, its basic melody repeated time after time with instruments coming and going, alternating drum fills, a new extension to the melody appearing and then disappearing, and then a return to the song's soft beginning. Then it all begins again, with slight variations along the way.

Some rock journalists have wondered why a song featuring a koto would be called 'Chinese Song.' After all, the koto is a traditional Japanese instrument, usually with thirteen strings and thirteen moveable bridges. Yet while the koto hails from Japan, the instrument derives from the guzheng, a thirteen-stringed instrument that first appeared in China over two millennia ago. The guzheng was introduced to Japan in the seventh or eighth century, after which it transformed into the koto, which became associated with court music and romance, and was soon written about in Japanese literature.

'Chinese Song' may not be a wholly traditional composition, but it certainly has an ethereal quality to it. As I listen to it, I'm reminded of another story that Mark Alexander once told me:

> I remember when Skip was trying out all kinds of novel recording approaches for 'Chinese Song.' At one point, he had [engineer] Ed Bannon tape a mic to a fifty-foot garden hose at one end. At the other end, he had me trying to time percussion sounds, mostly handclaps and shaker sounds to the delay at the other end of the hose, in a different room. Trying to time the percussion to the long delay from the hose proved impossible, and Skip abandoned that approach. The garden hose as a delay chamber was not a new idea. But Skip had heard of it, so he tried it. Thus, ended my fifteen-minute career as a delay/

> percussionist. Notice that some of the guitar refrain lines are not dissimilar to 'Blue Sky' by The Allman Brothers. Not sure which predates the other. But we live in a twelve-tone musical universe, so similarities are bound to crop up.

After nearly six wordless minutes, the music gently comes to an end, giving way to a very different song, the chugging 'Roundhouse Blues.' Starting out in a train station in Wabash, Alabama, the lyric tells the story of a man who spends all his time trying to please his Southern belle. He seems content, though. More than content. He seems happy.

In the background, a sturdy bass and drums keep the rhythm pushing forward ever tightly. Above that basic rhythm, a fingerpicking guitar blends with an electric viola, giving the song a constant hum. Holding everything together, a jaunty lead guitar adds runs here and there, complementing the different rhythmic layers as the short song chugs forward. During the solo, multiple lead guitars converse freely with one another in the foreground, before giving way to a short run on the viola.

When I mention the song to Jerry Miller, the guitarist laughs. 'I really didn't know what the heck I was doing with that one. I don't even know if there even is such a thing as Wabash, Alabama!' Checking a map afterward, I find a Wabash River and Wabash, Indiana—but no Wabash, Alabama. It doesn't matter, though. Alabama is a perfect setting for a honky-tonk song about a Southern belle.

Less than three minutes later, 'Roundhouse Blues' gives way to 'Ode To The Man At The End Of The Bar,' a humorous story-song sung by Bob Mosley. Listening, I'm transported back to an earlier conversation with Jerry Miller.

'Now that's a funny one,' Jerry chuckles. 'I don't know where he came up with that. But he sure got a laugh out of it. You know, that line, "I puked all over the floor." It's just one of those stories that Bob no doubt experienced.'

As Bob continues telling this comic story in song, I smile. It *is* a funny lyric. It's a portrait of a barfly who marches to directly to a bar after work, day-after-day, drinking himself into oblivion, forgetting why he feels compelled to go there at all. OK, that may not *sound* funny, but it is—at least when it's told so matter-of-factly, from the barfly's perspective.

'That's my brother's song,' Bob remembers. 'He was in the air force. He sent me a song from a base, and he asked me if I could look at it. I thought, *Wow, what a dig. I wouldn't want to be in the air force!* And I figured I could play that on the drums … and I sang it, too,' he chuckles.

After nearly four minutes, Bob's story-song is followed by a funky, bluesy tune, 'Wild Oats Moan.' Don's singing is frantic on this one. When I ask him about it, however, he dismisses it as 'just a rock song, you know. Everyone does a song like that.' He hums the beat of the song, then adds, 'I like it, but I think it's inconsequential.' Yet there's something infectious about the song, not least in David Rubinson's congas. Circling the melody, Jerry's lead guitar and Gordon's viola converse with one another, trading off, alternating between lead and rhythm, dueling across pentatonic scales.

The song ends with Stevens stepping back into a rhythmic mode, playing his viola percussively. It's as through the song *demands* percussion in its closing bars. Throughout the track, Bob's bass is on fire.

Thinking about Bob, I'm reminded of something else Mark Alexander told me:

> The state-of-the-art of things back then was so primitive. Back then, they were still inventing the stuff you need to do those mobile recordings. So, as I recall, they had a one-inch Ampex eight-track recorder and a rudimentary eight-track recording console that may have been custom built. This makeshift control room had been the den adjacent to the kitchen. From there, a partition wall's door led to the former fifteen-by-fifteen-foot library, which became the recording room. Back then, there weren't even any books on how to build a small in-home recording studio. Since the room was small by studio standards, all they really knew to do was deaden the room acoustically, as much as possible, to minimize mic-leakage. Well, they deadened the dickens out of that room! They had layers of heavy blankets

> covering the ceiling and the four walls. The floor was already carpeted. It was so dead in there that when you did handclaps, they would just die, with no hint of reverberation whatsoever. This now-anechoic space kind of gave Mosley claustrophobia or something when he tried to do solo vocal tracks. Bob told Ed Bannon, the engineer, that his singing sounded better when he practiced in the metal camper shell on the back of his pickup, which was like being in a mini reverb chamber. So, in the wee hours one morning, Bob backed his truck up to the den windows and Bannon ran a boom-mic out there! It was just a cab-high camper, so Bob couldn't even stand up in the thing. But there he sat, doing his vocal takes for one of his tunes. I don't believe they ever got a keeper take, but they sure tried!

When 'Wild Oats Moan' ends, it's replaced by Peter Lewis's somber 'Horse Out In The Rain.' It starts as a simple melody, softly delivered with a guitar and viola, and then a second, heavier guitar joins in. Everything hangs with echo and reverb. As the melody begins again, a voice floats above the wavering guitars and viola, telling a story about a lone horse struggling to stand outside in the rain. The horse is dreaming of a time its spirit will run free, waiting for the summer. Lewis sings the sad, visceral lyric quietly, echoing above a haunting melody, the dreams and pains of a tired horse.

Like a breeze, the first verse flies away and is replaced with a second layer that tells us more about this poor, tired animal trying to endure its pain as it waits. Maybe *that's* what that the *20 Granite Creek* project was all about. A time of creating and waiting. Yet perhaps it was more. Maybe it was a journey of retracing a path once taken, recovering something that has been lost along the way. What if it was lost again?

My thoughts turn to Moby Grape's eastward trip—that day in June when the members of the band boarded a jumbo jet heading for New York City. Thinking about this flight, I begin to replay the opening bars of 'Chinese Song' in my head once again …

EASTBOUND DREAM

The winding staircase that leads from the main deck to the upper deck of the jet is narrow. A man with longish blond hair ascends the steps with determination. With broad shoulders and a loose-fitting button-up Hawaiian shirt, he stands with his back arched. He has, after all, spent months in the marines. Today, he wears jeans though, a new uniform of sorts. Upon reaching the second level, he strides through the lounge and stops at the bar, which stands at the far end of jet's spacious upper floor. He nods at the bartender.

'What'll it be?' the bartender asks.

'A beer.'

'What kind?'

'Any kind. I don't care which.'

The bartender removes a bottle, opens it, and pours the beer into a glass.

'Here,' he says, handing the glass to the man with blond hair.

The traveler raises his glass. 'Thanks,' he says, before taking a gulp.

There is a brief silence.

'I'm John Smith,' the bartender says, holding out his hand.

'Bob Mosley,' the traveler replies, and the two shake hands.

'Is this your first time heading to New York?' the bartender asks.

Bob pauses. 'I've been to New York before. With my band.'

The bartender leans forward. 'What's the band?'

'Moby Grape.'

'One of those groups from San Francisco, right?'

'*I'm* not from San Francisco,' Bob tells him, 'but that's where we formed the band.'

'Do you know the guys in The Grateful Dead?'

'We used to jam with them.'

'Who's the biggest name you performed with?'

'I don't know. Hendrix, maybe.'

'You're kidding.'

'We played the Earl Warren Showgrounds. It's down in Santa Barbara. It was in July or August of '67. It was right before his first album came out. We played with him at Monterey too. That was a month or two before. Well, we didn't perform with him on stage, but we were on the same bill. He blew everyone away.'

'Didn't you break up? I remember your first album, and then the second one—the one with the giant grapes on a beach.'

'We broke up a few years ago.'

'And you're recording a new album in New York?'

'No. We're going to do some shows. At the Fillmore.'

'The Fillmore. I saw Janis Joplin perform there. Did you see her ever?'

Bob considers this question. 'She was at Monterey, too. She performed twice that weekend. Her first performance was good but I don't think it was filmed, or something like that. There was some sort of deal made where she got a second timeslot on Sunday, as a sort of second chance. I wish we had a Sunday timeslot.'

'And now you're playing the Fillmore.'

'We are.'

'Is everyone in the band on this flight?'

'See that guy sleeping over there?' Bob asks, pointing at the bearded man with his legs stretched out, 'That's Peter Lewis.'

'Well, good luck. I hope your shows go well.'

'Thanks.'

Bob scans the room. The upper deck is half full, and for the most part its passengers are either dozing in their seats or engaging in quiet conversation over drinks, cigarettes, or both. A haze of smoke hangs in the upper reaches of the room, giving it a dreamy appearance and feel. It's as though this room, filled with travelers, is floating above the clouds, immersed in an artificial haze.

Bob slumps down into a chair directly across from Peter. He sets his glass on the table beside him and regards it. It's mesmerizing. The beer moves in the glass as the plane buzzes forward. Bob thinks about the band's upcoming shows. Just a couple of months into their reunion, Moby Grape are already bound for the burning spotlights of New York. Not only are they under scrutiny for daring to put on the first real rock reunion, but they're also under scrutiny for being a band that was hyped—or seemingly hyped—beyond measure when they debuted in '67.

For the Grape, New York is like standing at the foot of a mountain. Returning to the Fillmore East, a place where things went so wrong in '68, they need to impress their fans and win over their detractors. It's a tall order. Bob knows this, as he silently looks at his glass of beer. He looks across the lounge at Peter and closes his eyes.

CHAPTER FOUR

THE SHOWS

On May 22 1971, Moby Grape played a show at Brooks Hall in San Francisco, followed, eight days later, by another at the Hollywood Palladium. Then, in mid-June, they played two more at the Fillmore East in New York, followed by five at the Fillmore West, back in San Francisco (June 22 and 24–27). By any reckoning, these would have been high-profile shows. Yet with Bill Graham announcing the closing of the Fillmore East and Fillmore West in the imminent future, Moby Grape found themselves preparing to step into a spotlight that was only getting brighter.

Unfortunately, things didn't start off well.

If you peruse the June 19 1971 issue of *Billboard*, you will find an unflattering concert review written by one George Knemeyer, sharing his thoughts on Moby Grape's May 29 show at the Palladium. 'It would be nice to say that Moby Grape's first appearance in over two years was a triumph,' he began. 'Nice, but untrue. It was mostly a disaster as the group just wasn't rehearsed enough.' Later, Knemeyer added, 'The original members of Moby Grape are back, aided by Gordon Stevens on electric viola who was inaudible throughout the set. The sound was very muddy and vocals buried most of the time, chiefly caused by the group and not by the Tycobraye sound system.' Of the songs and the band's condition, he offered the following observation: 'The new songs were the best, or rather, the best rehearsed. The band still needs about three months more practice before it can rightfully regain its onetime title of America's best rock and roll band.'

Re-reading Knemeyer's article, I listen again to a fan recording of one of the songs from this concert. On this live version of 'Chinese Song,' electric guitars replace Spence's koto. Moby Grape are playing well, and the audience reception is very positive when the song comes to an end. Stevens's viola is audible, despite what Knemeyer wrote. While the tone of his review was negative, Knemeyer was clearly a fan of the band. Yet his call for three months of rehearsals was wishful thinking, because Moby Grape didn't have three months. They had three weeks, which wasn't nearly enough time.

•

Moby Grape arrived in New York for their two shows at the Fillmore East on June 18 and 19. One of America's premier venues, the Fillmore East was located at 105 Second Avenue. Built in the 1920s, the four-floor theater was designed in a medieval revival style by Harrison Wiseman. Starting out as a Yiddish theater called the Commodore, it later transformed into a movie house called Loews Commodore, then into the Village Theater, a popular concert hall. When Bill Graham took over the venue in the spring of '68, he dubbed it the Fillmore East—a twin for his renowned San Francisco beacon, the Fillmore West.

The façade at the entrance to the Fillmore East was small, with a large rectangular marquee above it. It covered so much of the sidewalk, in fact, that it provided shade on sunny days or shelter from the rain. Passing through the venue's small entranceway could feel like a scene from *Alice's Adventures In Wonderland*, because it led into something much larger and grander on the inside. Long and narrow, the Fillmore East had a capacity of 2,700, split between three large sections on its main floor and a vast balcony overhead. It had seen many important shows over the past three years, yet by the summer of 1971, Bill Graham was tired and ready to close its doors, along with those of all the other venues he ran.

With the venue's end date set for June 27, Moby Grape arrived in New

York immersed in the hoopla that surrounded their own return, as well as the historic concert hall's final send-off. Ever-present were the cameras and crew from NBC, flittering around, recording everything they could.

Amid all this excitement, if you looked up at the marquee on one of those warm June days, you'd have read the billing as follows:

18–19 B.B. Moby Grape
24 Johnny Edgar
25–27 Allman J. Geils
That's All Folks

For Moby Grape, this was a return, and a possible new beginning.

Writing for *Rock Magazine*, Bud Scoppa sketched this pivotal moment in Moby Grape's history in a vivid piece that appeared in the magazine's August 17 1971 issue. With excitement, Bud captured the band's arrival in town and blistering rehearsal and anticipation before the night show. Then, with sadness, he went on to recount the band's crushing evening show and wonder about Moby Grape's future.

Regarding the reunion, Jerry Miller told Bud Scoppa, 'If it wasn't for Rubinson, it wouldn't have happened. Financial backing and good communication.' About the recordings for the album, he added, 'It's in the can, mostly. We got fifteen tracks.'

Fifteen? I wonder as I read this. What are these *fifteen tracks*? There are only eleven songs on *20 Granite Creek*.

Of the songs the band performed at the rehearsal, Scoppa noted, 'There were a couple things in rehearsal that sounded like they didn't quite click into place.'

'But that won't happen tonight,' Rubinson replied.

'The new stuff sounded really fine today,' Scoppa added optimistically.

'Yeah,' Rubinson agreed. '"Gypsy Wedding" is a killer.'

Asked about the band's future, Rubinson told Scoppa, 'It's taken awhile to get everybody together. And when you've gone through all that it's taken, it appears to me that there's no way to throw it aside. It would be very hard to put three new people in the band.' Then, explaining the rationale behind their early tour, he added, 'We're not gonna make any bread on these gigs, really, except for the weekends after this. But when you come in and you play and the whole band is there, *boom*, you know, the mill starts rolling.'

Awaiting the evening performance, Bud would reflect, 'If the Grape were gonna go over big this weekend—if they were going to make it again as a great rock and roll band, Spence would have to produce. It would be he that audiences would remember if they played well.'

At this moment, Moby Grape stood at a crossroads. They were together again, their future filled with possibility. If their short run of shows at the Fillmore East and Fillmore West proved to be a success, who knew what the future might hold?

It wasn't to be.

In painful detail, Scoppa went on to chronicle the band's night show. 'I suffered a mild form of heartbreak while all this was going on,' he confessed near the end of the article. 'Well, they *were* great in rehearsal, and I can prove it: I made a tape of an hour of it, and it sounds fine to me. Not professional (recording-wise) of course, but it's clear enough to tell that the Grape were playing their asses off at 5:00, even if they lost them at midnight.'

Writing in *The New Rolling Stone Album Guide* thirty-three years later, Scoppa sharply recounts the reunion album and disaster at the Fillmore East again. 'The '71 reunion album *20 Granite Creek* seemed to promise that the band was ready to get back to business, until a disastrous set at the Fillmore East during which Mosley snapped his fingers rather than playing bass and Spence stared into space, arms akimbo, causing the others to leave the stage, one by one, mortified and disgusted.'*

If Moby Grape had fifteen songs in the can by mid-June 1971, as

* Something's tugging at my mind. I can't help but wonder how accurate Bud Scoppa's two accounts of the Grape's return to NYC are. While he's clearly a sympathetic critic, both his reflections draw from his recollections of the events at hand. The reflection in *Rock Magazine* was written within months of his experience with the band, and his piece in *The New Rolling Stone Album Guide* was written over three decades later. Yet memory is elusive. Our long-term memory is fluid, as we sometimes reconfigure memories to fit the context within which we share our memories. We are also prone to reshape our autobiographical memories into proper narratives, compressing, revising, and adding to experiences with conscious and unconscious abandon. Any

Rubinson told Scoppa, then three of the extra four tracks not included on *20 Granite Creek* may have been played at the Fillmore East—Peter Lewis's 'There Is No Reason,' as well as a pair of Skip songs, 'We Don't Know Now' and 'Sailing.'

Don Stevenson remembers 'Sailing.' 'That was a great song,' he tells me. '*Sailing on a sailing ship*,' he recites. 'That was really cool.' When I ask him about Peter's 'There Is No Reason,' he starts to hum the tune. 'I do remember that one,' Don says. He's surprised it isn't on the album. 'Maybe it was a Rubinson choice. Because one of the things we didn't do, which I always liked, was we didn't keep track. You know, no one ever said, OK Bob, you've got three, you don't get anymore. We didn't do that. And some bands do. So leaving some of the songs off the album must've been a choice by Rubinson, or Reprise, because Peter could've had five songs on the album.'

In a recent interview with Raoul Hernandes for the *Austin Chronicle*, Peter Lewis recalled, 'I'd go stay with [Skip] in Santa Cruz and play music all weekend … In the middle of all that, "Sailing" came up in one of our jam sessions, and I wrote this bridge to it, about a guy sitting on a beach looking at the ships. 'Cause Skip could write a hook, he just didn't have any verses. The bridge just sort of finished the song.'

What became of the recordings that were left off *20 Granite Creek*? Do they still exist? Are they safely tucked away in some storage facility? I wonder.

•

time we reshape or misremember our experiences as we recollect things, our ability to recall with accuracy is hindered. It's possible that Bud's memories were, in part, shaped by these influences on memory. On one level, his recall may have been shaped by his *storytelling context*—in the first case, his venue was a music magazine, and in the second case it was a rock encyclopedia. On another level, to tell the story of his experiences with the Grape, Bud fits events into a proper narrative, with characters, a series of events, a setting, a problem, and a resolution—or, *hoped for resolution*. To be honest, I don't *only* wonder about Bud Scoppa's memory. I wonder how memory shapes *everything* I encounter, whether in print or in conversation. I also wonder how memory shapes this book I'm writing—because I'm navigating Moby Grape's past through people's memories, decades after the events unfolded. There's an ever-growing pool of research on aspects of human memory. I direct you to the work of the following researchers: Neil Burgess, Eleanor Maguire, and John O'Keefe; Mark Mayford, Steven A. Siegelbaum, and Eric R. Kandel; Peter S.B. Finnie and Karim Nader; Marya Schechtman; Charlotte Linde; and Elizabeth F. Loftus.

History and myth tell us that the Grape's afternoon rehearsal on June 18 was amazing. Their evening show was notoriously horrendous. Their show the following night was apparently good—not great, but not a disaster. So what happened? Had this return to the stage in New York come too early for the band? Were the band under-rehearsed? Were expectations too high? Was the pressure too much? After all, they had only just started their reunion a couple of months earlier. Would it have been better for Moby Grape to become recording artists first, rather than a performing band?*

Perhaps it was a combination of all these things. Maybe there was something else happening as well. Perhaps Moby Grape had stepped into the plot of Alan Sillitoe's iconic *Loneliness Of The Long-Distance Runner*, with Bob and Skip together taking on the role of Smith, who stops running and stands adamantly at the finish line, refusing to cross it and win the race. New York's Fillmore East *was* a finish line of sorts—and perhaps Skip and Bob, like Smith, just couldn't bring themselves to step over it.

Facing an uncertain future with hope diminishing, Moby Grape flew to San Francisco for their shows at the Fillmore West. After that, they returned to the Santa Cruz Mountains to wrap up their album for Reprise. In these trying times, they finished recording under the guidance and support of David Rubinson.

---

* I have a recording of one of the Grape's Fillmore East shows during that ill-fated June. They played well, if not spectacularly. Amid cheers and applause, Bill Graham excitedly introduces the band. 'It's like being in a time machine,' he says, 'and it's going in the right direction … here is Moby Grape!' The band energetically jumps into revved up renditions of two tracks from their debut, 'Fall On You' and 'Hey Grandma.' Amid calls for '8:05,' they quickly shift into a thumping version of 'Trucking Man,' a staple of their shows in late '68 and early '69. Then, after introducing Gordon Stevens and tuning up their guitars for a moment, they play Peter Lewis's new song 'Apocalypse.' As the show unfolds, the band continues to focus on their Granite Creek material, playing 'Road To The Sun,' 'Roundhouse Blues,' 'Going Down To Texas,' 'Gypsy Wedding,' and even a couple of songs that didn't end up on the album. At the midpoint of the show, Bob sings 'Ode To The Man At The End Of The Bar' a cappella. The audience listens intently, alternatively laughing at Bob's punch lines and cheering on his vocal bravado. The show closes with Skip singing two songs, one old and one new. Once again, 'Omaha' proves to be a showstopper, while 'Sailing' provides a glimpse into a possible future for the band. At the show's end, as the hum of a single guitar's feedback reverberates, the audience claps noisily in excitement and appreciation.

CHAPTER FIVE

'I MET A GUY NAMED STEVE.'

May 2017. It's been seven days since my last meeting with Don. Today, we sit in the same café on Eglinton Avenue to discuss Don's time in Moby Grape. As it turns out, this will be our last conversation devoted to *20 Granite Creek*. This time, it's Don who opens the conversation, and he does so by telling a story.

> Back when we were doing *20 Granite Creek*, I met a guy named Steve. We were at Jerry's, I think. Out of all the houses we had in Boulder Creek, Jerry's house was the most difficult one to get to. He had a private road that went up to his house, and it wound, and turned, and it had bumps and it had potholes. You know, it was like—it was a terrible road. I had my Checker at that point, so it was a little easier for me to get there—well, a lot easier than when I had my MG. I'd say to Jerry, 'Why in the hell don't you do something about that road?' and he'd say, 'I want to keep the bill collectors from getting up here. Only my friends would come up here to see me.' [*Laughs.*]
>
> Sometimes we'd have fried bread for breakfast with his wife, who he used to affectionately call 'My Bride,' and we'd get out our

guitars and start playing. Anyway, one time I was up there and there was this guy called Steve Hope there. He was a videographer. He had a video camera with a battery pack. That was totally unique back then. I'd never seen one before. He'd videotape us and play it back and we'd watch ourselves play and sing. His big dream was to have an exhibit in a room with a wall filled with television screens and then on each of the screens he'd be showing different videos that give snapshots of that time, the late 60s and early 70s—the various movements, and the politics of the time, and protests, and hippie nymphs in a field, and rock'n'roll—you know, all the stuff that was going on at the time. It would be a whole cultural wall of videos. That's what it was supposed to be. And with the technology he had, it was possible.

So we invited him to come down to 20 Granite Creek and film us. He had two dogs—big Dobermans. I liked the guy, but those dogs made me nervous. One day, I can't remember what exactly happened, but his van wasn't there. It had broken down or something. He had his dogs with him, those big Dobermans. He didn't want to let them loose on the property, and he didn't want to tie them up, either, so he asked me if he could keep them in my car, and I said, 'Sure.' It was supposed to be for a short period of time.

We went into the house and we were playing, and when I came back out, those dogs had torn up all my upholstery. They went crazy! They tore up everything. In my Checker! They tore up all my upholstery in my backseat. I had to go to a junkyard to find new pieces for my backseat. When I saw that, I told Steve to take his dogs out of my car, and I told him to get off the property before I exploded. I was ready to explode. So that was the end of Steve filming the sessions. I'd love to see if he still had that footage.

The image of a wall filled with television screens reminds me of Nicolas

Roeg's film with David Bowie, *The Man Who Fell To Earth*. But Roeg's film came out in 1976, five years after *20 Granite Creek*. It sounds like what Steve was planning to do was of its time, I observe, but also ahead of its time.

I ask Don if he has any idea of where that footage is now.

'Not a clue,' he says. 'I wish I did.'

My mind then turns to the postproduction phase of the album, and whether Don was present when it was mixed.

'No,' Don says. 'I think Peter was there, though. But if he was, I certainly don't think he appreciated what was done with "Horse Out In The Rain." That song originally came out amazing. You should've heard it when it was played, and all the parts were equal. And Gordon plays a part in there where his violin just cries.' Don hums the song to himself. 'You know, the viola just weeps. I think Peter was there for a part of the mixing, but maybe not all of it.'

I wonder, then, if there was any form of goodbye when it all ended?

> It didn't end in one fell swoop. It wasn't like the end of *Cheers*. People left one at a time. I remember Bob was disgusted. He got in his truck and left. I think Peter kind of endured it. Whenever we were recording, he endured it. So he was living up in Boulder Creek. He sold his house by that time and left.
>
> You know what? I just remembered something. There was a time when Bobby Moore was staying at Peter's house, when he was out on the road one time. He was one of our road managers. Very cool guy. Peter shot himself in the foot one time, literally, one time when he was out in the woods with Bobby. Bobby would be on a horse and he had his horse trained so that he could shoot his gun to get his horse. Bobby would be out walking with his gun, he was like a woodsman. That's how he got killed. He was chopping down a tree and another one somehow came crashing down around from behind and hit him. So we had a huge wake right at Peter's house for Bobby. It was like an Irish wake. We danced, played, sang, we roasted a whole pig, bikers

were there, everybody was there. It lasted for days. That was right around the time we were making *20 Granite Creek*.

Was there ever an idea to make another album after *20 Granite Creek*, I wonder? 'I think it was, like, *Stick a fork in it, man*,' Don replies. 'Bob was disenchanted. Skip was going off to do something else. It was like Humpty Dumpty. And we've attempted to put Humpty Dumpty together again over the years, but it's been difficult.'

It's too bad it didn't work out, I tell him, before going to explain how *20 Granite Creek* was the second Moby Grape album I bought. It was the band's fifth album, I tell him, but for me—in terms of my own discovery of their music—it was the second. And it's still one of those albums I can easily listen to from start to finish, I say, without ever wanting to fast-forward through a song. It's got brevity and variety, and everyone's playing is on form …

I pause for a moment, and then my mind turns to something that happened to me over twenty years ago. When I lived in Korea, in 1996 and '97, I had a mixtape I made with the first Moby Grape album on one side and *20 Granite Creek* on the other side. One time I left it at a phone booth at the airport. It was in my Sony Walkman. It was right after I got back from a trip to Japan. When I went back to the airport, my Walkman had been turned in to the lost and found, but the tape was gone. I missed the tape, but how could I get mad at someone for taking it?

Returning to the band's story, I suggest to Don that it must've been difficult, breaking up all over again, after everyone went to so much trouble to get back together and write and record again.

'It was.'

We sit in silence for a moment, lost in thought. I gaze out the window. A line of cars is stopped at a standstill on the road outside. Returning my attention to Don and the chronology of events I'm untangling, I ask, finally, if he has any regrets about the reunion. When he replies, he speaks with care.

'There's a lot of stuff that happens but forget about blaming. I'm not going to blame Matthew. I'm not going to blame Skip. I'm not going to blame anyone. Who's to blame? I don't know. Look in the mirror, that's probably the best thing that you can do.'

That's a good philosophy, I tell him.

Looking out of the window, I notice that the traffic on Eglinton Avenue has thinned out and the line of cars is gone. Each one of those cars is heading to a different destination. And this exact configuration of cars will never again form a traffic line in front of this café.

•

Later that evening, I telephone Jerry Miller, to see if he has any more to say about the Grape's shows in May and June 1971.

> I remember more about the early days, to tell you the truth. Back when we were playing in San Francisco. We had a lot of fun anytime we got on stage. I remember one time driving from Marin County to the old Fillmore. I had a '64 Impala, and I was coming over the Golden Gate Bridge, and as soon as I got over the bridge with all my stuff in the trunk, I got a flat tire. So I got down on my hands and knees, and I got all greasy because I had to change that damn flat tire. Then I was running late for the show—and you don't want to be late for Bill Graham. When I got a bit closer, and I'd almost got to the Fillmore, and I had *another* flat tire. So I pulled the car over a few blocks away and I had my amplifier and guitar and I was running down the street with them. That amplifier was heavy! I got in the building and I ran up the stairs with my amp and my guitar—this was in the early days, before we had a roadie. So I made it up those stairs and got all my stuff set up, and instantly, without having time to wash up, I had to jump onstage. I can just imagine people in the audience watching me perform, saying, 'Look at that lucky son of a bitch!' But they didn't know what I went through to get there. I didn't have time to change or anything.

Jerry chuckles, and I find myself laughing with him. I'll bet the audience had no idea what happened, I tell him. 'Not at all,' he laughs.

I ask him what he recalls of mixing and overdubbing the album at Pacific Studios in San Mateo, after returning from the shows in June. 'I do remember we worked there,' he says, 'but I can't remember much about that studio. I don't think I spent much time there.'

Well, I observe, it's getting close to fifty years ago now.

> It's unbelievable how long ago it all was. You know, I remember when I was a kid. People talked about the war, which was over with by that time, in the early 50s. I'd say to people, 'That was such a long time ago.' But it was only ten years ago at that time. And I was ten. I remember exactly, because I was born in '43. I was born on the day my dad invaded Sicily. The Invasion of Sicily was July 10, 1943. I watched it on TV, in a documentary. My dad was in the navy. He worked in underwater demolitions. He'd put that big underwater helmet on his head, you know, underwater deep-sea diver's stuff. All that equipment. He'd get geared up and go put mines on ships. Crazy stuff, you know. But he liked it. And he said that his biggest regret was getting out of the navy. *That* was a real long time ago.

The line goes silent for a few seconds as I consider Jerry's words. Throughout our conversations, I've been asking Don and Jerry to peer into their respective pasts. Some of the images appear clearer than others. One hazy element of the band's reunion is the period where things shifted from the mobile studio at 20 Granite Creek to Pacific, a small recording studio in San Mateo.

Mark Alexander told me he remembers being in the studio when the news of Jim Morrison's death was announced, which was on Friday, July 9, two days after the singer was buried.

> I remember being in the control room at Pacific Studios with some of the band members and David, when we were informed

of Jim Morrison's death. All of us were broken up by the news, and kind of in shock. For some reason, I remember David's reaction most vividly—it hit him extremely hard. With obvious pain in his voice, he said, 'What a waste,' and he went on to lament all the others, such as Jimi and Janis …

•

As the summer of 1971 unfolded, Moby Grape continued to work on their fifth album. In the August 7 issue of *Billboard*, Shirley Lewis Harris reported, 'At Pacific Recording Studios, San Mateo, Catero Sound Co. is finishing new release on Warner Bros of the original Moby Grape.' The album was finalized over July and August, with its release planned for mid-September.

San Mateo is a mid-sized city about sixty miles north of Granite Creek. It takes about an hour and a quarter to reach it when driving north from Santa Cruz. In 1971, Pacific Studios could be found at 1737 El Camino Real, just north of the Highway 92 overpass. Boasting 'wall-to-wall carpeting and theatrical lighting,' according to a contemporary report in *Billboard*, it was the first studio on the San Francisco Peninsula to offer sixteen-track recording facilities.

If creating *20 Granite Creek* was a sort of relay race, then the work at Pacific Studios marked the anchor leg of the trek. Somehow, amid all the chaos and excitement, Moby Grape managed to produce an album that's intricate, eclectic, and fresh.

So we have an album borne out of hope, a work of great promise, and a disaster at the Fillmore East. Numerous questions remain. What will critics say? What will sales be like? How will the future unfold? This was a path Moby Grape had treaded before.

CHAPTER SIX

THE RELEASE

Moby Grape's *20 Granite Creek* was released on Reprise Records in mid-September 1971 to little fanfare, disappointing sales, and mixed reviews. It was a busy month in the music business. Alongside *20 Granite Creek*, albums first released in September 1971 include *Imagine* (John Lennon), *Future Games* (Fleetwood Mac), *Cahoots* (The Band), *Electric Warrior* (T.Rex), *Goin' Back To Indiana* (The Jackson 5), *Harmony* (Three Dog Night), *Santana III* (Santana), *Welcome To The Canteen* (Traffic), *The North Star Grassman And The Ravens* (Sandy Denny), *Rock Love* (Steve Miller Band), *Bark* (Jefferson Airplane), *Ko-Ko Joe* (Jerry Reed), *Look At Yourself* (Uriah Heep), *Pilgrimage* (Wishbone Axe), *Seven Tears* (Golden Earring), *Street Corner Talking* (Savoy Brown), *Talk It Over In The Morning* (Anne Murray), *From The Inside* (Poco), and *Labelle* (Labelle).

On September 18 1971, amid this stack of new releases, *20 Granite Creek* entered the *Billboard* chart at #184.* That week's issue of *Billboard* also included an advertisement for 'Gypsy Wedding,' the single that opens the album.

* A yardstick for record sales success, the *Billboard* album chart initially appeared in 1945, though it was released irregularly until a 'Best-Selling Popular Albums' chart was first published ten years later. While the chart started out at a meager five albums, it soon grew to fifteen and eventually ballooned to thirty, to 150, to 175, to 200.

Drawing from Moby Grape's well-known narrative, the ad read as follows:

> Moby Grape was born with a bang and died with a whimper, but greatness never seemed more than a single or an album away, Moby Grape was reborn with a whisper. The same membership, plus one. The same producer. And greatness within reach in the form of an explosive single, 'Gypsy Wedding' (REP 1040), which is the kickoff for the Grape's greatest album, *20 Granite Creek*, new and now on Reprise.

The following week, *20 Granite Creek* inched up one spot to #183. Disappointing. On October 2, it moved up three more places, to #180, and the next week it climbed to #179. Things could have been worse, but the LP's showing was a letdown nevertheless. On October 16, *20 Granite Creek* reached its zenith: #177. The following week, it disappeared from the *Billboard* 200 altogether. Its five-week run with a peak of #177 was a far cry from the half-year chart runs of the band's first two albums, *Moby Grape* (which peaked at #24) and *Wow* (which peaked at #20). This wasn't the sort of chart action that Reprise wanted. It wasn't what anyone wanted.

20 Granite Creek's showing on *Billboard* was dismal, but context is everything. How well did other acts from the 60s perform on the US charts in 1971? The solo Beatles, The Who, and The Rolling Stones were all doing very well. But what about the others? In terms of the old guard from San Francisco, numerous acts were still active in '71, releasing albums with varying levels of success. Janis Joplin, who sadly passed away the previous autumn, reached #1 with *Pearl*. Jefferson Airplane made it to #11 with *Bark*, and The Grateful Dead climbed to #25 with a self-titled live album, commonly referred to as *Skull And Roses*. With a pleasant surprise, Lee Michaels had his most successful album in 1971, reaching #16 with the simply titled *5th*. A year earlier, he had covered Moby Grape's 'Murder In My Heart For The Judge.' Less successful on *Billboard* were The Steve Miller Band and Quicksilver Messenger Service. The former got to only #82 with their sixth album, *Rock Love*, while the latter managed a high point of #114 with their sixth record, *Quicksilver*. Country Joe & The Fish, who broke up the year before, only got to #111 with their final release, *CJ Fish*.

In terms of sales, then, *20 Granite Creek* put Moby Grape in the lower echelons of San Francisco's old guard. To be fair, though, they weren't the *only* 60s act having a hard time on *Billboard* in 1971. The Byrds might have climbed to #40 with *Byrdmaniax*, but they only made it to #152 with their subsequent release, *Farther Along*. And when The Flying Burrito Brothers put out their self-titled third album in June, it peaked at #176. Hot on the tail of their 1970 hit single 'Lola,' The Kinks' soundtrack to *Percy* didn't even chart, and the country-tinged record *Muswell Hillbillies* only reached #100.

While Moby Grape captured the mellow vibe of country-rock—a sound that was soon to become predominant across the USA—they were far too eclectic to be defined as a country-rock band, although some reviewers did just that. Over the next few weeks, music critics' comments on *20 Granite Creek* would vary wildly.

Although *20 Granite Creek* did not perform well on the *Billboard* 200, the album received a very positive early notice from the magazine in the form of a succinct four-sentence review in its September 11 1971 issue.

> A little bit of rock, a little bit of roll, some acid and an order of chitlins fill this album to the brim with jams from one of the first high energy groups. Moby Grape is all there and streamin' through the jungle at full speed. 'Gypsy Wedding,' 'About Time,' 'Goin' Down To Texas' and 'Wild Oats Moan,' aptly display Grape at its best. There's a lot of nostalgia here, but the music is strictly 1971.

Three divergent responses to the album appeared on September 19 alone: one positive, another mixed, and the third negative. Writing for the *Greenville News*, Jeanne Harrison was upbeat about the album. After discussing new releases by The Who and Joan Biaz, she added, 'Moby Grape's *20 Granite Creek* is also well worth spinning.'

Writing for the *Chicago Tribune*, Lew Harris was also positive, though more reserved, describing the album as 'a bad case of Procolharumitis. Much of the album is quite good, especially "Roundhouse Blues," which sounds like something unearthed from the Sun record files, but it's just another case of a top-sounding group that has turned itself into just another band of rock'n'rollers.'

Finally, in the *Philadelphia Inquirer*, Jack Lloyd gave a scathing two-sentence assessment of the album. 'Moby Grape, which never quite made the grade as a top rock group and then split up a couple of years ago, is together again on a new Reprise album titled *20 Granite Creek*. Unfortunately, the LP does not offer anything worth getting excited about.'

Two days later, a positive review of the album appeared in the *Miami News*, with reporter Susan Bring noting, 'It is rare that a group breaks and then reforms; but the quality within the Moby Grape allows them the latitude to experiment and pick up together again smoothly.'

The *Los Angeles Times* review of *20 Granite Creek*, which appeared on October 17, was the most cutting of all. Reviewer James Brown starts off negatively, and then things quickly go from bad to worse. He opens by making a general comment about the notion of rock band reunions, and of playing country-flavored music. 'If there's one thing the world doesn't need, it's a reformed rock band gone country. That, unfortunately, is what the Moby Grape has become.' In Brown's mind, Moby Grape had gone from a once-great act to a complete mess. 'From San Francisco's hip-rock underground of the late 60s, the Grape has been miraculously transformed into a third-rate imitation of a group trying to imitate the Band.' Summing up, he sees their new album as a document of the shamble they have become. '*20 Granite Creek* has such little originality and interest going for it that it finally becomes a game to see how much alike each and every song sounds. For the technicalities, the musicianship is competent, the vocals are dreadful, and one song, "Apocalypse," is passable. A waste—J.B.'*

With the gracefulness of a yin-yang symbol, *Rolling Stone* offered a very

* When I tell Don about this review, he breaks out laughing. 'We can be criticized for a lot of things,' he says, 'but having all our songs sound the same isn't one of them.'

different review, awarding the album five stars in its October 14 issue. This review wasn't just *very different*—it was the complete opposite of the one in the *Los Angeles Times*. In his lengthy review, Robert Meltzer—who would go on to co-write songs for Blue Öyster Cult—is bursting with compliments. Regarding 'Ode To The Man At The End Of The Bar,' he writes, 'It's fast and almost happy and either way it's one of the swellest drinking songs in the history annaldom … you know the story, it's happened to you, it's happened to me, it's happened to all of us.' Of Peter's bouncy travel-song 'Goin' Down To Texas,' he adds, 'He's going with the girl that he just met, they're gonna see her family *in her new Corvette*! That's all right.' But he saves his best comments for Skip Spence. 'The longest terrific amazing cut is also the only Skip Spence cut on the album. Skip's never done a bad cut and if you count all the cuts on his own *Oar* that's an awful lot of cuts.' Near the end of the review, Meltzer pines for a copy of Scoppa's Grail-like bootleg of Moby Grape's famed New York rehearsal. 'It would be a real treat if someone got ahold of Bud Scoppa's real tentacle of a tape of the Grape's pre-Fillmore practices session.'

Unfortunately for Moby Grape, this sparkling review would not boost sales. Besides, by the time the October 14 issue of *Rolling Stone* hit newsstands, the band had already split up—again.

•

Over the years, retrospective reviews of the album have been positive. Reviewing the album for *The Village Voice* in the fall of 1971, Robert Christgau initially gave the album a B- rating. Ten years later, however, when re-evaluating the album for his book, *Rock Albums of the 1970s: A Critical Guide*, he raised his score to a B+. In his 1981 review, Christgau states, 'At first I thought this reunion album lacked magic, but these guys sound remarkably whole for a band that failed to take over the world in 1967. You can hear the country undertone now, but you can also hear why you missed it—at their most lyrical these guys never lay back, and lyricism is something they're usually rocking too hard to bother with, though their compact forms guarantee poetic justice.' Sounding wistful about the band, he adds, 'Full of hope as they foresee their doom, stoned and drunk and on the move and yet always together, and above all intense, they should have at least taken over the country. All they really lacked was a boss, and what could be more American than that?'

Currently, the album holds a sparkling four-and-a-half-star rating on allmusic.com, the leading music guide of today, where critic Matthew Greenwald states:

> By the end of the 60s the Grape was all but finished—or so everyone thought. After an aborted attempt at a Peter Lewis solo album, producer David Rubinson was able to help engineer this reformation of all five original members, along with extra member Gordon Stevens on various stringed instruments. Written and recorded at the Grape's communal house in the Santa Cruz mountains, the results of the experiment rendered *20 Granite Creek*, an album that is rightfully the successor to the first album …
>
> One of the most shining examples is Peter Lewis's funky and fast 'Goin' Down To Texas,' which clearly illustrates the power Moby Grape had in this, one of the original three-guitar lineups. Skip Spence, who was one of the more interesting writers in the band, contributes one song, the delicate and gorgeous oriental-sounding 'Chinese Song.'
>
> Of course, it didn't sell anything. A true crime in a never-ending saga.

While the initial reviews for the album were mixed, the likes of Melzer, Christgau, Scoppa, and Greenwald have all subsequently agreed that *20 Granite Creek* is a worthy album. Yet critical success doesn't sell units, and nor for that matter does it keep a band together. As another critic, Dave Stephens, deftly observed in 2016, 'The good news was that the magic was back, and the bad news: no one took any interest.'

CHAPTER SEVEN

AFTERMATH

Early autumn 1971. A lot has happened over the past few months. In June, the USA ended it trade embargo on China, the last fifteen members of the group Indians of All Tribes (IAT) were forcibly removed from Alcatraz Island after a nineteen-month occupation, the *New York Times* began to publish the Pentagon Papers, and the first Hard Rock Café opened in London, England. The following month, the UK increased its troop count in Northern Ireland to 11,000, construction on 2 World Trade Center was completed, and the Apollo 15 mission was launched. Also, a security guard was murdered at a Who concert and Jim Morrison died in Paris. In August, George Harrison oversaw the Concert for Bangladesh; and, amid outbreaks of violence, thousands fled Belfast and Derry for the Republic of Ireland. That same month, the first gay rights demonstration was held in Canada, on Parliament Hill, and King Curtis was murdered in New York …

Moby Grape's reunion wound up in August 1971. By December, the members of the band had scattered once again to pursue their own individual paths. After the release of *20 Granite Creek*, Skip Spence formed a new band, The Yankees. In 1972, they recorded two songs by Spence at Pacific Studios, 'All My Life (I Love You)' and 'The Space Song.' Over the years, he would dabble with the band Epicenter, but he generally moved away from music. Collaborating with San Jose musician Brian Vaughn, he would make a late return to songwriting in the 90s, when commissioned to record a song for the album *Songs In The Key Of X: Music From And Inspired By The X-Files*. While the hypnotic 'Land Of The Sun' wasn't included on the album, it would later be released on *More Oar: A Tribute To The Skip Spence Album*, which boasts a diverse cast, including Tom Waits, Robert Plant, Mudhoney, Robyn Hitchcock, and Beck. By the time of its release, however, Spence had passed away, having lost his battle with lung cancer on April 16, 1999, two days shy of his birthday.

Gordon Stevens returned his attention to his family music store, Stevens Music, as well as his jazz playing and other projects. He opened a recording studio in San Jose, Open Path Music, and remained musically active in a wide variety of ways over the years.

Peter Lewis set aside his plans for a solo album until 1995, when *Peter Lewis* was released. In the early 2000s he joined The Electric Prunes, appearing on *Artifact* in 2001. Two years later, he released a live album with David West entitled *Live In Bremen*, with a second live collaboration between the two, *Live At The Lobero Theater*, following a decade later. Today, he performs regularly with his daughter, having appeared on her self-titled debut album, *Arwen*, in 2015. He released his fourth album, *Just Like Jack*, in 2017.

When Bob Mosley left the Grape, he returned to the Red Noodle nightclub in Hawaii and resumed playing with his own band, Snake Leg. He recorded a solo album for Reprise with his band in 1972, but the resulting *Bob Mosley*—a powerful performance with support from the Memphis Horns—failed to chart. The following year, he formed the Darrow Mosley Band with Chris Darrow, recording three demos and sending them out to record companies.* While the sampler failed to generate interest at the time, it would eventually be released decades later as the *Desert Rain* EP. Later in the 70s, Bob recorded an entire album's worth of songs with members of

* Chris Darrow played in Kaleidoscope and The Nitty Gritty Dirt Band prior to his short-lived collaboration with Bob Mosley. Both bands shared the bill with Moby Grape in the late 60s.

The Crickets and Elvis Presley's backing band.* Unfortunately, these songs would also remain unheard for nearly a quarter of a century, until they were put out as *Never Dreamed* in 1999.

Throughout the summer of 1977, Mosley played with Neil Young in The Ducks, alongside Jeff Blackburn (guitar) and Johnny Craviotto (drums), playing shows in and around Santa Cruz. Over the next few decades, he released two albums, *Live At The Indigo Ranch* (1989) and *True Blue* (2006).

When I ask Don about Bob's first album, he tells me:

> I love 'Gone Fishing.' He never uses that voice. If I knew he had that voice I would've said to Bob, 'Don't start at 10. Start out at, like, 3, or 4. Use that voice because you can. Then go up another octave.' It's mellow and raspy. Fantastic. Then, at the end of that song, he goes up into his powerful mode. I mean, a lot of those songs on there are great. With those horns.† 'The Joker,' which opens the album, is awesome. He has kind of an Otis Redding show band thing going on, like Sam & Dave.

Jerry Miller stayed in Boulder Creek, biding his time and plotting his next musical venture. He reemerged in 1972, first with The Jerry Miller Rock Ensemble, then with Swiftly To Loose, and finally with Miller-East. These three outfits would all play in California and Reno throughout 1972. Miller later formed The Jerry Miller Band, and over the years has released *Now I See* (1993), *Life Is Like That* (1995), and *Live At Coles* (1998). More recently, he contributed his distinctive lead guitar to *This Is My Love*, the 2014 debut album by Open Blue, a band led by his son, Joseph Miller. During the course of our conversations for this book in 2016 and 2017, he was playing weekly gigs in and around Seattle and Tacoma while completing a new solo album.

---

* From 1969 to Elvis's passing, James Burdon was lead guitarist and leader of the TCB Band. Glen D. Hardin played keyboards with the band from '70 to '76, arranging numerous songs along the way.

† 'Those horns' are played by the Stax Records icons The Memphis Horns.

After *Granite Creek*, Don Stevenson spent some time living on 8th Avenue in Santa Cruz.

> We had the open flea market. That's where I was with Mary after we left Granite Creek. I played with Swiftly To Loose, with Jerry. I was the drummer in Swiftly To Loose. We were with the rhythm player from Steve Miller's old band. And we had an amazing violin player. We played some great stuff. It was in early '72. After Swiftly To Loose, I worked the summer with my friend Mark Alexander. His uncle Pete owned a concession company. We worked fairs all around California. I traveled the fairs and slept in my Checker. I bought the Checker Cab with some of the money I got from Reprise. It was an amazing car. It had a Warner Gear three-speed manual transmission, it had sixteen-gauge sheet metal, and a great big Chevy engine in it. It was indestructible.

In late 1972, Don returned to Washington State, where he formed a gospel band. He played with Holy Smoke into the late 80s. In 2010, nearly forty summers after *20 Granite Creek*, he released his first solo album, *King Of Fools*. Produced by Gordon Stevens, the album was recorded at Open Path Music, with contributions from Gordon and Jerry Miller. I caught many of Don's shows around Toronto throughout 2017, during which time he was putting the finishing touches to his second solo album.

Meanwhile, David Rubinson continued to work with Bill Graham, with Fillmore Incorporated growing into San Francisco Records and Fillmore Records. Five years after *20 Granite Creek*, he built a recording studio, the Automatt. Over the years, he produced a great many artists, including Herbie Hancock, Santana, Patti Labelle, The Pointer Sisters, and Taj Mahal. Along the way, he continued to collaborate with engineer Fred Catero, yet as far as his collaborations with Moby Grape are concerned, that path had reached an end. In 1982, David suffered a massive heart attack that prompted him to step away from the music business. He moved to the south of France in 2009, and today pursues permaculture.

•

20 Granite Creek started out as a new beginning, but it quickly became an ending. By the autumn of 1971, the hopes of everyone involved had extinguished as Moby Grape split apart for a second time. Yet, as before, their story wasn't quite finished.

As 1971 neared its end, the temperature in the Santa Cruz Mountains dropped. While the members of Moby Grape had once again scattered to pursue their own musical paths, they would never truly be apart. Over the next few decades, they would somehow manage to reform in a variety of configurations, all of which took place amid courtroom dramas and life crises. It's as though the band was a phenomenon of nature—something that splits apart but then somehow naturally draws itself back together again. Sometimes, when that happened, they would rekindle their old magic, reminding people of what the all the fuss was about back in '66 and '67.

Peter, Jerry, and Bob toured together throughout 1974 with Jeff Blackburn (guitar) and John Carviotto (drums).* Two years later, Jerry and Bob worked with Michael Been on guitar and John Carviotto to record *Fine Wine*. In 1977 and '78, Peter and Jerry performed with Cornelius Bumpus (saxophone), John Oxendine (drums), and Chris Powell (bass). They even had Bob at one show, and Skip at a few others. Skip contributed one song to *Live Grape* (1978), which was recorded at the Shady Grove and the Inn Of The Beginning. The album doesn't feature the name Moby Grape anywhere on its packaging, however, because by the late 70s, not for the first time, ownership of the band's name was in dispute.

In the early 80s, Moby Grape reconnected for yet another reunion—this

* Moby Grape's May 8 concert at Ebbets Field in Denver was released over four decades later (with recordings taken from a KLMF-FM broadcast) as *Ebbets Field* (Keyhole Records, 2017). The liner notes for this release feature a 1974 article published in *Zigzag*. While the notes do not identify an author, the piece offers a fascinating glimpse into the band's status in terms future hopes and current litigation (over ownership of the name Moby Grape, and royalties), three years after *20 Granite Creek*, two years after Bob's solo album, and one year after a court decision that ruled in favor of Matthew Katz.

time, surprisingly, with ex-manager Matthew Katz's involvement—though Don and Jerry would appear on only one track, with Skip participating only as a composer. The album borne out of this project is called *Moby Grape '84*.

By the end of the decade, the band had reconvened yet again for another reunion album, as well as multiple short tours on the West Coast. Because of heightened legal conflicts over such things as royalties and the ownership of the band's name, however, the band members once again refrained from using the name 'Moby Grape' on the album, instead calling themselves and the record *The Melvilles*.

This period of activity continued into the early 90s. Over the next quarter-century, Moby Grape would play in a variety of venues, including New York's famous (and now defunct) Wetlands and Austin's bustling SXSW festival. Yet their recording and touring work has been sporadic. After Skip Spence passed away in 1999, his son Omar would occasionally take his place in the band. Around a decade after Skip's passing, the band recorded an album of fifteen songs, new and old. It remains unreleased.

•

It *was* a retreat, of sorts. In the Santa Cruz Mountains, Moby Grape moved away from the fluorescent lights and vast rooms of the recording studio and tried to tap into a communal, back-to-the-country atmosphere in their rented home at 20 Granite Creek. Yet it was far more than an exercise in communalism. It was rock's first full-on reunion album.

For nearly fifty years, *20 Granite Creek* has been a lost chapter in the Moby Grape story. It's not only a part of Moby Grape's larger narrative but a sharp demarcation line between the band's late-60s and early-70s iterations. *Granite Creek* is itself a full story, a tale of hope, talent, excitement, conflict, and disappointment.

Contemplating the spirit of *Granite Creek*, Don reflects, 'It was kind of hopeful. We had a feeling that maybe something good could happen. On one level, we felt that nothing was going to happen, but we also had this hope—a feeling that something good *could* happen.'

•

Granite Creek is a success and a failure. It's a rebirth and a re-death. It's at once a triumph and a disaster. The album is a powerful and richly varied sequence of songs, and, clocking in at under thirty-three minutes, it's a tight work, too. Although it has oscillated in and out of print over the years, its place in rock history is assured, just as Moby Grape's place is assured.

Musicians from Bruce Springsteen to Chrissie Hynde to Burton Cummings and Randy Bachman to Beck to Black Rebel Motorcycle Club to The Black Crowes to Robert Plant sing the praises of Moby Grape. These folks aren't stingy with their praise, either. And, when they perform live, they sometimes treat their fans to their own personal favorite Moby Grape song.*

After I started working on this book, Burton Cummings called me to talk about Moby Grape. Back in August 1968, The Guess Who performed with Moby Grape at the Canadian National Exhibition in Toronto. It was a time when The Guess Who were young and impressionable, and Moby Grape were famous. During our conversation, Burton says, 'They're really loved by musicians, particularly guitar players. When I mention Moby Grape to people when I'm traveling, I notice that a lot of guitar players love that band.'†

•

For Moby Grape, *20 Granite Creek* was about recovering something that had been lost. Yet by the time the album was released, it had been lost again. The album is the story of a small group of young men who struggled to work together, make music, and make something of their future. This struggle mostly took place in a big house, tucked away in the Redwood

* Bruce Springsteen sometimes performs 'Omaha' at shows, and writes in his memoir that the band are 'one of Steve's and my all-time favorite groups.' Chrissie Hynde performs 'Murder In My Heart For The Judge' regularly at shows. Burton Cummings and Randy Bachman performed '8:05' on their 2006 CBC television special, *First Time Around*. While Beck has covered Skip Spence's entire *Oar* album, the Black Rebel Motorcycle Club have covered 'I Am Not Willing' numerous times. Over the years, Robert Plant has covered four Moby Grape and Skip Spence songs, including, '8:05,' 'Naked, If I Want To,' 'Little Hands,' and 'Skip's Song/Seeing.'

† My interview with Burton Cummings was conducted on December 24 2016.

covered mountains of Northern California. In a sense, Moby Grape's time in Santa Cruz is a repeat and a magnification of their San Francisco years. Yet it's more than that. It's an ending of sorts, because the band would never again function with their original lineup.

Moby Grape's story is far larger than the narrative you've just read. As intriguing as *20 Granite Creek* is, it's really the band's second act—a denouement of sorts. The second part of this book tells the story of Moby Grape's first act—their meteoric rise and heartbreaking fall. The tale of Moby Grape's genesis, their stunning debut, and their difficult path from San Francisco to the end of the road in Nashville, Tennessee …

PART TWO

MOBY GRAPE

THE ARK, THE BALLROOMS, THE PLACE AND THE TIME: THE FIRST RISE AND FALL OF MOBY GRAPE

CHAPTER EIGHT

ON THE ARK

The story of Moby Grape's first rise and fall is a tale of five musical alchemists in late-60s San Francisco. It's also an epic tragedy. In literature, tragic heroes are people who achieve a certain modicum of greatness but are capable of more. Somehow, somewhere on their path, they make an error of judgment. Sometimes they make a series of errors. Ultimately, this error—or, series of errors—leads to their downfall. As you read about Moby Grape's first incarnation, keep this idea in mind. Don't let go of it. But don't fixate on it either, because there's much more to the band's story.

Something else we need to keep in mind is the matter of myth. We use myths to explain the world around us—our customs, our histories, even nature itself. Sometimes a myth reveals something about our humanity, and other times it focuses on the physical world. Myths are popular stories, and they are old stories—and, because they carry the weight of received wisdom, they are often held to be true. Yet they are not factually true. While myths may convey certain general truths about humanity, they are not true in terms of pure fact.

Entangled within the Moby Grape narrative are many myths. We have received wisdom and mythology, and we also have the actual events themselves. Additionally, we have multiple perspectives of these things from different people who saw or experienced them, as well as our own interpretation of those perspectives. It's complicated, but that's what makes it so interesting. Where do the myths end, and where does reality begin? And what can we learn from the myths themselves? Keep pondering these questions as you read on.

•

Let's start at the beginning, or at least *a* beginning: the moment the members of Moby Grape signed their management contract on a ferryboat in a popular Sausalito harbor, most likely on September 8 1966.

A little over a month earlier, The Beatles had released their most experimental and eclectic album to date, *Revolver*. On August 29, they performed their final proper concert at Candlestick Park, in San Francisco. A few days after that, Alabama governor George C. Wallace signed into law a bill that would put the state on a collision course with the country's policies on desegregating public schools. And on September 6, Hendrik Verwoerd, South Africa's prime minister and the architect of apartheid, was stabbed to death in Cape Town.

That same day, September 8 1966, was proclaimed by UNESCO, an international organization based in Paris, France, to be International Literacy Day—a date to be celebrated worldwide from hereon. And at 8:30pm that evening, a new science-fiction program would make its debut on NBC-TV. Its first episode depicted an away team visiting a research station on planet M-113 run by Professor Robert Crater and his wife Nancy. The away team's doctor had a relationship with Nancy many years ago, and instead of seeing her in her present, aging form, he envisions her as she appeared in the youthful beauty of the distant past. It is as though he is hallucinating. Something is amiss. Eventually, the team discovers that Nancy is a shape-shifting alien, desperate and lonely. She injures and kills numerous crewmembers before coming face to face with the doctor, who nervously points his weapon at her.

The episode was titled 'The Man Trap,' and the show itself was called

Star Trek. It went on to run on NBC for three more years, with its final episode showing on June 3 1969. Moby Grape had broken up five days earlier, after completing their final recording session on May 29 1969, in Nashville, Tennessee.

September 8 1966 was a warm day in San Francisco, marking the end of a long cold spell in the city. From July 13 to September 7, the city experienced fifty-seven consecutive days of cooler-than-average temperatures. Against the odds, every day of August dipped below the average low.

That afternoon, five musicians made their way from various points in the Bay Area to Waldo Point Harbor, at the northern end of Richardson Bay. The harbor is about ten miles north of the well-known Haight-Ashbury district, a trip that takes approximately fifteen or twenty minutes, depending on traffic. As the musicians drove from their various homes, heading northward on the Golden Gate Bridge, they would have passed Alcatraz Island, jutting out of the bay on the right. Beyond the bridge, their route would veer gently to the right as Highway 101 runs through the greenery of Golden Gate National Park.

During World War II, Sausalito's waterfront had been used as a construction site for Liberty ships. In the decade that immediately followed the war, Waldo Point Harbor transformed into a floating home marina. In time, as San Francisco became the hub of the beat generation, the marina attracted a small artistic community. And on this September afternoon in 1966, bobbing up and down in the harbor, or shifting in the mud, was a small fleet of crafts—houseboats, barges, and even a large sidewheel ferryboat. This ferry, known as the Ark, had become a music club, gathering place of sorts—though it wasn't originally designed for this purpose.

Before the Richmond-San Rafael Bridge, which stands to the north of San Francisco, was built, a small fleet of ferryboats chugged across the northern edge of the San Francisco Bay, shepherding passengers back and forth from Richmond to San Rafael. Commissioned in 1915 and completed the following year, the SS *Charles van Damme* was the first to carry cars, cattle, and people between the two cities. Near the end of the

Great Depression, however, the ferry was laid up, and, eighteen years later, in 1956, it was decommissioned. A salvage company purchased the boat and stripped it for parts, such as its brass fittings, the following year. In 1959, Dolon Arques bought the boat at auction and had it brought to Waldo Point Harbor in Sausalito.

In 1960, flamboyant restaurateur Juanita Musson transformed the first floor of the ferry into an eatery. For a few short years, it became a hub of sorts, attracting a variety of celebrities who traveled north of the Golden Gate Bridge as they caroused following late-night performances in San Francisco. Some of the luminaries who passed through Juanita's Gallery include Robert Mitchum, Joseph Cotton, and Noel Coward. Also known to frequent the restaurant were The Smothers Brothers, The Kingston Trio, and Jonathan Winters. Yet Juanita's business sense did not match her jovial nature, and after three short years the Internal Revenue Agency seized the restaurant due to an accumulation of back-taxes owed to the government.

For the next three years, the ferry sat slowly deteriorating at Gate 6. But while the SS *Charles van Damme* was down, it certainly wasn't out. In 1966, the ferryboat once again opened its doors, this time refurbished and transformed into a nightclub. As a performance venue, the Ark featured a variety of established and up-and-coming stars as performers or guests, including Santana, Janis Joplin, Bob Dylan, and Jimi Hendrix. Otis Redding also performed here—and he was in Sausalito when he wrote the infectious classic '(Sittin' On) The Dock Of The Bay.' The boat was once again a destination point—for California and for international artists alike. Yet it was also very much a local hub. In its short lifetime, the Ark hosted 'battle of the bands' competitions for nearby high schools, and its blending of amateurs with rock royalty gave the venue a distinctive aura in the San Francisco scene. The band at the center of this book personifies this uniqueness, so it's unsurprising that their story entangles itself with the history of the Ark.

For a time, during the autumn of '66, the artist Jim Mazzeo did the lighting for numerous Moby Grape shows on the ferryboat club. When I spoke to him in 2017, he described the layout as follows.*

> It was dark. The floor was not level because it was a ferryboat that was dragged up on the mud. Sometimes the mud would get two or three feet of high tide water around it, and it would almost look like a boat! But most of the time it was smelly old mud, and sludge. It had sort of a walkway, a gangplank that you'd take from the mud. When you went inside it was real dark, it was kind of a low ceiling, it wasn't high, maybe a nine-foot-high ceiling—which is high for a boat, but not very high for a concert hall, or a light show, or any of that stuff. It held about—I don't know if it held more than a hundred people. Most of the time there was twenty or thirty people in there. Most of the bands that were playing in town, and after they finished their gig they'd take the bridge over to Sausalito and go over and jam with a bunch of cool local musicians, and they'd get free food in the morning. So, whoever was in town, they'd be done by eleven o'clock, and boom—they'd be over to the Ark. And the doors would open at about ten, eleven o'clock and it was just starting to get rolling. We didn't serve booze, so we just would stay open till about three or four, until there was nobody around anymore.
>
> So it was dark and it was wide, because ferryboats are wide—

* I conversed with Jim Mazzeo multiple times throughout 2017. All quotations from Jim throughout the book draw from our conversations and correspondences. To read about Jim and view some of his art, I direct you to his website, jamesmazzeoartworks.com. At one point, Jim told me about something that happened in the autumn of '66 that doesn't quite fit into the main text, so I'm including it here: 'Did I tell you about the day Bob Mosley and Skippy Spence and I went driving through Haight-Ashbury to buy some weed? As we were driving down Haight Street in front of a bakery the bakery blew up. We had just bought three ounces of really good pot, but when the bakery blew up we got stopped in traffic right in front of the exploded building with glass from the windows all on the street in front of us. We couldn't go anywhere, so Skippy said the cops are going to be here any minute and we better get rid of this weed. He and Mosley and I decided it was time to eat it, and we ate about half an ounce by the time the cops got there. But they didn't stop us or look in the car to question us. They just told us to drive on out of there and leave, so we did, of course. Thirty minutes later, as we digested the weed we ate, we all got really, really high—like being underwater for eight hours. They had to go back and play, and I had to go back and do my light show for them. And we were *whacked out*!'

> they've got to be thirty or thirty-five feet wide. It was probably about nine hundred square feet, maybe a thousand square feet on the first floor. There was an upstairs area, which had offices. And on the third floor there was a wheelhouse way up at the top. The caretaker, this guy Brian McMahon, slept up in the wheelhouse.

A small venue, the Ark often hosted performances from late evening to dawn. Generally, shows ran from 9pm to 2am, and 2am to 6am, when a *huevos rancheros* breakfast was served to weary but hungry customers—both performers and spectators. While musicians were rarely paid for performing, those who undertook the 2–6am shift received a complimentary breakfast. On some weekends, matinee shows ran from early afternoon to dinnertime.

The Ark was never a desired *endpoint*. It was a place to start out and make a name for oneself, before reaching for larger, more lucrative venues, such as the Avalon Ballroom or Fillmore Auditorium. These thoughts must have crossed the minds of the five musicians from Moby Grape as they sat at their table inside the dimly lit Ark on that warm Thursday afternoon.

Within a few weeks of this meeting, this ambitious and eclectic group of musicians would become a virtual house band at the Ark, writing and rehearsing a set of songs that they'll go on to record the following spring on an album that will later earn the band critical accolades and cult status.

Thinking back to the band's early days at the Ark, Bob fondly recalls, 'It was a fun time. We played there constantly, every night. And we played original material, which was our first chance to do that in a club setting. It was a lot of fun, doing that.'

The songs written, arranged, and refined in the Ark collectively form what's regarded by some to be one of—if not *the*—best albums to come out of San Francisco in the 60s—or ever. But notions of forming a stellar set list and getting a record contract were still only dreams for these five young musicians as they sat laughing and chatting at their table.

While they sat there, a tall, slightly heavyset man with longish hair and a trim, slightly Van Dyke–style goatee sauntered into the Ark and looked around. Striding over to the table carrying a stack of papers, he set the papers down and began to speak with the musicians about their content. The musicians signed the papers and shook hands with the man. The papers outlined a personal management contract that would bind the group to this man, their new manager, Matthew Katz, who in recent months had arranged their first rehearsal in his office, as well as their upcoming stint at this Sausalito club.

Little did anyone know at the time, these musicians would become an underground sensation in a matter of weeks. Little did anyone realize, the band would soon be wooed by a contingent of record-company executives. These five musicians would have been pleasantly surprised to hear that day that the following spring they will briskly record an album that will become a cult classic. Yet they'd be troubled, too, to hear that they will sign a problematic addendum to their management contract in the autumn, and acrimoniously split with their manager within a year. And they'd be distressed to hear that the agreement they've just signed—along with its subsequent addendum—will lead to decades of disagreements and courtroom battles.

Recalling the contract *addendum* nearly three decades later, Peter Lewis told Jud Cost that Katz had turned up at the Ark with a document that stated that he owned the name Moby Grape, although he said this was only necessary so that he could 'do business' on the band's behalf. An argument ensued, Lewis recalled, but the band ended up signing the document—largely, he said, because 'the threat was that if we didn't sign it, that was the end of his paying for the [band members'] apartments. And we couldn't have gone on without that.'*

* 'Matthew was renting an apartment for Skippy and Bob on Sacramento Street for a lot of money—$250 a month—which enabled Bob to stay and do his thing,' Lewis told Cost. 'And he was taking care of Jerry and Don, too. I didn't need it because I had this insurance policy that gave me $10,000 when I turned twenty-one, so I could get out of Hollywood and not be Loretta Young's son anymore, but Peter Lewis. And it was my money that kept the band from having to get other jobs to survive.'

According to Lewis, while all of this was going on, Neil Young was sitting playing his guitar in a corner across from the band. 'I think Neil knew, even then, that this was the end. We had bought into this process that we should have known better [than] to buy into. Matthew brought the spirit of conflict into the band. He didn't want it to be an equal partnership. He wanted it all.'

If signing their management contract and then signing the contract addendum represented a beginning of sorts—no matter how many complications that paperwork would precipitate—then the band's initial formation process marked the true beginning of the band—their zero point. Yet for Moby Grape, like all other bands, there is no absolute zero point. Moby Grape's beginning isn't a singular event. It can't be. After all, no single event exists in isolation. In Buddhist philosophy, this is called *pratityasamutpada*. It's sometimes called *dependent arising*. Within the Buddhist principle, all *dharmas*, or things, are borne in a state of dependence. Within this dynamic, physical states and mental states are endlessly shaped by preceding conditions, interactions, and relationships. Moby Grape's origin is no different. The Grape's formation didn't occur at one precise moment in time, but rather it unfolded over an ongoing period.

NORTHBOUND DREAM

It's September 1965. The Vietnam War continues. With more and more troops being sent into combat, the US Marine Corps announces it will reduce the length of training of new recruits from twelve to eight weeks. Following this significantly shorter boot camp, troops will be flown to Vietnam at a much faster rate. Four days after this announcement, the word 'hippie' enters the American lexicon via the *San Francisco Examiner*, journalist Michael Fallon becoming the first person to use the word in print, in a piece focusing on the Haight-Ashbury neighborhood.*

In three months' time, promoter Bill Graham will rent a building at the intersection of Geary Boulevard and Fillmore Street and call it the Fillmore Auditorium. On that December evening, it'll house a benefit for the San Francisco Mime Troupe, the radical theater group Graham is managing. Further north down the steep hill of Fillmore Street, past Sutter Street, California Street, and Sacramento Street, beyond Pacific, Broadway, and Vallejo, something else is already brewing.

This part of town is largely residential, with old homes on both sides of the street, most of them built around the turn of the century. Sprinkled between them are numerous shops and businesses, and sprouting out of

* For more on the emergence of the term 'hippie,' see Sarah Hill's *San Francisco & The Long 60s*.

some concrete slabs on the sidewalks are differently sized trees, adding a touch of greenery to this urban scene.

On the right side of the street—the east side—is a medium-sized building, some sort of performance space, located at 3138 Fillmore. The building itself is relatively small—much smaller than the city's larger ballrooms, which will also soon become landmarks in America's growing counterculture scene. To the right of the entrance is a small cabinet bearing concert handbills, advertising upcoming shows and bands at the club. Over the next few years it will bear such local names as Big Brother & The Holding Company, Quicksilver Messenger Service, Sopwith Camel, Country Joe & The Fish, It's A Beautiful Day, and The Chambers Brothers. Then, after establishing a homegrown cartel of sorts, it will expand its performance roster to include bands from farther away: The Steve Miller Blues Band, The Sparrow (Steppenwolf), The Doors, and Electric Flag. Of course, it will become most closely associated with the band at the center of its creation: the Jefferson Airplane.

The club consists of one large room, about eighty feet long, without a lobby or front foyer. The lighting throughout is dim, except for the small stage area at the front, where it shines intensely, the focal point amid a barrage of music, smoke, and the hum of multiple conversations all happening at once. The ceiling is nearly twenty feet high at the back, but closer to the tiny stage at the front it seems to dip to about eight or ten feet. The layout of the club will later be remodeled, but in mid-September 1965, the entire back part of the room is an open dance floor, and closer to the stage the floor is littered with small cocktail tables. Along the left wall is a mural of the Four Horsemen of the Apocalypse—all carrying musical instruments. (Some will say that the artwork was painted by Jefferson Airplane, but no one seems to know this for sure.)

Soon, this place, the Matrix, will be a landmark of the San Francisco scene—a place where bands will play for a weekend at a time or weeklong stints with shows often fusing together folk, rock, and other genres. The club and its design and format will help bands advertise, attract a local following, and polish their material and performance. This isn't a place for poetry readings, sipping espresso, and sitting on stools on the stage. Not exactly. With its bar and a small legion of cocktail tables, it *could* be such a place, but it's altogether something different. It's an intimate space yet it's removed from what the San Francisco nightlife has offered in the past. It's something closer to the popular Red Dog Saloon, which opened a few years earlier in Virginia City, Nevada.

In a matter of months, the Matrix will quickly become a popular hangout for young writers, artists, fans, and musicians themselves in and around the Bay Area. And a few years later, in late 1971, Hunter Thompson will immortalize the club in a comical flashback sequence in his gonzo travelogue *Fear & Loathing In Las Vegas.**

The Matrix is San Francisco's newest club. Not long ago, before it was renovated, it was a pizza shop. Then one of those local musicians, Marty Balin, teamed up with some investors to transform it into a performance space. Gone are the old tables and chairs, the countertop and cash register, and all the old remnants of its days as a pizza parlor.

Marty is quite happy with all that. After all, he owns a quarter of the club, and his new group, the Jefferson Airplane, have become the house band. Yet despite the great turnout at the club, he can't relax. His mind is occupied. His band needs a new drummer—not just any drummer but someone to fit into the band.

Scanning the room, Marty's eyes move across the various individuals and groups, quickly stopping at a small cluster of twentysomethings. Holding court in a quiet corner of the room is a radiant young man with dirty blond hair. He's wearing a leather jacket. His laugh is infectious—this is clear in the reactions of the people standing around this man. This young man is completely in the moment. He grins broadly as he talks, laughs, and charms the people who surround him. With a perpetual smile, this jovial imp, a Peter Pan of sorts, is youthful, zestful, and alluring. People clearly enjoy being around him. He looks like a modern bohemian.

Slowly, Marty wades his way through the packed room and soon strikes

---

* For more on the rise of the Matrix, see Jeff Tamarkin's *Got A Revolution!* and Sarah Hill's *San Francisco & The Long 60s*.

up a conversation with the young man. With an air of confidence mixed with excitement, he tells the man about his band, how they started the club, how they're starting something new for the city, and for musicians.

'We need a new drummer,' Marty explains. 'For our band.'

'Wish I could help, but all the drummers I can think of are in bands.'

'I was thinking about you.'

'It's not really an option,' the young man demurs. 'I don't play the drums.'

'You can learn,' Marty offers.

'You know, I've been rehearsing with some guys for around a month now.* Did you catch our practice this afternoon?'

'I did. But we need a new drummer, and I think you'd be a good fit.'

'Well, I have played some drums over the years, but I'm just a guitarist now. And I sing. I don't want to be sitting down playing the drums when I perform.'

'Think of it this way,' Marty persists. 'If you join our band you'll get a chance to relearn the drums. And you wouldn't start right away. As the drummer you'll drive the band,' Marty insists. After a few seconds of silence, he asks, 'What's your name?'

'Skip Spence.'†

•

Many tales of the Grape depict Skip Spence materializing one mystical

---

* This rehearsal band will soon become Quicksilver Messenger Service.

† Marty Balin has told this story many times over the years. In a piece published in *Relix* magazine, he explained to Jeff Tamarkin, 'Skippy was this beautiful kid, all gold and shining, looked like a little Buddha and I went, "Whoa!" because I always go by people's vibrations, my first intuition on people. I know immediately. And I just saw him and said, "Hey, man, you're my drummer." And he said, "No, I'm a guitar player." I said, "No, no, no, you're my drummer." I gave him some sticks and said, "Go home and practice and I'll call you in a week." I called him in a week and asked him if he could do it because I'd fired this other guy and I had no drummer. And he said, "Well, I'll give it a try." And he was great.' When Jeff asked why Skip parted with the band, Marty replied, 'During the drug days he just got too drugged. Too many pretty women. He just went off one day. We went to a gig and somebody said, "Hey, Skippy went to Mexico." I said, "No, we got a gig tonight." But I found out he had gone to Mexico, drugged out, so we stopped his bank account.'

night at the Matrix, as though he were some sort of nineteen-year-old psychedelic apparition. He wasn't. He was a young musician with friends, family, and a past.

Imagining myself in the Matrix on this September evening, I hear these imagined words as they are spoken. I hear Skip tell Marty he was born thousands of miles away, in Windsor, Canada. I hear him explain that his dad was a war hero who worked as a machinist and musician, and how he passed away a few months ago—how Skip himself has played in various bands since he got out of the navy.

The scene described above isn't the precise origin of Moby Grape. Such a thing doesn't exist. Yet it marks a key step in the path *to* Moby Grape. After arranging to meet Marty for a rehearsal, Skip would go on to perform and record with the band he encountered that night, Jefferson Airplane—and befriend their manager, Matthew Katz. Then, in the spring of '66, Skip parted ways with the Airplane after missing a show when he wandered off to travel in Mexico.

Playing with the Airplane gave Skip a certain cachet of sorts. When the band's debut, *Jefferson Airplane Takes Off*, was released in August '66, it featured two songs he co-wrote with Marty, 'Blues From An Airplane' and 'Don't Slip Away.' Although his tenure with the group would last only about half a year, it linked him to Katz, who in turn would work with Skip to form the band that eventually morphed into Moby Grape.

In a rare 1994 interview with Johnny Angel for *Relix*, Skip described the genesis of Moby Grape succinctly. 'I was broke at that point, and I had nothing to do then,' he said. 'I'd spent my last $500 in Mexico, and I got hooked up with Peter Lewis and Bob Mosley by my manager Matthew Katz, who managed me in the Airplane.'

CHAPTER NINE

IN SAN MATEO

The Frantics' 'Human Monkey' was recorded in the early months of 1966 for Action Records, a company based in San Mateo, California. It opens with three taps on the snare drum. Quickly, the drums are joined by a thumping bass and layers of guitar. For twelve seconds the song darts forward, a nimble guitar solo at its center, as through the musicians are aligning themselves, finding their way along a pathway that blends the crunch of garage rock with the harmonies of pop. Soon, a soulful voice joins in, inviting listeners to 'come on in and join the Human Monkey.'

In just over two minutes, 'Human Monkey' offers constant interplay between layered guitars, a revved-up bass, and a Hammond B-3 organ. The chorus features harmonies, soft and high, that contrast with and respond to the evocative cries of the lead vocalist. As the song continues, the backing harmonies engage in a call-and-response interplay with the lead singer. Throughout the song, a lead guitar offers crunching power and short runs that punctuate the melody as it chugs forward.

'Human Monkey' is a song about a dance. Well, on the surface it *seems* to be a song about a dance. Songs about dance crazes, whether real or made up, are rare these days. Yet long ago, when the rock and pop music industry was a young, its universe in its infancy, there was a whole subgenre of songs telling listeners the names of new dances, how to do them, and even the story of the dances.*

The lyric to 'Human Monkey' isn't exactly about a dance, however. It's a play on the entire subgenre of dance craze songs. Sure, the words detail a dance *of sorts*. Yet this is something different. It's all about rules, and the way rules get us to conform to expectations of one type or another.

All you got to do is just play by all the rules
When I say jump, you've got to jump so high
When I say do, you've got to do or die
Yours is not to reason why, you fool.

Think about these words for a moment. Consider how the song itself is a parody of all the dance songs that waltzed through the charts in the decade before its release. From this perspective, there's something biting going on beneath the song's cheerful appearance.

After thumping forward for an intense 130 seconds, the song fades down as the chorus is repeated one last time. Written by Don Stevenson and Jerry Miller, 'Human Monkey' was released by Action Records in July 1966, backed by another original tune by the band, 'Someday,' that would reemerge in a much different form after Don and Jerry rewrote it with Skip Spence. By the time 'Human Monkey' was released, The Frantics had splintered, with three of their members moving on to form the short-lived rehearsal band Luminous Marsh Gas. But the single itself remained, left behind like an artifact.

•

* Back in the 50s and 60s, some of these songs whirled up the charts. In November 1959, The Olympics' 'Hully Gully' first appeared in record stores, eventually climbing to #70 in the US charts. The following year, Chubby Checker's iconic release 'The Twist' reached #28 on the *Billboard* 100. Two years later, Dee Dee Sharp's 'Mashed Potato Time' made it all the way to #2, only one spot away from the coveted summit. In late December, *Billboard* ranked it as the #3 song of the year. While these sorts of dance craze songs appeared less frequently in the charts as the 60s wore on, they never disappeared altogether. A song called 'Do The Freddie' by the Manchester band Freddie & The Dreamers, for instance, climbed to #18 in 1965. Later that year, not to be outdone, Chubby Checker released a reply of sorts, called 'Let's Do The Freddie,' which rose to #40.

One afternoon in early 1966, five young musicians with tidy haircuts traveled to San Mateo. Because they weren't playing a live gig, they weren't wearing their matching hound's-tooth suits, and that pleased them. Nevertheless, they arrived in town with a sense of purpose and determination. They had, after all, come to San Mateo to record a new 45—their first with their new lineup. As the five musicians lugged their equipment into Action Records and set up to record, none of them had the slightest inkling that the end of their band was only months away. They were just excited to be there.

San Mateo is a small town about twenty miles south of San Francisco and almost forty miles northeast of San Jose. It is a unique place, less crowded than its neighboring cities. Covering an area of nearly sixteen square miles, it offers a Mediterranean climate, with warm, dry summers and mild, damp winters. It is a relatively quiet city, known for its vast 670-acre Coyote Point Park, which blankets the city's northeast corner, jutting into the San Francisco Bay. Long ago, Coyote Point was an island in the bay, but over the centuries it morphed into an overgrown peninsula, with a tightly packed cluster of towering eucalyptus trees.

As the 1960s unfolded, San Mateo's population jumped from 70,000 to nearly 80,000. Along with this population growth, the city's infrastructure expanded. In 1963, the College of San Mateo opened a hilltop campus boasting a total of 5,000 students. In early 1966, two new recording studios sprouted up in the city, Pacific Studios and Action Records. Opened as a four-track studio by Fred Cohn and Raymond Turner, Action Records would later offer an eight-track option and advertise itself as 'a production company which sells masters.'

Working against the clock, the five young musicians continued to set up their instruments. The Seattle band—predominantly a rhythm & blues outfit originally founded as The Four Frantics in the mid 1950s—had been led by Chuck Schoning for over a decade. Chuck played organ, most recently a B-3, taking the keyboard lead on the keys and covering the bass with his pedals.

Jerry Miller had been playing lead guitar in the band since 1963. The previous summer, just before The Frantics relocated to California, Don Stevenson joined on drums after Jon Keliehor was injured in a car accident.*

Thinking back today, Don recalls how The Frantics came to relocate to the Bay Area:

> We came down right around the time The Byrds were playing on Broadway, in San Francisco. There were rumors that people were sleeping overnight on the street to get tickets to get to see them. I was enamored with The Byrds at that point. Really enamored. So somebody came in, and listened to us playing at the Top Hat, and they offered us a gig down in San Francisco on Broadway—right where The Byrds were playing! That's when we went down to San Francisco. We didn't go to visit—we had a gig. And we got there just in time for Carol Doda. She was the first person in modern history to take her top off and expose herself for other people's pleasure. She had just done that, and it was catching on all on the Strip.
>
> So, when we got there, The Byrds had left a month before.† I can't remember the name of the place we were playing. They had go-go stuff going on with dancers and everything. It was in between songs, like, 'Could we get a pound and a half of music please?' It was like ordering a hamburger or something. You'd play a song and stop—but as the drummer I'd have

* According to Keliehor, writing at pnwbands.com, 'When Joe left the band, guitarist Jerry Miller joined. His playing was a little lighter in style, and he had a mellower, more liquid sound, similar to that of B.B. King. He too was an excellent soloist. They both loved Freddie King tunes. Miller and Johansen were fantastic to play with. ... Deciding to expand their influence outside of Washington State, The Frantics traveled to San Jose, California, in May 1965 to audition for a club. The audition was successful, and The Frantics moved to San Jose in July 1965. On the way my little Volkswagen Beetle was introduced to the front end of a large, fast-moving truck. I was admitted to the emergency room of a nearby hospital with a ruptured spleen. The band were stopped at the California border, and told the news of my accident. They returned to Seattle to contemplate things, but eventually went on to San Jose while I recovered. The Frantics survived for another year. Their new drummer Don Stevenson, along with Jerry Miller and Bob Mosley, found their way back to California, toward the formation of Moby Grape.'

† To learn about The Byrds' fascinating rollercoaster career, see Johnny Rogan's thoughtful and engaging two-volume set *Byrds: Requiem For The Timeless*.

> to keep playing, so the dancers could do their thing to a drumbeat.
>
> We lasted for about two weeks before we quit. We did not go to California to back up topless dancers. That was our introduction to San Francisco. Quite a way away from Haight Street.

Influenced by the music of The Beatles and The Byrds, The Frantics decided to recruit a new bass player early in 1966. With Bob Mosley, they would be getting much more than just a bassist. A lettered high-school athlete and surfer, Bob had a long history of adding his soulful vocals to numerous bands over the years, among them The Misfits and The Joel Scott Hill Trio.

Jerry first saw Bob perform with the latter group, possibly at Le Poupée, in San Jose. 'He was such a great bass player, and he was so in time with Johnny Barbata on drums,' he recalls. 'That's what I like—when the drums and the bass are synced. And they were playing good. And we didn't have a bass player. We had Chuck Schoning on the Hammond organ. With The Beatles and everything, you know, you've got to have a bass—especially if you can get one who can sing like Mosley.'

Don recalls:

> When we met Bob, he was with The Joel Scott Hill Trio, with Joel and Joni Lyman at the San Francisco International. I went to see one of their shows. They were so good. And Bob looked like a surfer god—that was my image of the guy. And Joel Scott Hill and Joni Lyman, and I think Johnny Barbata was playing drums—he later joined The Turtles. Like Jerry said, they were just an amazing band. They were playing all covers, but they were just kicking ass, and Mosley played bass so good, and I couldn't believe it. And he sang like a monster. So we had some gigs around San Francisco at the time, and we had convinced him to come down and play with us. Nobody sang like Mosley.

> For some reason, he came and joined us. He was every bit as advertised.

•

After setting up their equipment at Action Records, The Frantics recorded a basic track, with their newest member taking center stage. While 'Human Monkey' was written by Jerry and Don, and would often be sung by Don at shows, Bob took lead vocals for the single. He belts out the lyrics in a way that is penetrating. This is not the kind of voice that can be ignored. It's the kind of voice that shouts, 'Here I am!' The band sounds excited to showcase their new singer—*and* their new garage-pop sound.

Remembering that day in San Mateo, Jerry fumes, 'I had my beautiful amplifier stolen there, an old 1956 Deluxe amplifier. I had my own PA that went with it, too. And it all got stolen! People say, Don't worry about it, you can leave your stuff in the studio. But don't ever do that! Because people are walking in and out of studios all the time. Boy, that was a lesson.'

•

This spring day was the first time that these three future members of Moby Grape recorded together in the studio, yet it was also an ending. Within months, Bob had left The Frantics to join The Vejtables. Then, in June '66, he left that group to form a new band with a fingerpicking guitarist he met at an airport—Peter Lewis.

After Bob's departure, The Frantics transformed into Luminous Marsh Gas, a four-piece outfit featuring Chuck, Don, Jerry, and newcomer Richard Fortunato on guitar, as Jerry recalls:

> Marsh Gas was Richard Fortunato on the twelve-string and Don and myself and Charlie. Just the four of us basically. And we never did anything. Well, Richard later went into a band called Fields, and Charlie went into Quicksilver. But we never did anything as Marsh Gas. Then, Bob called up to say he had gotten together with Peter Lewis, the son of Loretta Young. I'd

> seen Peter perform before, and he was a good player—and Bob told me that they needed a drummer. So there we were, all ready to go and we knew a lot of each other's stuff. It was just after that that we had our first rehearsal.

As the summer of '66 continued to unfold, Bob suggested Don and Jerry join his new group, which now also featured Skip Spence as well as Peter Lewis, and was being guided by Matthew Katz. Thinking back to the band's first rehearsal, Bob tells me, 'We all meshed together pretty well for just a bunch of rookies.' Describing these events in a 1976 interview with the *San Diego Reader*, he recalled how he had decided to leave the Joel Scott Hill Trio around this time after Lee Michaels was asked to join on organ. 'I didn't like organ at the time,' he told reporter Ted Burke. 'I liked the trio sound, with a driving lead guitar, a solid bass, and a drummer who knows all the chops. The organ just filled up the band's sound too much for my taste, so I quit.'

Some of Bob's final performances with this group took place at the San Francisco International, where 'two guys from Seattle' happened to be in the audience, he recalled to Ted Burke. After the show, they told him they needed 'a bass player who could sing.' Then, following his stint in The Frantics, Bob made his way to Los Angeles with the aim of finding 'a folk-type musician, someone who can do all that fancy picking stuff. I got a hold of Peter Lewis, who I found out later was Loretta Young's son. I thought, *oh boy, now's my chance to get into the Hollywood scene* … Anyway, he knew a dude named Matthew Katz, a drummer named Skip Spence who was just fired from the Jefferson Airplane, and we all went up to San Francisco, where we met Miller and Stevenson.'

CHAPTER TEN

ON SUNSET STRIP

Running for twenty-two miles, Sunset Boulevard winds alongside the mountains that bind Los Angeles to the north. Like a natural water spring, it begins in Downtown LA and then snakes to the northeast, circuiting through Hollywood, before bending southwest toward the blue waters of the Pacific Ocean. Three centuries ago, it was a cattle trail; by 1966, it had become a bustling tourist attraction.

In West Hollywood, a small portion of this meandering boulevard became known as Sunset Strip. Though it was smaller than you might think—a mile and a half long in all—at night, especially on weekends, it was a busy avenue of lights, glowing under the cover of a starless, dark sky. Far too bright for anyone to see any stars when they cast their eyes upward. Cars upon cars would wind in and around each other, moving toward their various destinations, all merging in the glow. Sometimes, a car would slow down, its driver becoming captivated, even mesmerized, by the flood of sounds and bright lights emanating from the many clubs along the roadway. Most of the buildings were older, some of them remnants of ages past, an age of Hollywood glitz that had since fled to the neon lights of Vegas and elsewhere.

The Strip was at once hypnotic and sharp, the volume of people socializing, partying, and listening to music continuing ceaselessly. Visitors would be lulled as they grew more and more accustomed to the waves of background noise, and then jolted by the staccato sounds of loud laughter or sharp voices jutting out of the busy night. As a hub with an ever-changing set of venues within it, Sunset Strip itself would also become a venue, the two words alone enough to conjure up images and a whole cache of word associations in the hearts and minds of those who knew something, anything about it. In the 1940s, it was Bogart and glamour. In '66, it was Dylan, The Doors, and change.

The streets were alive, and they'd been bustling for a long time, offering nightlife and drawing in crowds for some four decades. During prohibition, Café La Boheme boasted drinking, dancing, and gambling for local socialites to enjoy before a 1934 raid closed it down. Reopening the same year, the club was redubbed Café Trocadero, or the Troc, and offered jazz, gambling, and dining to a bevy of moguls, Hollywood A-listers, and social-climbers. During that time, the likes of Samuel Goldwyn, Cary Grant, Nat King Cole, and Fred Astaire stepped through its doors.

Perhaps the most famous of the Strip's earlier clubs was Ciro's, which drew a mix of executives, celebrities, and gangsters in white gloves, scarves, and cigarette holders. It was the scene of luxury, brawls, and a three-strike rule on fighting. It ran for seventeen years, from 1940 to 1957. Opening one year later, the Macombo had a Latin-American décor, exotic birds in cages, and was a short walk away from the famed Garden of Allah apartment building. It marked the rise of Ella Fitzgerald before finally closing its doors in 1958.

As the 1950s gave way to the 1960s, Las Vegas became the new glamour capital of America, attracting the Strip's old clientele. Meanwhile, the Strip itself transformed into something different. There were new clubs with a new clientele and a new ambiance. As the youth of LA and Hollywood began to tread up and down the Strip, a variety of rock'n'roll clubs sprung up, one of which, Pandora's Box, featured such acts as The Beach Boys, Sonny & Cher, and The Byrds. First opening in 1962, it would be demolished half a decade later, shortly after the curfew riots of November '66—the Sunset Strip Riots.

In 1964, two years after Pandora's Box opened, the Whisky A Go Go cast open its doors, offering a stage for acts and glass cages for go-go dancers wearing mini-skirts and boots. The Whisky featured some of the biggest names in the music business, from The Doors to Love to Frank Zappa & The Mothers Of Invention, to name a few. But while the Whisky was itself a sort of beacon, there were others nearby. A few steps away was the London Fog, which opened in 1966 and served as the home of The Doors before they become the house band at the Whisky. These new clubs were a world away from Ciro's and the Macambo, which had closed less than a decade before.

Within this different reality, one club still straddled the old world: a place where the past and present could co-exist, and where the divergent worlds of 1940s Sunset Strip, Vegas, and 1960s Sunset Strip might all co-mingle.

Just blocks away from the Whisky and the London Fog was Gazzarri's. Owned by Bill Gazzarri, the club first opened as Gazzarri's Hollywood A-Go-Go in 1963, before *re*-opening in February 1967, simply as Gazzarri's. A future LA legend, Bill Gazzarri wore a white fedora, chomped on cigars, and advocated for poker playing in rock clubs—and for a 'Rock 'n' Roll Sidewalk of Fame.' (To his everlasting frustration, those dreams would never come to fruition, though not for any lack of effort.)

Initially working as a construction contractor, Gazzarri leaped into the world of entertainment in 1961 with an Italian restaurant on La Cienega Boulevard that featured his mother's cooking and the singing of Johnny Rivers and Vikki Carr. Two years later, he set up shop on Sunset with his own Gazzarri's Hollywood A-Go-Go. With the large sign outside advertising the name of the club and a shining billboard below featuring the names of performers alongside the word 'cocktails,' Gazzarri's was a place that mixed the old with the new. Behind the stage was a brickwork design covering the lower half of the wall, around it a curtain design that called back to the regal décor of the 1940s. Yet it was also the home of the new. In 1965, Gazzarri told the *Los Angeles Times*, 'Many adults are hesitant about trying the new dances at first, but after they watch kids on the floor for a while, they lose their bashfulness.' He went on to add, 'The young people actually provide the floor show.'

In the days before TV screens in nightspots, Gazzarri filmed his dancers, encouraging them to hurry back to try and catch themselves cavorting on one of the club's large screens.

•

On a Sunday afternoon in early spring 1966, a young man set up his guitar and PA equipment on the stage at Gazzarri's. Tall and thin with longish dark hair, Peter Lewis was now the lead guitarist and vocalist in his own band. Beforehand, he'd played with The Cornells, a surf band, alongside a small collective of celebrity offspring. The band reached a certain level of success, performing at the Hollywood Bowl and releasing an album and a handful of singles in 1964, but over time they'd moved in different directions, pursuing different dreams and goals.

After studying to be a commercial pilot at Perdu University, spending time in the national guard, and working for a short time as a pilot, Peter returned to music. It was his passion. And yet on hearing albums by Bob Dylan and The Byrds, he knew that surf music was not a part of his future. Years later, in an interview with Jud Cost, Peter would reference the mischievous character from Kenneth Grahame's *The Wind In The Willows*, describing his transformation as follows: 'When I saw The Byrds it was like when Mr. Toad found the motor car.' It was an epiphany of sorts—and this feeling of discovery is what inspired him to form Peter & The Wolves, a folk-rock outfit based in LA.

Stepping around the stage, three musicians joined Peter in setting up the band's gear: Ron Morgan (guitar/vocals), Tony Bellamy (bass), and Bob Newkirk (drums). As the band began their set, two young men with long hair stepped into the club, their hair, clothes, and nonchalant air setting them apart from the sparse crowd in the room. Making their way around the various cocktail tables, these young men—so different from everyone else in the club—looked as though they'd come to the wrong place.

As they stepped closer and closer to an empty table by the stage, the two men became aware that sets of eyes were following their movements throughout the room. Before sitting down, they casually glanced around, quickly noticing that many of those around them were wearing suits, and nearly everyone had short hair.

'I thought, *wow, that's strange, to see a guy with long hair in this place*,' Peter later recalled, in a 1996 interview with Craig Morrison. (In 1966, the length of one's hair made a difference.)

The two men sat down to watch the show. They were impressed with what they saw, and afterward approached the stage to chat with the musicians as they packed up their gear. Introducing themselves as Lee Michaels (keyboards/guitar/vocals) and Johnny Barbata (drums), they explained how they were playing with Joel Scott Hill—and looking to rework their lineup.

Not long after that, Peter joined the trio for a day, sitting in for a sick Joel Scott Hill at the Action Club in Santa Monica. 'When Joel got back,' he recalled to Craig Morrison, 'I met him at a point when I was just beginning to write songs and I wanted to get in a band with other songwriters, or people that could do original music. Joel and I and this drummer that was in Peter & The Wolves that went with Joel at some point [Bob Newkirk]; he was going to be in the band, and we needed a bass player. Joel said, I know this guy Bob Mosley who's really good but he's crazy. I said, Great, man, crazy's happening!'

Before long, the lineup of both bands had shifted. Everything was in motion then, with Peter's path now set to converge with that of a young bassist and vocalist from San Diego: Bob Mosley.

'At this point the Joel Scott Hill trio was Joel, Bob Mosley, and Johnny Barbata,' Lewis explained to Cost. Then, after Lee Michaels came on board, Bob quit. 'He didn't want to play in a four-piece band,' Lewis recalled, 'and they weren't making that much money anyway.' At this point, Mosley joined The Frantics, and eventually ended up down the coast in Hollister, 'playing acoustic guitar in a bar.' Then Barbata and Michaels came to see Peter & The Wolves at Gazzarri's. According to Lewis, 'They were looking for a folk-rock thing to add a different vibe to the Trio, and they'd heard we were pretty good.'*

For Peter and everyone else who would soon form the Grape, everything was in flux. Lives, events, and people were all moving forward—in transition, too, and always in a state of becoming, but they were now set on a course, their destination a small office on California Street, San Francisco, where the Grape would have their first rehearsal. In a way, things weren't just moving—they were converging.

Peter looked back on his meeting with Bob in his 1996 interview with Craig Morrison:

> [Joel Scott Hill] called Bob and I went out to pick him up at the airport. I remember Bob sitting at the bar with a goatee, completely unhip for those days, with his hair combed back and cut real short, kind of like a military guy, with white Bermuda shorts, a tennis shirt and sneakers, drinking beer with his bass leaning up against the bar. I could sense his vibe, of 'don't talk to me, and don't fuck with me or I'll kill you.' He was on the edge, intense. I had long hair and bell bottoms and no shoes or whatever, and I guess he looked at me and I looked at him and went, 'Wait, wait a minute!' I said, 'You're Bob Mosley,' and he just grabbed his bass and followed me. I had to take him someplace, so we got into my car, driving back to Hollywood, and he hadn't said anything to me. Halfway to Hollywood, he says, 'I can sing anything up to high C and sing like a motherfucker. What can you do?' We got to where we were going to practice, and the first thing he did was play 'Big Boss Man.'

•

* Speaking to Cost thirty years later, Lewis described Gazzarri's as 'the un-coolest club on the Strip. It was mostly people there with sharkskin suits and their hair slicked back, and you knew if you had long hair you had to be cool or they'd kick your ass.' Many of the venues Peter & The Wolves played, he added, 'were owned by these sub-mobsters, local enforcers. It was hard to get your money. But they were making the effort to get some of the people in there who were hanging out at the Whisky and the Trip to see Love and The Byrds.'

As the spring of '66 gave way to the early summer, Peter and Bob started rehearsing with Joel Scott Hill and Bob Newkirk in LA. When I ask him about 'Fall On You,' Bob recalls, 'I recorded that song with Peter Lewis down in Hollywood when we got together.' Skip Spence, meanwhile, was in San Francisco with Matthew Katz, who was looking to form a new band around his spirited charge, now ready to leave the drums and return to the guitar. Bob Newkirk connected Joel and his band with Matthew Katz, who offered to bring them to San Francisco.

When Joel met Matthew, he was unimpressed, so Peter and the two Bobs trekked to the Bay Area on their own, to meet and rehearse with Skip.* Elsewhere in the Bay Area, Don and Jerry were playing in Luminous Marsh Gas, their rehearsal band, which rose from the embers of The Frantics. By now, it was summertime, and Moby Grape's very first rehearsal was only a few weeks away.

* For more, see David Fricke's liner notes to *Vintage: The Very Best Of Moby Grape* and Jud Cost's three-part series on the band for *Ptolemaic Terrascope*.

CHAPTER ELEVEN

'WE HAD RAZOR CUTS AND MATCHING SUITS.'

December 2016. A cold winter evening marks my first long conversation with Jerry Miller. We talk about his time in The Frantics and his early days in California, and because memories and personal stories don't always conform to chronology, Jerry also tells me about experiences and songs that stretch way beyond that timeline.

'Don and I started writing together a little bit when we were up in Seattle,' Jerry tells me. 'Not very much. We didn't really get going until we got with the Grape. And that was just inspiring—with Skippy and Bob and everybody adding harmonies on everything. That was just plugged in right. Of course, Don and I wrote a little bit with Skippy and with Bob as well and Peter, too.'

I ask Jerry to explain how he and Don approached writing songs together.

> Don was a drummer. Basically, I'd come up with something—usually I'd have the beginning of a tune. But not always, mind you. With '8:05,' for instance, I was at the crossing gate at the Golden Gate Bridge and I asked the guy in the booth what time it was and he said, of course, '8:05.' So I'm riding in my '50 Oldsmobile Rocket 88 Futuramic, going over the Golden Gate

Bridge. I was singing to myself, '8:05, I think I'll drive off this bridge.' I needed a bridge, actually—for the tune [*laughs*]. So I went directly over to Don's and he helped me with the bridge and added a few things. That's a time where I had most of it myself. But then on 'Changes,' Don had most of that himself, and I helped him with little bits of putting it together.

Our conversation then turns to the recording of 'Human Monkey' with The Frantics, who featured Bob Mosley in early 1966.

We recruited Bob from the Joel Scott Hill Trio. He'd left the Misfits by then—that was his old band from San Diego. So he came into The Frantics and we got into a nightclub. Back then, The Frantics was me, and Don, and Chuck Schoning—who played the organ, he'd play the basslines with his left hand and he'd play treble with his right hand—and Bob Hosko, too, who played saxophone. Chuck and Bob have both passed away now.

Back then we could do stuff like 'Hold On, I'm Coming' by Sam & Dave, and we did all the Righteous Brothers songs, and we did The Beatles. At that time, the Top 40 was worth playing! It was great! [Songs like] 'Shotgun' by Junior Walker—we played all those tunes. We were playing at a place called the Dragon a Go-Go in Chinatown. We had razor cuts and matching suits, so we could change all the time. We were doing that for a while. Then, we heard about the Fillmore and the Avalon and a couple of other places there. So we had to go snoop around and see what was going on. Around that time, we caught a little bit of Peter Wheat & The Breadmen and Sopwith Camel and all those bands—The Grateful Dead.

Jerry pauses for a moment.

I missed a really important part. At one point, when we were in

> The Frantics, back before we met Bob Mosley, back when it was just me and Don and Chuck and Bob—Bob Hosko, that is—we were playing at the Hunter's Inn in Santa Maria. After we finished that gig we decided to head back home because we didn't have anything to do. So we were on our way back to Seattle. We just happened to stop into a place to have a bite in Belmont. It was called the Inn Room. A band called The Warlocks were playing there, before they became The Grateful Dead. There was Jerry Garcia and a guy named Joe Larpy McLean, and Sam Salvo, a few other guys. And I got to talking to them, and they offered us a place to stay, rather than going home. So we ended up in this beautiful Victorian place on Ralston Street in Belmont. We got to stay there for a while. You know, had we not stopped in that place called the Chalet at the Inn Room we would've just gone back home to Seattle, and there wouldn't have been a Moby Grape. And it was in a little off-the-wall place in Belmont, too!

They would get to know some of the other Bay Area bands of the time, too. 'We used to go to Sly Stone's house,' Jerry recalls. 'He turned me on to Albert Collins and some wonderful old stuff, like George Benson. We met him when he was a DJ. We used to go up to KSOL quite a bit and hang out and talk. He was a really nice guy, him and his brother Freddie. He had a Gibson L-5 like mine.'*

When I ask how The Frantics' 'Human Monkey' single ended up being released by Action Records, Jerry expresses surprise. 'I didn't know that song ever got out! I'll be damned.' Chuckling to himself, he adds, 'I'll bet it didn't go far.'

•

January 4 2017. On a windy evening I drive south, leaving midtown

* Jerry still has the Gibson L-5 electric guitar he bought in 1962. Called 'Buelah,' Jerry's L-5 was stolen in the spring of '67. With his trusted friend Tim, Jerry went on a long adventure to recover the guitar. More on that story later.

Toronto, heading all the way to Queen and Bathurst. Long ago, this was Toronto's garment district. Now it's at the center of the city's fashion industry. Over the years, Queen Street West has been gentrifying, all the while losing pieces of its past identity.

Just west of Bathurst, on the north side of Queen, is a small club called the Cameron House. Built in 1920, the building started out as a working-class hotel and eventually transformed into a space for music and art, firmly rooted in its bustling downtown community. Table seating is sparse, like a bare-bones saloon. Yet it's a place of vitality and history. Musicians who've gotten a start at the club over the years include Blue Rodeo, Ron Sexsmith, and The Barenaked Ladies. On this cold night, however, I'm there not to catch a new up-and-coming act but to see a rugged songwriter in his seventies who played at Monterey and all the various Fillmore venues when they marked the apex of the rock world.

Approaching the building, I hear a band. The music is melodic, and loud. Stepping into the room, I'm struck at how crowded it is. I order a Stella Artois. The band continues to play. Don Stevenson is set to perform at eleven with his friend Tim Bocavonti. Two tables in the seating area are filled with their friends.

Before Don is set to go on stage, I step over and introduce myself, having first got in touch with him through Jerry. Don guides me to his own seat and urges me to take it for the show.

For over an hour, I'm surprised. Don hits all the notes he reached so long ago. His voice is still there. While Don plays a few older tunes with Tim, he mostly plays new ones. I recognize a couple from his recent album, *King Of Fools*. But there are a great many songs in the set that are unfamiliar to me, like 'The Letter,' 'Low Strollin',' and 'Regret.' These country-tinged songs tell stories—real stories about people and situations you might see in coffee shops, or on busses, or on the street. All the while, Tim's delicate guitar lines compliments Don's rhythm guitar and singing, sometimes adding ornament, other times holding down the foundation.*

* Over the years, Tim's playing has led him to share the stage, or the studio, with such diverse artists as Burton Cummings, Dave Swarbrick, and Jerry Lee Lewis.

When the show is over, Don and I chat briefly, before agreeing to meet the following week.

•

Feeling slightly anxious, I step through the entrance of the café. Espresso in hand, I sit down at an empty table. Not long afterward, a spry older man bounds through the front door, orders himself a cappuccino, and heads over to my table.

We begin our conversation by looking at an old photograph of The Frantics. Don inspects the image in silence. 'That's a long time ago,' he says, pausing for a moment before identifying one of the fresh-faced young men in the picture as Jon Keliehor.

> He was the drummer in The Frantics before me. There's Chuck. And here's Bob Hosko, who was a wonderful horn player. And Jon Keliehor, his mother—I don't know if she was a medium, but she was someone who supposedly had mystical powers. We went to his house one time, back when Jon was playing with the Frantics and I was playing in a band called the Playboys. So I went over, and we went to a little session at his house. One of the things that happened along with other predictions and things that she saw and said … she came over and went up like this, took hold of my arm, and said, 'I see you on television. I see you on television and I see your musical future on television.' And I just went, 'Cool!'

As Don recounts this story, I think back to some of the Moby Grape television performances I've seen: on *The Steve Paul Scene* in the summer of '67, *The Mike Douglas Show* in January '68, *The Jerry Lewis Show* in October '68. These performances mark very different phases in the band's short lifetime, like dispatches from the band's journey.

Continuing his story, Don describes how he ended up being invited to join The Frantics after Jon Keliehor's enforced departure.

> I'd played with Chuck and Bob on and off and they asked me if I'd quit The Playboys and come and play with them. They offered me more money, and I knew them. I knew they were great players, and that's when I met Jerry.
>
> Something really funny happened one of the first times I met Jerry. He has a false tooth. And when we'd go in some places and they'd check your ID and everything, with a light, his false tooth would turn blue. It was pretty funny. One time he'd left his tooth at home and I saw him and he went in his pocket and he couldn't find his tooth. He went into his wallet, and pulls out a little piece of something. It looks like a rag, and he puts it up to his nose, and he's kind of rubbing it with his fingers. And I go, 'What the hell is that?' And he says, 'This is my binky, man. This is a piece of my binky. I still have a piece of my binky!'

Don bursts out laughing at the memory, and then I ask him how the single, 'Human Monkey,' came about.

> 'Human Monkey' came from the time we were playing at the High Hat. That was when we were still up in Seattle. The High Hat was owned by the Colacurcios, and they were *connected* people. I think that's pronounced right. That was in the day we'd play six nights a week at the same place for months. And people kept coming out and dancing and having a good time. It was a great way to get your chops; just go from one six-night-a-week gig to another six-night-a-week gig. I'd played a lot in Seattle too. I had a time where I'd play six nights a week at the Royal, and I'd pack up and then I'd play six nights a week at an afterhours place in another part of town. So I just got a lot of playing in.

As I listen to Don, I remember reading about Frank Colacurcio in the *Seattle Times*. Described as a 'one of Seattle's most notorious racketeering figures' and a 'strip club magnate,' his obituary, penned by Steve Miletich, reported that he had benefited during the 50s and 60s from Seattle's 'rougher edges' during a time when 'police turned their eyes from vice and criminal activity in exchange for payoffs.' Don's memories of the High Hat fit right into this nefarious snapshot. 'They almost had us indentured,' he says. 'On Friday nights, when we got paid, we had to pay the bar bill, and then we also played Yahtzee.' Don chuckles to himself. 'And it seemed that all my money just ended up being enough to make ends meet. They always won.'

It was around this time that Don and Jerry began writing songs together.

> There was a place down there called Chambers Creek where we'd go. And lots of people would go there—people who were in the know. It was kind of a secret. There was a big rope that you'd use to swing over the creek and drop off into it. At the same time, we were at Chambers Creek, we were writing 'Human Monkey.' We wrote a song called 'Chambers Creek,' too. We did that little recording after we moved down to the Bay Area—and I can't even remember hearing it. We did that when we were playing at the Phonics, I think.

I tell Don what Jerry had told me about the musical hotbed of the Bay Area in the mid 60s, and how they'd run into people like Sly Stone from time to time.

> Well, Sly was a disk jockey. Periodically, he frequented our place, when we were living down on the peninsula. He'd come over, stop by, and say hi. I remember one time, I think we were living in Redwood City. This was before we were in Moby Grape. Sly came over. I was sleeping on the couch and I woke up and there were two monsters staring at me. He had two Great Danes, one named Bummer and the other named Stoner. Two big Great Danes. I was just sleeping on the couch and I looked up and there were these two huge monsters just drooling and

> staring at me! Sly saw I was scared, and said, 'Calm down, man, it's just Bummer and Stoner.'
>
> Sly would come down, and we would know him from the recording studio. He was a friend of the guy we lived in the house with, a guy named Yo Larry. Larry had a glass eye, and he'd get stoned on acid and take his eye out and put in a shamrock. He'd turn the lights off—whoosh! Switch from his glass eye to the shamrock, and then—whoosh! He'd switch the lights back on.
>
> So we had social times with Sly, and I do remember when we later played with him when we were in Moby Grape. I remember it well because his drummer used to drive the place. I don't know how the hell the guy did what he did! It's amazing to watch somebody doing something that you can't figure out how it was done! He could do stuff with his foot pedal, independent of his arms, and it used to knock me out. Sly was a music fan, and I was a big fan of his band.

Turning his mind back to The Frantics, Don recalls how The Troggs were recording at Action Records at the same time. 'They might've been recording that big hit they had … "Wild Thing," that's what it was called. That what a huge hit. "Human Monkey" just didn't take off like that one!'

By the time 'Human Monkey' came out, of course, The Frantics were no more; by then, Don and Jerry were playing in Luminous Marsh Gas together. 'The Marsh Gas was short-lived. Maybe a couple of months. That's right when we went to do the audition for Moby Grape. It was something I'll never forget—the audition. After that, we kind of put Marsh Gas on the backburner.'

SOUTHBOUND DREAM

January 2017. Walking home one evening, I am carrying in my backpack a small notebook and five well-worn art books.* Together, these books offer a glimpse into a vibrant landscape. The art scene exploded out of the Bay Area, and over the decades it transformed from an influential force to something to be cared for, curated, and studied. It's easy to forget that some of the 'Big Five' poster artists of San Francisco—Wes Wilson, Alton Kelley, Stanley Mouse, Victor Moscoso, and Rick Griffin—didn't go to art school, and happened upon 'rock art' by happy accident.

My thoughts turn to the poster art of the day, which bloomed out of a period when music and poetry and art and other media from the Bay Area seemed to simultaneously converge inward and explode outward. One such image that's locked in the foreground of my memory features a majestic peacock, standing tall, with its head twisted to the side, facing the left side of the page. Behind the peacock's neck, to the right, are the heads of three smaller peacocks looking in different directions. To the left of the peacock,

* Two of the books are staples on rock poster art, Paul Grushkin's landmark *The Art Of Rock* and the more recent *Classic Rock Posters* by Mick Farren and Dennis Loren. The three other books focus on the 1960s and the San Francisco scene: Ted Owen and Denise Dickson's astute *High Art*, the thoughtful *High Societies* by Sally Tomlinson and Walter Medeiros, and the comprehensive *Art Of The Fillmore* by Gayle Lemke.

in the upper left quadrant of the page, the words 'Byrds, Byrds, Byrds' descend in a wave, sweeping diagonally across the page, cutting toward the bottom right quadrant. Continuing to the right side of the peacock is a second cluster of writing. Like writing on a scarf, it weaves its way down the bottom right quadrant of the page, with the name 'Moby Grape' kicking things off, followed by information about the third act on the bill, the dates, times, and locations of the shows. The poster, designed by Wes Wilson, was not the sort of thing that came out of Madison Avenue. It was something else altogether. Looking at a tiny image of this iconic poster on my phone, I try to recall what Wes told me when we spoke about it a few weeks earlier. 'I just wanted to do a bird, so I drew up a bird,' he casually recalled. 'It's pretty much that.' Although Wes didn't catch Moby Grape performing before he started to design posters for their shows, he has fond memories of their talent. 'Moby Grape was a good band,' he said, simply but firmly. 'They were good.'

Later, flipping through the thick *Classic Rock Posters*, I examine image after image, scanning the short descriptions of the individual works. My eyes are glued to one particular poster that shows a witch gleefully looking at the brew she's stirring in a large cauldron. A fire glows beneath the cauldron with words in flames. In her hands she clutches a guitar, which serves as her ladle. This is one of my favorite Moby Grape posters. It promoted a gig they played on Halloween in 1977, during one of their reunion phases. Looking at the poster, I think about Jim Phillips, the artist who designed it. Known for his skateboard art, Jim was recently inducted into the Skateboarding Hall of Fame. When I corresponded with Jim, he told me about his process of designing the famous 'Moby Grape Witch.' 'Macbeth's "Double, double, toil and trouble" did come to mind,' he told me, as he cast his mind back to events that transpired nearly four decades in the past.

In David Fricke's liner notes to *Vintage: The Very Best Of Moby Grape*, he describes Moby Grape's first gig outside of the Ark, at the California Hall on November 4 1966, as 'a Katz-produced fiasco; Peter Lewis says the band played to five people and several hundred empty folding chairs.' Something nags at me, though. I can recall seeing the poster for this show, with the mirrored image of a yogi—but I also remember seeing a poster for another, earlier show at California Hall, on October 28. What happened at that show, I wonder?

•

October 28 1966. *Fresh Cream*, Cream's debut album, was released in the UK today. Yesterday, *It's The Great Pumpkin, Charlie Brown*, a Halloween-themed special, aired for the first time on CBS. Three days ago, the People's Republic of China completed its first successful nuclear test in the Lop Nor desert. That same day, Luna 12 began to orbit the Moon, as the Soviet Union started to photograph potential landing sites. Two days before that, Che Guevara flew to Moscow, leaving Cuba for the last time. On October 16, Bobby Seale and Huey P. Newton created the Black Panther Party in Oakland, California, the same day that Grace Slick made her first public appearance with the Jefferson Airplane at the Fillmore, in San Francisco. A few days before that, John Lennon met Yoko Ono for the first time at the Indica Gallery in London, England. One week from today, The Beatles will return to EMI Studios to begin work on 'Strawberry Fields Forever,' a new composition by Lennon …

On Friday, October 28 1966, the temperature in San Francisco has reached a high of sixteen and a low of eight. The street is calm—not silent, but calm. On the corner of McAllister, just east of Polk Street, is a vast courthouse designed in a neoclassical beaux-arts style, with terracotta masonry and a granite façade. Completed in 1922 after barely a year of construction, the building marks the tail end of the architectural movement in the United States. Reaching up more than seventy-five feet across six floors, it is more than three hundred and twenty feet wide.

Like this courthouse, two key ballrooms in the city display a variety of beaux-arts features—long flat roofs, raised first stories, arched windows, symmetry, polychrome, and a bevy of sculptures, murals, and mosaics. It's ironic that the Fillmore and the Avalon visually share so much with the state's supreme court, a symbol of authority, that these ballrooms—spaces of change, rebellion, and counterculture—are housed in such traditionally designed structures. It's a marked contrast.

Resting on the sidewalk is a sheet of paper, the middle of the page dominated by a drawing of a topless woman wearing a dress that flows across the left side of the page, her cascading long hair flowing below her hips. The woman's dress makes her look a bit like a mermaid. She's drawn two dimensionally, with her arms outstretched. Within her dress, and its colorful organic shapes, are the words 'Dance Concert.' Below her left hand, in the top right quadrant of the page, is a disc that bears the words, 'East Vision Productions.'

The woman's disproportionally large eyes are half closed, showing off her long eyelashes and enormous, pouting lips. On her forehead is a third eye. In various philosophies—including Hinduism, Chan, and Zen—a third eye represents a deeper form of consciousness. It's never externally visible (unless portrayed in art) but extends one's vision beyond the ordinary perception of sight. This heightened sense of sight extends from the mind, and the interplay between one's awareness of their surroundings, and the surroundings themselves. With the third eye, awareness is rooted in the subconscious.*

The woman is looking to her left, perhaps at the words that are written below her left arm, which list the four performers at the upcoming show: Moby Grape, Lee Michaels, West Coast Branch, and American Dream. Below these names, painted dark blue, is the name of the California Hall, the location of the event, and the date of the show, October 28. Written in very small letters below that are the name of the artist (who is simply known as 'Marjorie'), the time of the show (8:30), and the intersection of the venue (Polk and Turk). Splashing across the page are the colors of purple, blue, pink, black, and white.

This handbill isn't just announcing a performance. It's more than that. The handbills and concert posters that appeared in and around the Bay Area in the late 60s were works of beauty, *about* things of beauty. And the things of beauty weren't just rock'n'roll shows—these were events where

* See, for instance, Ravindra Kumar's *Kundalini For Beginners*.

light, music, dance, and youth intermingled in some of the city's oldest halls. Within these halls could be found a sense of change, and a reality of change. Shows weren't just places to listen to a popular new band, these were places to pursue a different level of consciousness.

McAllister Street, where this piece of paper is flapping in the wind, is two blocks south of California Hall. Dominating the north side of Turk Street between Polk and Van Ness, the large hall is made mostly of yellowish brick with ornamental detail-work along its edging on each floor of its outer walls. Construction of it was completed in 1912, its design modeled on a Heidelberg castle. Funded by the local German Association, Das Deutsches Haus received best wishes from Kaiser Wilhelm himself. At that time, over forty German societies and lodges called it home, in the days when, according to writer and historian Joel Selvin in his book *San Francisco: The Musical History Tour*, 'Polk Strausse was the main commercial street for San Francisco's many German immigrants.' With the onset of World War I, the building was soon renamed California Hall.

Today, October 28 1966, Moby Grape's manager, Matthew Katz, has arranged for this fifty-four-year-old building to be the venue for the band's debut outside the Ark. They have been writing, and rehearsing, and jamming solidly for around two months now. At this point, they're just another drop in the ocean. Along with an expanding cluster of artists, the members of the Grape have been jamming with others at the Ark and the Heliport, sometimes from midafternoon to sunrise. The collective of musicians includes Big Brother & The Holding Company, The Grateful Dead, The Sons Of Champlin, Lee Michaels, and others—and these are only the more established local bands. Hundreds of bands are springing up across the Bay Area, with some later estimates suggesting that up to 1,500 bands are vying for gigs and attention in and around San Francisco during this period.*

With five songwriters, five singers, five-part harmonies, electrifying performances, and the kinetic presence of Skip Spence, Moby Grape are a unique proposition. There's something special about them. Yet there are no

* To read about some of these bands, see Bruce Tahsler's *The San Francisco East Bay 60s Scene Then and Now*.

guarantees. At this point in time, they are a young band with a cartload of potential—and their future is one very much of uncertainty.

These are Moby Grape's realities on this Friday evening, October 28 1966.

Shortly after 9:30pm, after Lee Michaels's performance ends and the musicians pack up their equipment, the lights dim and Moby Grape jump into their opening number. With a fuzzy bass, a distinctly jingle-jangle guitar, and prominent harmonies, this electric-folk song sounds very much of its time—until, that is, the band leaps back into the past, when the song's repeated chorus rolls around, with a kazoo, some scat singing, and a peppy sing-along. All the while, flashing across the stage and backdrop are brightly colored lights, continually changing in flashes and bursts.

Spinning and spinning like a merry-go-round, the song blends a lo-fi Byrds sound with the music hall cheer of Ray Davies. It's 'Good Time Car,' the first—and only—single released by The New Tweedy Brothers, released in 1966 by Dot Records.

There have been so many car songs over the years. Back in the 50s there was 'Maybellene' by Chuck Berry. In the early 60s The Beach Boys released a trove of catchy car songs, mostly about hot rods, including 'Fun, Fun, Fun,' 'This Car Of Mine,' 'No-Go Showboat,' 'Our Car Club,' 'Little Deuce Coup,' and 'Custom Machine.' As the 60s unfolded, more and more car tunes zoomed across the airwaves, like Ronny & The Daytonas' 'Bucket T,' The Beatles' 'Drive My Car,' and Wilson Pickett's classic 'Mustang Sally.'

'Good Time Car' didn't just continue a branch of songs, however; it put a new twist on the whole subgenre. It's a sort of music-hall car song, set when the sunny days of summer are getting shorter, and are about to give way to the autumn:

We're riding in my car
Well, it ain't got much but it's the best by far
I'm happy as can be
Just riding with my girl and me.

This car song doesn't zoom—it bounces. Its creators, The New Tweedy Brothers, came and went in the blink of an eye after moving to San Francisco from Portland, Oregon, in 1966—one single and one album. With a small print run and a hexagon-shape design, the album was destined to become a collectable, but that was immaterial to the band. They had no way of knowing their poorly selling album would become a relic of sorts. With low record sales and fewer gigs, this band of troubadours would reach the end of their path by the end of '68. And that was it.

•

Somehow, it's nighttime. At the intersection of Sutter and Polk is another old ballroom in the beaux arts style: the Avalon, run by Chet Helms, represents the main competition for Bill Graham and the Fillmore.

The entrance opens and four figures burst into the street, hurrying east in a flurry on the north side of Sutter. Who are they, and why are they in such a rush? On the wall at the front of the Avalon is a concert poster designed by Stanley Mouse that features a large Spanish galleon navigating a turbulent sea storm, reminiscent with its white-capped waves of Hokusai's woodcut, 'The Great Wave Off Kanagawa.' Written prominently on the ship is the year 1967, and above and below the galleon scene are the details of the shows. It's New Year's Eve—still 1966, barely—and Moby Grape are playing at the Avalon at midnight.

CHAPTER TWELVE

'IT WAS PRETTY MUCH LIKE A WORKSHOP.'

February 2017. In the early evening, I dial Jerry's number. Nervous and expectant, I wait as the phone rings. It's late afternoon in Tacoma, and Jerry has an evening show tonight. He answers after the fifth ring, and he begins our conversation by telling me about Moby Grape's first rehearsal.

'We got together at Matthew Katz's little studio office on California Street in San Francisco,' he says. 'It was a small building, and we were up on the second floor. And there was Skippy standing there. It was the first time I met Peter and Skip.

'We all plugged into our amplifiers and Skippy grabbed his guitar and right there I thought, *This is different. This is way different than anything else. Boy!* And on the way home, me and Don were just high fiving each other saying, This is something that could work!'

Filled with curiosity, I ask if he remembers which songs they played together that day.

> Sure. There was 'Fall On You.' I think that was the very first one. That was Pete's tune. And we did a version of 'Someday,' but it was very different from the version we recorded for the first album. And, of course, I like my blues stuff, so we had

to throw in a little Sonny Terry and Brownie McGee in there. Because me and Don were doing a lot of R&B. We were doing a lot of Sonny Terry and Brownie McGee stuff. That old stuff. [*Laughs jovially.*] But that's where it started for the five of us, right there in Matthew's office. I relate to it like in *Indiana Jones* where he has sort of a staff in his hands, and the beam of light through a hole in the ceiling, and the light goes around. It's like when you've really got something special and you know it.

That first rehearsal at Matthew's office was just a get together—but it was magic. It wasn't long after that that we started playing at the Ark. It was within the month at least, or maybe a couple of weeks. But our first gig, our debut, was at California Hall. It was our coming out party. We only had about a hundred people out for those shows. It was a good turnout, but in California Hall it looked really empty.

I pause for a moment, collecting my thoughts. From everything I've read and heard, it sounds like the Ark—an old paddleboat in Waldo Point Harbor, in Sausalito—was a really unique and important place for Moby Grape, and an important step in the band's development. I ask Jerry about the first time the band played there.

Well, the first time we played in the Ark was just like all the other times. Whenever we'd play at the Ark, we'd come in and set up and have a little confab with Matthew, or whoever else was involved. And we would talk about publishing and what that meant. You know, a lot of us didn't know much about publishing, unfortunately.

Sometimes I'd drive to the Ark. Otherwise, we'd have to catch the train and walk across the bridge to Sausalito. Both of us had a car at the time. I had a '50 Olds Rocket 88. We'd take that, me and Don. Me and Don and our wives and kids were all living together in San Carlos. Sometimes Don and I would

> catch the train from down in San Mateo to San Francisco, and then we would walk all the way to Sausalito. We would rehearse from six in the evening to six in the morning, with breaks and stuff. But people would come in. Right next door was a place called the Heliport. That was in Sausalito, right next to the Ark. And that's where everybody would practice, the Quicksilver, Big Brother, and Janis, Lee Michaels—you know, everybody would be up there. Everybody! The Dead, the Airplane, the Sons Of Champlin. They all had different cubicles at the Heliport for rehearsing.

When I first read about the Ark, it sounded like a magical place, slightly unreal. In my imagination, it was something that somehow *belonged* in the Bay Area—a place that could only come to be in those months that led up to the Summer of Love. Over the years, I've perused old photographs of the S.S. *Charles Van Damme*, but none that showed what it was like on the inside. Pondering this, I ask Jerry to describe it.

> The Ark was lopsided. It was a ferryboat called the *Charles Van Damme*. And the floor wasn't even, as if the floor was like—a marble would roll down it. But it had a little stage. They had afterhours food, and we could play all night long and change around with different bands and people would come up there and play. But we had basically control of the situation. It was nice. Matthew set us up with some guy named Martinez, or something like that. It was our basic rehearsal spot. We did shows at night. Sometimes we'd go on all night long—and into the morning. Buffalo Springfield would come up there—Neil and everybody would be playing and would go up and play. We were smokin', too!
>
> So it must've been interesting at the Heliport as well. Back in the 40s it was an old Second World War ammunitions warehouse, and then, by the time you got to Sausalito, it'd been

> converted into a rehearsal space. It kind of looks like an office building, or a school from the outside. But it was really like a music community.
>
> When we were at the Heliport we'd go from room to room to see how loaded we could get. We'd just get more and more loaded. [*Laughs.*] And there was all kinds of good weed around. We smoked all we could. Sometimes we'd play at the Heliport in the afternoon and then go over to the Ark in the evening. Sometimes we'd play from eight thirty at night to two in the morning at the Ark, sometimes longer. Sometimes we'd be around there for breakfast. They had a nice little breakfast there.

Thinking back to the Grape's early days, I wonder about what it was like to shift from the sort of music The Frantics were playing to the new territory the Grape dived into—how they managed the transition from R&B to the their new sound.

> We wanted to get in on all the changes going on. Out went the three-piece suits. Out went the razor cuts. We let our hair grow and we could wear what we wanted. There was a place that made little psychedelic clothes that was cool. It was nice not to have to wear an itchy old hounds-tooth suit!
>
> Things didn't really start happening until we hit the Avalon and the Fillmore. Then, we developed a lot of new friends. But we still had a lot of old friends from The Frantics, too. People would love to come around and see what was going on. The band was so good. It was something. If you saw us once you'd want to see us again. But we worked really hard. We spent a lot of time rehearsing, over and over again with the background voices, and all the harmonies.

When they first started out, the band would move from place to place as they rehearsed and wrote the songs that would eventually form their debut album. 'I remember going over to Skippy's one day, and he was working on "Omaha" upstairs. He didn't know what to call it, so he just said, "Omaha." I think Don and I wrote most of the other stuff over at Don's place, over on Alcatraz—he lived on a street called Alcatraz. [*Laughs.*] We'd write anywhere—in the car, sometimes!'

In those days, as Moby Grape started playing their first shows, Jerry was playing a Gibson L-5, made in 1961—'I still have it, and as a matter of fact I'm going to play it tonight at my gig'—through a '59 Fender Bassman amp. As he tells me this, I start to mentally go over the names of some of the musicians the Grape shared the bill with during their first run of shows in late '66 and early '67.

There's the James Cotton Blues Band, for whom Moby Grape opened in November 1966, the first time they played at the Fillmore. 'It was quite an honor to play with him. He was a big time old Chicago bluesman.'

Steve Mann, the amazing fingerpicking guitarist who opened the band's shows at the Matrix in December '66: 'He was wonderful! I have his first album right here. Him and Taj Mahal. It's a rare, rare album. They recorded it in Berkeley. As a matter of fact, I do "44-Blues" and I do a couple of tunes from Steve Mann's first album in my shows. I might do one tonight. He had a tune called "Holly" that he was working on forever. You know, I thought he was dead forever. Then, I found him on the internet and there he was, and I read about him. And before I could get a hold of him he passed away. He was good friends with Mac Rebennack in the old days—that's Dr. John.'

The Charlatans, with Dan Hicks on drums, and their old-timey clothes that made them look like they were from the 1800s: 'I remember them arguing with Bill Graham before a gig one time. They were badass, you know.'

We then turn to the band's shows at the Santa Venetia Armory during this period. 'We did a couple of benefits there,' Jerry tells me. 'We did one for a teacher who needed a transplant, I think. The kids at the school sent us a letter asking if we could do something for their teacher. We said okay. We got some accolades for that.'

Reflecting on his favorite venues to play during this period, Jerry flits between two legendary stages:

> It's hard to say between the Avalon and the Fillmore. They were both great places to play. But if I had to pick one it would be the Fillmore. We played at the Fillmore more. The Avalon didn't last as long.
>
> You know, Bill Graham always stuck with us. And he was so ashamed of us when we fell apart. David Rubinson, too. But we had no business going to New York in the first place. It was just too much. We should've stayed on the West Coast. They told us, 'You'll save money if you stay at the Albert Hotel.' It was just a pigsty. There were cockroaches, and we were walking around there on the edge of the building—more than ten flights up, wandering from room to room on the ledges. It was crazy! We could've fallen and broke our necks! That was crazy ...

•

Later that month I meet Don again. Leaving Yonge Street, I cut through Sherwood Park and then head south on Bayview to a café shortly before Millwood Road. I sit down at one of the many empty tables, and in a short while Don joins me.

We start off by talking about his first audition with Moby Grape, which took place before they even had a name for the band, when Peter, Bob, and Skip were looking for a drummer but ended up with a two-for-one package deal: Don and Jerry.

> Bob knew two of us—and Peter was playing with Bob. Matthew had Skippy, who he wanted to build a band around. So when we went up to the audition we just played songs we all knew—cover songs. It was like, well, you've got Mosley playing bass, you know, and Jerry's a monster on guitar. It was just amazing!

> And when Jerry and I drove back down … you know, at the rehearsal, we were being kind of cool, like, they'd say, 'What do you think?' and we'd reply, 'I don't know, man.' But when we got in the car we were high-fiving each other! So, that's how we felt about it! I guess everyone felt the same way.

Before long, Matthew Katz would set the band up at the Ark, but first, as Jerry had also explained, they rehearsed and wrote together at each other's houses. 'We were writing like crazy,' Don says. 'When we had a song, we'd just start contributing, changing it, saying, What about this? What about that? And put in harmonies. There was that energy—that musical energy. That's the thing that I miss about having a band. When we were rehearsing at Skippy's house there was a huge amount of contributions from everybody—and nobody was worried about who gets what in terms of credit. It was a very special thing.'

Moving to the Ark, still dry-docked at Gate 6 on the harbor, they quickly settled into a routine of playing and jamming right through the afternoon and evening into the night, taking turns with some of the other bands from the scene who were honing their sounds on the Ark, too.

> We had a regimen at the Ark. It was almost like a job. We had to show up and we all moved down there. Me and Jerry, and I think Mosley lived around Sausalito. We'd come into the Ark in the early afternoon, and we'd all hit the freezer. There was a freezer full of really bad food—like frozen chicken with some kind of bizarre center. [*Laughs.*] We'd heat up some food and then we'd rehearse. There were the other bands that were there too, like Lee Michaels, and Buffalo Springfield and Janis [Joplin] and others. There was a time where you'd rehearse and practice and play. Then, somebody else would take the stage and they'd practice and play, and we'd go do vocals at the other end of the Ark. It was pretty much like a workshop. It was almost kind of like a living space, and at night it became an afterhours club. It

was a showcase for the bands. Different record companies came in to check out who the different bands were.

I remember a time later on—this was after '66—sitting down and talking with Janis one time, on one of the upper decks where the public didn't go. So we were up in one of the upper decks sitting and talking, and she had already had some success at that point. They were out touring, and they were doing really well, and she was—she was *pining* a little bit. Like, being home, and you're on out on the road, and it's kind of lonely. I remember having some conversations with her in New York like that too—at a club called the Steve Paul Scene. Janis was with us there one time, and Tiny Tim was there and B.B. King was there. Janis was like a girl—she was like a little girl. She was kind of like a girly girl. Suddenly, everybody thought that she was like Aretha Franklin. She wasn't ready for all that stuff. She was a little bit overwhelmed by it all. She'd kind of go, 'Hi boys! Heya fellas!' She had Southern Comfort. That was her drink of choice.

I remove a piece of paper from my backpack and hand it to Don. It's a printout of the earliest known poster for a Moby Grape concert, hand-drawn by an artist who went by the name Marjorie in black-and-white, and then painted with purple and black ink. The floral design is comprised of a bunch of organic shapes that flow out of a circle in the center. In the circle is a little ferryboat, representing the Ark, and in a ring around the circle are the words 'Rock Boat' and 'Gate 6, Sausalito.' Around it, in petal-shaped areas, are the words 'High on the Vine,' 'Light Voyage,' and 'Dance,' as well as the more important details: that the shows will run from Tuesday to Sunday, October 11–23, from 8:30pm to 2am. The top half of the poster lists the name 'Moby Grape' and the bottom half 'Lee Michaels.'*

'I remember playing more after-hours—more than just 2am,' Don says,

* On the band's name, Peter Lewis later explained to Jud Cost, 'Bob and Skippy had come up with the name, the punch line to the joke: What's eight tons, purple and floats in the sea?'

after looking at the poster for a moment. 'Everybody would come out of the Avalon and the Fillmore and come over to the Ark.' The Ark would remain open until six in the morning, and the bands that were still there would eat breakfast together.

> We'd chow down on that and then go home and crash. It was really intimidating, playing those early morning shows. It's funny, because Jerry and I are kind of like—if we were the East Coast, we'd be, like, Philadelphia. And then Peter's more Hollywood, and Mosley's a surfer guy, and Skip's from outer space. [*Laughs.*]
>
> I came from the school of rhythm & blues, and I wanted to play jazz, and all that changed when I heard The Byrds for the first time. Jon Keliehor turned me on to The Byrds, and that's when I realized that there was something more than just the B-3 Hammond organ trios with guitar, which is what I had done a lot of up to that point—Etta James, and all that stuff, which was really cool. But switching over to that kind of music … you know, I'm still kind of a hardcore rhythm & blues guy. When people would come over from the Avalon and the Fillmore at two or three in the morning, I'd look out there and, to tell you the truth, I was—I don't know if 'intimidated' is the right word, but everyone was so stoned and they all had hair sticking out everywhere. They looked like water buffalo sitting out in the crowd. And you'd sit there and you'd play and you'd think, *this is a strange experience.*
>
> I'd played afterhours clubs before—the Black & Tan, stuff like that—but this was different. The audience at the Ark looked like woolly mammoth and buffalo—and it took a bit to adjust to all of that. It freaked me out a little bit.

I remind Don of something I'd read about a young band who opened for the Grape at their second-ever show, at the California Hall, called West

Coast Branch. They had formed after finishing high school in Inglewood, California, and got a regular gig at the Flying Jib in Redondo Beach, not far from where Buffalo Springfield were playing at the time. In the autumn of '66, after releasing a version of Willie Dixon's 'Spoonful' (predating the Cream version), they headed up to the Bay Area for a week of shows. One of the guys in the band, Chuck Marchese, later described it as like playing the French Riviera—so much so that a few of them ended up renting a room and staying in the city for a while.*

'It was pretty seductive,' Don chuckles.

I then show Don another printout of a poster, this time for Moby Grape's shows at the Avalon Ballroom of December 23 and 24, where they shared the billed with The Steve Miller Band. The poster itself, with its vivid green and red design, was the work of Victor Moscoso—one of the major poster artists of the era—and has since become known as the 'Hippie Santa Claus' poster.†

One of the shows that stands out for Don was the band's New Year's Eve '66 set at the Avalon Ballroom, on a bill that also featured Country Joe & The Fish.

> We were playing at midnight—on January first. And it got close to midnight and Mosley was nowhere to be found. [*Laughs.*] So we had to go out to try and find him. Maybe it was around eleven o'clock, and we were all in the dressing room, and Bob wasn't there. So we went out and walked around the neighborhood and we found Bob sitting in a bar, drinking—having a beer. He

* To read an interesting snapshot of the short career of the West Coast Branch, see Erik Bluhm and Paul Gammage's 'West Coast Branch,' as published at westcoastfog.com.

† In his introduction to *The Art Of The Fillmore*, Walter Medeiros lists five general characteristics of the art from these posters: (1) posters are 'handmade—drawn—unlike the 1960s commercial style of photos and typeset lettering' ... (2) 'The sheet is fully covered, rich in decorative line and/or pattern' ... (3) 'Lettering is compact, shaped into abstract forms, or undulating, stretched or warped. Otherwise, it may be finely rendered and elegantly decorative.' ... (4) 'Color is bright, often intense, sometimes with contrasting adjacent hues that cause the edges of the form to flicker, flow, or create an illusion of depth.' ... and (5) 'Imagery is often unusual, and unrelated to the event or to the bands on the bill. Images may be sensual, bizarre, or beautiful, philosophical or metaphysical.'

said, 'Don't worry man, I'm just having a beer.' So we came back in, and Bob brought this cool-looking old dude with us—he looked old to me at the time, but he was probably like I am right now.

When we got up to play, this old guy comes up on the stage and he says, 'I've got something to say.' And Jerry's like, 'Yeah, go right ahead, man, whatever you've got to say.' The old man goes up to the microphone and he goes, 'Hey everybody, I want all of you young people to know that you're wonderful. You're doing amazing things. I'm an old guy. My time is slipping by, and when I'm going down, somebody else is coming up. You guys are all coming up. I just wish all of you love and happiness for this New Year!'

I thought to myself, *how cool is that*? Bob had just met him in the bar, and then he came with us to the gig. So we played our gig and we played 'Old Acquaintance Be Forgot' and all that stuff. It was a New Year's Eve I'll never forget. It was pretty cool. And Bob made it to the gig!

CHAPTER THIRTEEN

THE PROMISED LAND

As the New Year approached, Moby Grape found themselves in a strong position, with bookings plentiful, shows selling out, and a number of record labels wooing them. The 'What Goes On?' column in the February '67 issue of *Crawdaddy* summed up the situation they found themselves in:

> The most exciting and most sought-after (by record companies) new group on the West Coast is San Francisco's Moby Grape. The Grape have enormous impact on an audience. Three guitars, a very talented bass, and a drummer (all of whom sing well), they come on like a flash flood. Guitarist Skip Spence—who used to be drummer for Jefferson Airplane—radiates joy in all directions, turning on the group, turning on the audience, turning the whole performance into an event, a celebration. The Grape's music is excellent and is likely to get better—the group is only a few months old, and when they *really* get together, they'll be frightening.

'There were numerous people who were pursuing us,' Don recalls, 'and it was just happening all around San Francisco. Because that was the hub where everything was happening at that time. It was probably like the way Seattle was when grunge became big. All the record companies were coming to San Francisco trying to pick some band that was going to be successful.'

On January 13, Moby Grape played at the Santa Venetia Armory, sharing the bill with Country Joe & The Fish, Lee Michaels, Big Brother & The Holding Company, and Morning Glory. That same night—and on the next night as well—they played the Avalon Ballroom with The Charlatans and The Sparrow. Around this time, they flew to Los Angeles, where they'd been invited to audition for various different record companies in an informal hotel setting.

By now, the band and manager Matthew Katz had narrowed the field to Columbia, Elektra, and Atlantic. 'We were down in Los Angeles to finalize a deal,' Don continues. 'We were in a motel down there—one that had individual little cabins. [Elektra's] Paul Rothchild came and heard us when we sang, and [Columbia's] David Rubinson came over and listened to us sing. We did a set just sitting there with our instruments in the hotel room. We just sang our set, and we had our harmonies bang on. It was nice. It was really fun to do that.'

'We were at the Hollywood Hawaiian,' Jerry adds. 'I remember sitting there playing, and we had our harmonies worked out. I think there was a guy there named Bongo Wold and his girlfriend, Sister Weird,' he laughs. 'Pretty weird people.'

Though Atlantic made an offer for the band, too, in the end it came down to a choice between Elektra and Columbia. It was a difficult choice, as Don recalls:

> Rothchild and Elektra offered us a really nice deal, as far as money and promotion goes.* I kind of thought that I had something to say about it, but looking back I had nothing to say about it. I didn't get to have any kind of input. I don't know

* Lewis later told Jud Cost that Rothchild said he would give the band 'anything you want' to sign with Elektra, even offering 50 percent of the company's stock.

what sort of deal Matthew worked out in the end. But David Rubinson impressed us. Paul did, too. But David said, 'Look, guys, here's what's going to happen: I'm going to record you guys and Columbia's going to make this the biggest thing that you've ever seen. And you guys won't be able to walk down the street in Mill Valley without people recognizing you. We're going to make you stars!'

Personally, I had that drive from the time that I was young for a lot of reasons. We all get raised in different ways. I always had that *I'll show you* mindset. And that was the answer. I thought, *boy, I'll show them!* [*Laughs.*]

I look at it now, after all these years, and I think that David Rubinson did an amazing job. I love what he did. He ended up being the only grown-up in the room for periods of time. But I wasn't happy with what Matthew did. It wasn't something that someone who had everyone's best interests at heart would do. As things turned out, everyone's had to spend their lives litigating. But I don't have any regret. I think Paul Rothchild would've been a great choice, too. Elektra did a great job with The Doors. I don't know how their affairs were handled, but, for us, things didn't work out.

In the end, the band and their manager were swayed by the combination of Columbia's clout and Rubinson's eagerness, but Elektra wouldn't give up without a fight. As Rubinson revealed to Gene Sculatti in 2007, 'Jac Holzman offered me a job at Elektra if I'd bring Moby Grape with me!'

•

Around this time, the journalist Richard Goldstein wrote a glowing piece on San Francisco for the *Village Voice*—and, in doing so, unwittingly accelerated the loss of the city's innocence, as his article would help fuel the mass migration to the city among American's youth. Surveying the signing frenzy in the Bay Area, he wrote:

> Talent scouts from a dozen major record companies are now perusing the scene, and grooving with the gathered tribes at the Fillmore and the Avalon. Hip San Francisco is being carved into bits of business territory. The Jefferson Airplane belong to RCA. The Sopwith Camel did so well for Kama Sutra the label has invested in a second local group, the Charlatans. The Grateful Dead have signed with Warner Brothers in an extraordinary deal which gives them complete control over material and production. Moby Grape is tinkering with Columbia and Elektra. And a bulging fistful of local talent is being wined and dined like the last available shikse in the promised land.

'It took off like crazy!' Jerry exclaims. 'We could've gone with any record company.' Looking back now, he suggests that Rothchild and Elektra might have allowed the band to 'stay loose—a lot looser … but I don't know if that would've made such a nice first album.' With Rubinson, he notes, they 'really worked hard' on their debut. 'When we got there, in the studio, we had everything pretty much done in about thirteen days. Hell, we went in there *rehearsed*! We had it pretty well down. Then we'd start the overdubbing—but we'd always go in there and just *play* first.'

On January 25, Moby Grape stepped into the studio for the first time to record two demos for Columbia: Peter's 'Looper' and Skip's 'Indifference.' A few days later, they returned to San Francisco for a January 29 show at the Avalon, a benefit event called *Krishna Consciousness Comes West*. Also at the event—which raised funds for opening a Krishna Temple in San Francisco—were Swami Bhaktivedanta (the founder of the International Society for Krishna Consciousness, or ISKCON), Allen Ginsberg, The Grateful Dead, and Big Brother & The Holding Company.

On February 6, they recorded another demo for Columbia in LA, Peter's 'Stop.' The label was suitably impressed; the following day, the band signed their recording contract, with the news shared at a press conference. 'Columbia was a prestigious label,' Don reflects. 'They had Dylan and The Byrds. That was a part of it. They were doing a good job.'

Of course, complications were in the works. Speaking to Jud Cost, Peter Lewis put a slightly different spin on the band's decision to sign with Columbia. 'We loved The Byrds, and that's why we went with Columbia—the worst place for us. You can sink or swim, and it doesn't matter to them.' According to Lewis, Columbia also promised to 'make every contract we had with Matthew unenforceable. But they couldn't do it.' Katz, he concluded, was 'too much of a prima donna to be a manager,' but because he had a contract with the band, he was the one the labels called. 'That's how he got back in the game.'

•

Shortly after signing their record contract, Moby Grape whisked back to the Bay Area for more shows. They performed at the Fillmore on February 12, sharing the bill with The Grateful Dead, Sly & The Family Stone, The New Salvation Army, and Notes From The Underground. The show was a benefit put on to support the Council for Civic Unity, a Bay Area organization involved in the Civil Rights Movement.

Two nights later, on Valentine's Day, the band returned to the Ark for a show with Big Brother & The Holding Company and Jack The Ripper, followed by a three-night run from February 17 to 19 with The Freudian Slips and All Night Apothecary. In the middle of these late-night shows at the Ark, they also played the Sausalito Auditorium on February 18, with Loading Zone. The following week, they played shows on February 24 and 25 at the Avalon with The Charlatans and Iron Butterfly, and the next night, February 26, at the Fillmore with Steve Miller and B.B. King.

In the midst of all that, Jerry recalls, they were making the final preparations for the recording of their debut album.

> We were going back and forth when we rehearsed the album. We were living in Marin County. Some of us had kids by then. We'd stay at the Hollywood Hawaiian in LA. It was nice—right in the middle of Hollywood, and we'd get to bump into everybody. I was doing a jam session one time with The John

> Dance Band and I looked over and I thought, *that guy looks familiar*. It was Huntz Hall! You know, from *The Bowery Boys*.
>
> We'd fly back and forth and play gigs at the Fillmore and the Avalon. I remember playing up in Sacramento, with The Turtles. We did a gig there that made Bill Graham really mad, 'cos we'd been booked to do two gigs on one night. So we played our first set at the Fillmore, and we'd got … I don't know if it was a helicopter or a little plane, but we jetted up to Sacramento and played with The Turtles and then hustled back to play the last set at the Fillmore. Bill Graham was not happy with that, and you did not want Bill Graham unhappy. You didn't want to be late with Bill. Bill was strict. And I didn't like that idea either. I thought it was bad. You know, you cut the draw at the Fillmore by splitting the bill. It wasn't a very good business deal in my view.

Reminded of this, Don shares another funny story about Graham. 'We'd play the Fillmore quite a bit,' he says, 'and Bill Graham was very strict with time. If we'd show up late or not play a great set … one time, he put a time clock right on the stage and gave us time cards to punch in and out. He did it as kind of a joke, but it was also to send us a message. So, if we were scheduled to start at 9:30, we'd have to punch in and really be there at 9:30—with a time clock right up there. That was pretty funny!'

•

Moby Grape might not always have started their shows on time—during one of our conversations, Don laughed frantically as he recalled how road manager Tim Dellara 'used a cattle prod one time to get us to go to a gig!'—but they were at the height of their powers at this point in early '67, in full command of their live performances and standing on the threshold of their first studio recordings. In a 2016 radio interview with Nick Black, Peter Lewis likened music in this sense to surfing:

> It's kind of like you're on this wave when you're playing music.

> You're between the past and the future. The past being where that thing is, like, rolling up, everything from the sea floor. And just pounding it to bits. If you don't stay on your feet, that'll catch you. But with a song … it's not life threatening, but … you gotta be where you are in the song. You can't think about the end of the song when you're in the middle of it …
>
> That's what it felt like when we were playing music in the 60s sometimes, up in those ballrooms: it felt like you were pulling the future toward you, not like you're moving toward it. And that's what music is really good at doing … that's the religion of music. When you get together with a bunch of guys that can communicate that way, I mean, it's better than anything else.

March 1967 would be another busy month for the band. On March 3, they played the Winterland, sharing the bill with Love, The Grateful Dead, Loading Zone, and Blue Crumb Truck Factory at an event, the 'First Annual Love Circus,' that ran from 7pm to 7am. Two nights later, they played another benefit concert at the Avalon, raising funds for the New Stage and the Straight Theater, this time on a bill with B.B. King, Country Joe & The Fish, The Sparrow, and The Grateful Dead.

Following this show, the band made their way back to Los Angeles to start recording their debut album, armed with a reservoir of tight, infectious songs, their arrangements and harmonies already worked out, and a producer, David Rubinson, who believed in them wholeheartedly. Working together at Columbia Studios on Sunset Boulevard for just a handful of days in March and April, they would create an LP that still stands as a classic of 60s pop.

The brisk recording schedule began on March 11 and 12, with 'Rounder' and 'Come In The Morning' recorded on the first day, and '8:05' and 'Fall On You' on the second. The first of these would fail to make the final album, but when I play an instrumental version of it to Don, he calls it 'a hell of a song. The instrumental is just great. It shows how funky it was and what a groove it was. And then the vocals were great when we did it live. But it didn't end up on any of our albums. It just got lost in the shuffle.'

Jerry chuckles when I ask about recording in LA, remembering how Moby Grape 'bounced back and forth' between the different Columbia studios, depending on who else was working there at the time.

> We were in Studio D at first to lay down the tracks. And then we went over to Studio A. The Beach Boys took over Studio D. I was over there one time when we got started and they were doing some sounds—like *bubadee-bubadee-bubadee*, and after a few days I went back there and they were still working on this sound, *bubadee-bubadee-bubadee*. [*Laughs.*] I remember Brian coming in with his Ferrari and his own little parking spot there at Columbia. He'd come in and he was all together when we were over at Columbia. Then The Byrds came in and did some stuff, and Don Ellis took over one of the studios and we went over and watched him record. My good friend Jo Johnson came poppin' in there. I think he was playing with Tamer Black.
>
> We had one session that was so cool. We had Dr. John playing piano and Chuck Schoning playing organ, and Andy Williams and Johnny Mathis came in … we were all playing and having a heck of a good time. We were doing 'Satisfied' and a whole bunch of Dr. John tunes, jamming like crazy. Later, I went up to the studio and into the control room, and David Rubinson looks at me and says, 'I hope you didn't think I was recording that.' [*Bursts out laughing.*] I said 'What? You didn't record that?' What a lineup! What a funky session. When David said, 'I hope you didn't think I was recording that,' I thought he was kidding!

After leaving the studio on March 12, Moby Grape would not return to Columbia for another forty-one days, but those forty-one days were busy ones. With another run of shows scheduled for the end of the month, they began to rehearse in earnest. From March 24 to 26, they played the

Winterland with The Chambers Brothers and The Charlatans, and then, on March 31 and April 1, they played the Winterland and the Fillmore with The Byrds and Andrew Staples.

'I've got a collection of those old posters,' Jerry tells me. 'I just love the fact that on some of the posters there's Moby Grape and Jimi Hendrix, Moby Grape and Traffic, Moby Grape and The Sparrow, and The Byrds. Those are all great memories. They're right here on my wall. We were like a family then. We'd go to Stanley Mouse's operation or any of the other studios and just watch them work. And *Rolling Stone* was headquartered in San Francisco back then too. It was a great time.'

Playing with The Byrds at Winterland was a landmark moment in Don's career—but a disappointing one, too.

> Musically, they changed my life. I loved them. [But] when we got to play the Winterland with them, they weren't that great. Maybe it was just that night. I'm not sure. We were on top of our game from constant rehearsal, and recording and playing, and because we were playing with The Byrds, we just went all out to rehearse and prepare. And we played a great show. Then, I heard The Byrds and it kind of broke my heart. It was probably just a bad night for them—but they were playing like how we later played sometimes. After a while, you take it for granted. On that night, we were not taking for granted at all. We were hungry and rehearsing and playing. I was disappointed, because I wanted The Byrds to play a great set as well. I just loved them.*

'We rehearsed for about four days,' Jerry recalls, when I ask him about these shows. 'And we were great. We were all dressed up and we were on fire!'

* The year 1967 was a complicated one for The Byrds. They released their fourth album, *Younger Than Yesterday*, shortly before their run of shows with Moby Grape. During this period, their singles stopped climbing the charts, and their audience changed from teens to more of an underground following. In the early summertime, they fired their managers, and by October, both Michael Clarke and David Crosby had left the band. When I remind Don of all this, he replies, 'There you go. I knew it had to be something.'

Less happily, this was also the weekend when some opportunist thieves came into one of the venues between shows and made off with much of the band's equipment, including Don's brand new Gretsch drum kit and Jerry's Gibson L-5, his beloved Buelah.

Casting his mind back to the spring of '67, Don recalls:

> I had wanted to get a set of black Gretsch drums, 'cos I loved Gretsch drums. I was playing Slingerland drums at the time, then I got this set of black Gretsch drums. We played Friday night and my drum sound was awesome. Beautiful. Then, on Saturday, we came to do the gig and all our stuff had been stolen. Somebody had come in in the daytime on the Saturday, and they had overalls on and a big truck, and they had all our equipment and they looked like they fit right in, like equipment guys. They took Jerry's amp, his L-5, they took all my drums and all the amps—all of the instruments. Everything was stolen!
>
> We got to the gig and we didn't have any instruments, so we had to play on somebody else's stuff. It was like having a moment with a woman you love, and for some reason she had to leave. She didn't want to but she had to. You should ask Jerry about the sojourn he had to go through to get his guitar back—including bikers and all kinds of stuff. He had all kinds of people out there looking for it. It was one of those things. They cleaned us out, and they looked authentic because they had overalls on and came in in a big truck—the whole deal. And I never found my drums.'*

Jerry picks up the story of his L-5, which at least has a happier ending.

> I told Matthew what happened and I said, 'I need ten $100 bills.' And he gave 'em to me. So I went to a friend of mine and

* Don never got another Gretsch drum set. 'Rogers gave me a set,' he tells me, 'so I could use those in photos and all that. That was right around the time of the Monterey Pop Festival.'

asked him to find the sleaziest guys around there. We figured [the thieves] were junkies. We started tracking them down. Soon I'm down a couple of hundred and I'm on the line, tracking it down. People would say, 'I've seen it.' By the time I got to the last hundred-dollar bill, my guitar was sitting there. But when we went to get it I had a pistol in my pocket. I was going to take my guitar—but I didn't want to take any chances. I didn't have to use it—and that's good! I wouldn't want to be sitting in jail forever!

We had a couple of real lowlifes in the backseat of my car when we went up to Thorn Lane in Santa Cruz. We walked in and opened the door, and I saw my guitar case sitting there. I had a picture of me playing my guitar with me—and he said, 'Aw, man, I'm glad it got back to the rightful owner.' And I said, 'Yeah, me too.' Then, we went back down to San Jose, and I had to get rid of those two guys who were sittin' in my backseat, doin' their junkie thing—and I had to get rid of that goddamned gun! And then I could breathe again. My wife was gonna kill me. When my guitar was gone I was just sour. I was not to be dealt with.

Skippy's guitar got stolen, too, but I couldn't find his. His got stolen from Jim Lendersmith's car—a red XJE. He went down to hear Sly & The Family Stone at the Winchester Cathedral, and while he was inside somebody came and busted the window out and took Skippy's guitar and my guitar—which was pretty irresponsible of him, to leave 'em out there! Finally, I had my friend Tim Dellara try to track down those nasty son-of-a-bitch guitar thieves. Tim ended up becoming our road manager.'*

---

* Listening to Jerry, I recall Tim's own recollection of these events—a psychedelic rendition of Antonio and Bruno's desperate search for a stolen bicycle in Vittorio de Sica's classic *Bicycle Thieves*. 'Jerry came to me and told me that his guitar got stolen. I told him I can put the word out that I'm looking for some stolen equipment. So I did that, and we got a couple of references, and one of them was some guy who came to my house one night and said, I've got this guitar. It was stolen. Do you want it? It was stolen from an all-girl band. It was a Telecaster or a Stratocaster. I called Jerry and told him about it and I asked, Do you want me to buy this from this guy to give her guitar back to her? And Jerry said yeah. It was, like, fifty bucks or something. So I gave them the money, and I wrote a little note and stuck it between the strings and the fretboard of the

•

Stolen equipment aside, at this moment in time it must've felt as though anything was possible for Moby Grape. Casting his mind back to the period and to landmark events like the Human Be-In at Golden Gate Park in a 2007 radio interview, Bob Mosley recalled, 'It was great. There was a gathering, you know … the Gathering of the Tribes. All the bands and all the people who came to hear the music were kind of like the same kind of … people in one place, with the music kind of holding them together.'

---

guitar. It said something like, *Here's your guitar back. Jerry bought it back from the guys who stole it, and we paid fifty bucks to get it back. It would be nice if you gave us the fifty bucks back.*

'About an hour later, I got a knock on the door, and these two guys were standing there—and they were obviously cops. They said, We saw this guy come in here with the guitar and he left without it, and we've been tracking this guy and we've been trying to pin him down. I'm thinking to myself, *I hope you guys don't ask to use the bathroom*, because I had a key of grass in the bathtub. I showed them the guitar, and fortunately I'd already written the note that was underneath the strings, so they bought my story.

'Eventually, these other guys came to me and said, We think we know where the guitar is. We think we know the guy that has it. We know his name, but we don't know where he lives, it's in Santa Cruz somewhere. He has a name like John Smith. In those days, you didn't have anything other than the telephone book. So I started calling people with that last name, and asking for a guy with that first name. It took about ten or twelve calls, and somebody said, Oh yeah, he's out in the other shed right now, we'll get him for ya. So he came in, and I thought to myself, *I've got to have a cover story here*. So I said, We're putting a band together and we hear you're a keyboard player and we're wondering if you wanna be in that band. He said, I do play keyboards but I don't want to be in a band. But are you guys interested in any guitars? I said, Not really … but what d'ya got? He said, I've got this Gibson. I said, You know, I don't know if we're interested in that or not … but, we could come and look at it. He gave me the address, and I said, We'll come over tomorrow. So I went to a friend of mine and I told him, We're going out to try and get this guitar back, and I think I need a pistol. And the guy said, Here you go. I think I told Jerry we better take some protection, because we don't know what's going to go on.

'We drove out there with two dudes who kind of turned us on to this lead. We were supposed to give them a reward. They were sitting in the back of the car. We came up to this place—it had a house, and there was a shack off it, where the son lived. We went in, and he was a dude who made jewelry—beads and stuff. We went in there, and said, What about this guitar? He brought it out, and it was Jerry's guitar, and I said, We'll give you a hundred bucks for it. And he said, Oh no, I need $250 for it. So I pulled out a picture of Jerry holding the guitar and said, In that case, we're just gonna take it, because it belongs to him. And the guy says, Good karma! Good karma! Great! This is wonderful! It's going back to the owner. Let me go get a joint and we'll smoke it. I thought, *Oh, God. Is he going to come back with a machete or something?* So I had my hand in my pocket. And he came back with a joint instead. Which was fine. We smoked it, and we put the guitar in the back of the car, and got in the car. As we drove away from that house, after this whole improbable thing, I turned to Jerry and said, You know what's in the trunk? And Jerry said, Yeah, my guitar.'

In his *Village Voice* article on the Bay Area scene, Richard Goldstein concluded, 'San Francisco is a lot like that grimy English seaport these days, in 1964. Liverpool rang with a sound that was authentically expressive and the city never tried to bury it. This is what is happening in San Francisco today. The establishment has achieved a much greater victory here than on the Strip: integration. The underground is open, unencumbered, and radiating.'

Like a hothouse, San Francisco had so much growing, from musicians to artists to magazines, and so many of them were challenging the status quo and exploring new possibilities. Monterey Pop and the fabled Summer of Love were still to happen, but they were both within reach. So too, of course, were the shadows of the Nixon presidency, the tragedy of Altamont, and chaos of Charles Manson—the yin to the yang—but as the summer of '67 approached, a sense of possibility was still in the air.

In April, Moby Grape continued to rehearse for the second and final leg of recordings for their debut LP, while also playing another clutch of gigs around the city: at Kezar Stadium on April 15 (with Judy Collins, Malvina Reynolds, and Steve Miller), and at Freedom Hall the following week (with Buffalo Springfield).

Then, across three days in late April—the 22nd, 23rd, and 25th—they returned to the studio to cut a barrage of songs—no less than ten tracks that complete the run of thirteen that will make up the album. Recalling the final day's session, Don tells me that Skip said to him as they prepared to sing the last of those thirteen songs, 'Someday': 'We need to breathe together to get our voices totally in sync. It shouldn't be two of us, it has to be like we're one voice.'

'"Someday" was just amazing!' Jerry exclaims when I tell him this.

> That was something I wrote on the bass, down in San Carlos, where me and Don and Paula and Cheryl and my kids were living. I started playing it on the bass, E to D and all that. So Don picked up on it too. But the magic—the magic part happened when we had the words and the melody and

> everything all worked out—but those harmonies! When we got down to Columbia Studios, I wasn't there when they added all those nice harmonies on it. But when I came in and heard it, it was so beautiful. We all helped each other quite a lot.

Over the next six weeks, the album will be mixed, the cover art finalized, and the release date confirmed.* On May 12, while mixing took place in New York, the Grape played another benefit show at the Fillmore Auditorium with Jefferson Airplane, The Grateful Dead, Quicksilver Messenger Service, Andrew Staples, and the Loading Zone. The show, titled 'Busted,' was arranged to raise funds to support the San Francisco Mime Troupe, who had recently gotten into trouble (again) for performing without a permit.

The following week, on May 19 and 20, the band played two more shows at the Winterland, this time with P.J. Proby and The Young Carousels. By May 20, the album's release was only seventeen days away, and the executives at Columbia had already turned their attention from production to promotion. They had something special planned for the marketing of the album—something that had never been done before.

Before we get to that, however, let's explore Moby Grape's debut album.

* When I ask Bob if he got involved in mixing the album, he replies, 'No, I didn't. It was Peter and Skip … the two younger guys,' he laughs.

CHAPTER FOURTEEN

MOBY GRAPE

Moby Grape's debut is a thirteen-song cycle. It's thirty-two minutes that race forward. With tremendous energy, the band charge ahead, blending styles, presenting contrasts and dualities, balancing those contrasts, sharing observations, pushing boundaries, expressing feelings, coping with worries and concerns, and feeling joyful and exuberant. It's a little over half an hour of excitement. After spending such a short time in this world, you feel as though you have been to a place of happiness, excitement, and joie de vivre.

Moby Grape is a thirteen-song album of freedom. It's also about free love, being in a place where people can love one another for a time, perhaps in the morning, and then part ways not sad but happy for having known and been with one another. It's a whole world, and within this world are feelings of happiness and despair. Feelings of purposelessness and sadness lurk in the midst, but through songs these five musicians find ways of coping, so they can look forward to the future while living in the here and the now. This suite of songs is a collection of contrasts, hope/despair, old/new, real/unreal, trust/mistrust, past/future, end/beginning, together/alone. The words and the music sometimes contrast with one another, and while the five singers often blend their voices into sweet harmonies, their voices sometimes contrast with one another too. It isn't simply an album of contrasts, however. It's a dialogue. The songs unfold in a sequence that represents a lyrical and stylistic conversation. The singers dialogue with one another from song to song, and within the songs themselves. As the album charges forward, it's filled with sharp, unexpected turns in speed and style, jumping from one genre to another, blending genres, changing tempo, changing key, and all the while holding everything together. It's an album of alchemy and exuberance. *Moby Grape* is an album made by five musical alchemists—six if we include producer David Rubinson. It's also an album of joyful exuberance, from the first note played on the guitar, and the first moment the band starts to sing. This is one of those rare albums that's both *of its time* and *timeless.*

•

It opens with a dash, as one buzzing guitar dives into the silence, crunching forward. It's soon joined by a bass, thumping the root note and mingling with the drums, which move along in a shuffle. Higher up, a soft, clean lead guitar sweeps across the mix, threading six notes—the last of them held in a vibrato. The drums speed up and multiple blended voices harmonize the first words ever sung on a Moby Grape album:

> *Hey Grandma you're so young*
> *Your old man is just a boy.*

The last words of some lines are held, extending into the instrumental follow-up, which includes a rollicking guitar, rapidly descending and then ascending like a Slinky. When the first verse ends, the song slows for a few short seconds, as though everyone needs to catch their breath—but soon everyone picks things up again and leaps into the second verse. With the second verse, the voices of Don Stevenson and Skip Spence paint more images of youth, zest, and happiness.

'Hey Grandma' is a song of contrasts—guitar work, harmonies, and lyrics. The grandma in the song isn't an older lady living a quiet life. This is a young woman, living free, with her partner, dressing in granny dresses and vintage clothing in self-assured joy. Her clothing contrasts sharply with her age. The song itself contrasts with so many contemporary tales of young women lost in the big city. Unlike the stories told in 'She's Leaving Home' (The Beatles, 1967) or 'Big Black Smoke' (The Kinks, 1966), or 'Young Girl Blues' (Donovan, 1967), this isn't the tragic tale of a lost woman. No, here we have something altogether different. This is a young, independent woman living in happiness and freedom. She's immersed in the here and the now.

When I ask Jerry about this song, he tells me:

> When I started writing that thing, I was just playing a little honkytonk thing in the key of D. And I just kind of—real laid-back—started singing ... just singin' it kinda slow. Then, when we took it up and started rehearsing it, we put a lot more energy into it. Of course, it really has to do with my grandma ... but it's also about the girls in San Francisco who liked to get their clothes from second-hand stores. So they had a lot of granny clothes. There was a lot of that in San Francisco then. So it's for all the girls, really. But when I came back home to Tacoma, my grandma was tickled that there was a song called 'Hey Grandma!'

'Hey Grandma' is a musical swirl—a swirl that introduces us to many Moby Grape trademarks: melodic pop, delicate lead guitar, thumping bass, trucking shuffle, percussive rhythm guitar, lyrical jokes, and delicate harmonies coming and going as though they are tied to certain frequencies in the lyric. The solo sweeps cleanly above the mix, leading everyone into the final vocals, as Don and Skip cry out 'Hey Grandma' over and over in a whirling electric chant. In this outro, the lead guitar repeats a hypnotic phrase; the bass sprints about, locking into a pattern that moves up and then hits that root note repeatedly, as though it's running on the spot. The fade-out is nearly a minute long, with harmonies, repetitions, some slightly countrified lead guitar, and, of course, a rhythm guitar playing percussively and flamboyantly.

After 166 fleeting seconds, this brisk song is over, and something quite different begins. 'Mr. Blues' is a song that swings. By no means is it swing music, but Bob Mosley's bass swings smoothly from note to note. It's also the first time we hear Bob's rugged, bluesy voice. His vocal delivery is striking in its power, yet sometimes it falters, at those moments where the narrator reaches a state of exasperation. Again, we have contrasts. Here, the self-assured strength of Bob's vocal performance contrasts with doubt and wavering exasperation. The lyrics tell the story of someone who's standing up to depression and despair—two hallmarks of the blues—yet the narrator isn't alone in his struggle. With an ongoing call-and-response between Bob and the rest of the band, the response harmonies are both unifying and supporting, the others' much higher and softer delivery contrasting with Bob's gruff, soulful lead vocal. The narrator is often alone in his struggle to fight the blues, but sometimes he's supported.

Speaking with journalist Steve Roeser about the song in 1999, Bob recalled, 'I had seen the Temptations at the Playboy Club in Los Angeles … and I listened to Marvin Gaye a lot, how he talked about, you know, being downtrodden. "Mr. Blues" was kind of like that kind of song. How you just can't be afraid of … all the trouble you get into, and all the trouble that you can't get out of. You gotta go on with it.'

'That was a great song,' Jerry tells me. 'I remember when Bob came in with that. I'm not sure exactly the inspiration Bob had for that one, but it's like what Otis Redding sang—it had a Motown, or Stax sort of effect. We liked that. That's always fun to play. That song was usually about third on the bill when we used to play.' When I ask him about the piano part, he tells me, 'Once in a while, Dave would play the piano, and once in a while I would play the piano. Like "Motorcycle Irene"—that had a little piano on it too.'

While 'Mr. Blues' might *seem* conventional, it isn't. It opens with a short introduction that never reappears, it doesn't have a chorus, and its outro is just wacky. As it draws to its end, it transitions into a closing section that doesn't appear in any other part of the song—an unexpected coda, like a breakdown of sorts.

From the soulful 'Mr. Blues,' we have a few fleeting seconds of silence before the next song, 'Fall On You,' begins with an electric chant—not unlike the one that closed out 'Hey Grandma.' Here, the voices of Moby Grape repeat a layered chant, crying out the words '*Yes, I know it's fallin*',' over and over again. It's like a handful of Gregorian monks have been scooped up and transported from the Middle Ages right into the explosiveness of San Francisco in the spring of '67.

On this third song on the album, we hear a third distinct voice—the voice of Peter Lewis. Peter's vocals are often softer than the voices of his bandmates, but in this song his delivery is frenzied, matching the urgency of the lyric. At times, his voice cracks, beautifully, in the pressure. After all, this is a song about debt, relationship troubles, and an ever-present sense of pressure. The harmonies both support and contrast with Peter's lead vocals. After catching his partner cheating on him, the narrator forgives her, but all the while he thinks about revenge. The song's tempo and vocal delivery tell us that the tension is still hanging around. Free love, this song shows, has its drawbacks.

Like 'Hey Grandma,' 'Fall On You' is an infectious song with a rapid melody and a frenzied vocal delivery. But where the narrator is cheerful in 'Hey Grandma,' here he is nervous. Lurking throughout the song are his worries about losing his love, running out of money, and getting hurt. It keeps coming back to his worries about his own feelings:

> *But all the time you're worried*
> *'bout the pain that's gonna fall on you.*

Peter wrote 'Fall On You' about a year before it was recorded, back in the days when he was playing in Peter & The Wolves and gigging in such places as Gazzarri's in Los Angeles and Frenchy's in San Francisco. As Jerry recalls, the band would often use the song as a set opener. 'That was the first song we started to play at Matthew's office, I believe. At our first rehearsal.'

When I tell Jerry that his guitar solo zips by in what feels like five seconds (rather than its actual twenty), he chuckles and says that it's one of the ones he's most proud of. 'You know, sometimes you'd have two or three runs at [a solo]—I think on that one it just came off. We'd been playing quite a bit and rehearsing quite a bit, so I had a pretty good idea of what I was gonna do.' Tightly arranged, the song runs to just under two minutes, ending as it began with a frantic return to the layered chant of '*Yes, I know it's fallin'*,' which repeats three more times before everything crashes to a halt.

With this, the album takes another sharp turn. '8:05' is a soft, almost country folk-ballad with rich harmonies throughout. It opens with a beautiful eight-second introduction played on the acoustic guitar by Peter Lewis, accompanied by Don Stevenson on tambourine. It's so smooth it *sounds* easy, but it isn't. The version of the song included on the *Vintage* compilation, with ten seconds of studio chatter preceding the song, offers a glimpse into the sort of hard work and sweat that went into the recordings.

When the singing begins, we quickly realize that '8:05' is sung by a fourth distinct voice in Moby Grape: the deeper drawl of Jerry Miller. He sings the first verse with Don harmonizing, accompanied by acoustic guitar strumming and Bob on bass. On the second verse, they are joined by drums and a folky, fingerpicked guitar.

The band's performance on '8:05' reflects the fragility of the melody and the lyric. The song tells the story of someone who is awaiting his love's departure. He can't bear to see her leave, and he can't understand how he will go on. But he can't prevent what is going to happen, either. It's immanent. In singing the song, the narrator pours his heart out, pleading with his love to stay, pleading with her, '*Don't fill my world with rain.*' He offers her his heart, which is all he can give. '*Please change your mind.*'

But '8:05' isn't just a ballad about longing. It is also a story about futility. It tells the story of a man who knows his relationship is doomed, and who is desperately trying to keep it alive at that final moment before it ends. By the end of the song, his love has left, leaving him to pick up the pieces and find a way to go on.

Just as '8:05' ends in sadness, the next song, another one by Bob, begins with happiness. Opening it, Bob beckons the listener in:

Come on in, people
we gonna tell ya 'bout good dreams and things to make ya happy.

The fifth song of the album takes us around another sharp turn. After the longing of '8:05,' 'Come In The Morning' offers Motown soul, with lyrics that express the utter joy of living in the moment and experiencing free love. When Steve Roeser asked him about the song, Bob shyly described 'Come In The Morning' as 'a song about, you know, having some young girl come by in the morning and wake you and make your day, you know.' Of his guitar work in the song, Jerry recalls, 'I had a couple of licks that I wanted to use in there. Those are also kind of soul licks. A little like Curtis Mayfield.'

'Come In The Morning' is a song about a fleeting relationship. It isn't about long-term commitment—rather, it's about being with someone in a moment, caring for that person, and living entirely in that moment. The singer calls for his love to visit him in when the sun is shining, and dreams are in their last fleeting minutes. Again, we have a song with contrasts. Here, the music of Motown is juxtaposed with the idea of free love. It isn't the sort of lyric you'd ever find on a Motown record—and that gives the song, and Bob's voice, something unique. The vocal delivery is pure soul, but the words themselves are firmly rooted in the counterculture. It's as though the emotional vibrancy of soul has materialized in San Francisco and possessed the band. 'Come In The Morning' is a song about living in a state where love—free love—is here to enjoy. Ultimately, it's about happiness and freedom, encompassed in the moment when Bob's voice wavers on the word 'need' during the song's final outro. It's one of the album's moments of sheer exuberance.

If 'Come In The Morning' is a joyful blending of Motown and the counterculture, then the following song moves the band into another sort of joy. 'Omaha' brings with it a charged, joyful state of pure energy. It's also here that we first hear Skip Spence sing the lead vocal on a Moby Grape song. Like the opening of 'Fall On You,' it begins with a charged chant, as Skip cries out, '*Listen, my friends*,' over and over, the rhythm of Don Stevenson's marching drums and Bob Mosley's pumping bass leading the charge forward.

'Omaha' is another song with heavy call-and-repeats that zap back and forth like electrical volts being sent from Skip to the other members of the band. 'Right at the beginning it's a Theremin and a backward guitar,' Jerry tells me. 'Skip came up with that idea.' The opening guitar line—'*Da-da-da-dada-da-dada-da*'—was Skip's too, he adds. 'It's catchy.'

Skip's words call for unity and understanding. This is a song of love and hope—not the free love of 'Come In The Morning,' but more of a *social* love. Skip asks his friends to listen, and he sings of a time where there is 'no more rain.' Here, images of the weather contrast with those in '8:05' and the later 'Sitting By The Window,' the tenth song on the album. Predating the power-pop genre, Skip gleefully calls out a series of catchy hooks:

Into the light
So outta sight
Bein' in love.

Listening to this song, I think about how the young Skip Spence is often described by those who knew him as a force, a person with a sort of glow. You can hear this in his vocal delivery, and in some of the outtakes from various Moby Grape releases, such as when he greets Arthur Godfrey with a bouncy 'How are ya, how are ya, Arthur.'

When I spoke with visual artist Jim Mazzeo about his time doing lighting for the Grape's shows, he told me, 'When Skippy would play at the Ark, or sometimes at the Avalon or the Fillmore, he would get a smile on his face that would literally lift his feet about seven inches off of the floor. And he would float. I swear to God. I know, everybody was taking a lot of LSD, but he would literally shine like a Golden Buddha, smiling. It was infectious—and, you'd really have to look hard, because you'd swear that his feet were not on the ground. He was just floating there and playing. He was just incredible.'

The seventh song on the album—and the last one written for it—is a fifty-eight-second ballad called 'Naked, If I Want To.' It's a question, or rather a series of questions. With Jerry and Don harmonizing, the opening lines ask:

Would you let me
Walk down your street
Naked if I want to?

This central image came from an acid trip, or an idea some people had while tripping. But before we delve into LSD and its place on the album and in Moby Grape's music, let's step back in time. Before trekking to California, Don and Jerry had been playing late night gigs and afterhours clubs in and around the Northwest Coast in their respective bands. When they journeyed down to California in 1965, LSD was not something these young sojourners knew much about. Yet by the time Jerry and Don were living in Belmont, the idea of using hallucinogens to obtain a deeper level of consciousness had not merely gained a foothold in a *faction* of America's counterculture—it was an idea that was rapidly gaining momentum.

An important precursor to this was the publication of Aldous Huxley's treatise on an experience he had while taking mescaline. His 1954 work *The Doors Of Perception* is not just the namesake of The Doors, it was text that interwove ideas of psychology, art, spirituality, and beauty. For Huxley, it was transformative. Following Huxley's path, Harvard psychology professors Timothy Leary and Richard Alpert started to research the effects of hallucinogens. In a 1963 lecture, Leary theorized, 'No matter how parsimonious our explanations, we must accept the fact that LSD subjects do claim to experience revelations into the basic questions and do attribute life-change to their visions.'

The following year, Leary and Ralph Metzner coauthored *The Psychedelic Experience*, in which they link consciousness with psychedelics and various hallucinogens, including LSD. 'A psychedelic experience is a journey to new realms of consciousness,' they write. 'The scope and content of the experience is limitless, but its characteristic features are the transcendence of verbal concepts, of spacetime dimensions, and of the ego or identity.'

While in his mid-twenties, budding author and night aid hospital worker Ken Kesey volunteered to take part in Project MKUltra, a CIA-funded study that examined the effects—such as mind-control and information extraction possibilities—of various psychoactive drugs, including LSD.* A few years later, in late 1965 and throughout '66, Kesey and his loose group of Merry Pranksters hosted numerous 'acid test' events as a sort of life-art/enlightenment experience. With the tagline 'Can You Pass The Acid Test?' these events advocated for and facilitated social experiences of taking LSD-25. While all this was occurring, former engineering student Owsley Stanley was producing his famous LSD in the Bay Area. He became Kesey's supplier in September 1965, and two years later supplied LSD for The Beatles while they were filming *Magical Mystery Tour*.

LSD was not just a small corner of America's counterculture landscape in the mid 60s. For some, it represented a route to a new level of consciousness. LSD was used recreationally (such as by some who took part in the acid tests) and it was also used in research (such as in studies conducted by Leary and Alpert). By the time possession of LSD was made illegal in the US on October 24 1966 (fifteen days before Ronald Regan was elected governor of California), it was firmly entrenched within the psychedelic vision of reaching for a new, different sort of reality—one that pushed beyond baby-boomer, postwar America. Yet it wasn't limited to America's counterculture. Paul McCartney famously spoke about taking LSD in a June 1967 interview for ITV. And the radiant Italian film director Federico Fellini took an LSD trip in 1964 under the guidance and supervision of Emilio Servadio, his former psychoanalyst—an experience that profoundly

* See, for instance, John D. Marks's *The Search For The Manchurian Candidate* and Martin A. Lee and Bruce Shlain's *Acid Dreams*. For an overview of the acid tests, meanwhile, I direct you to the astute Sarah Hill's *San Francisco & The Long 60s*, as well as Patrick Lundborg's *Psychedelia: An Ancient Culture, A Modern Way Of Life*.

ABOVE THE GRAPE HAVING FUN ON A PHOTO SHOOT IN 1967. **RIGHT** 'WE HAD RAZOR CUTS AND MATCHING SUITS': THE FRANTICS, EARLY 1966 VINTAGE, FEATURING JERRY, BOB, DON, AND CHUCK SCHONING.

moby grape
Night Voyage
Dance

DANCE
CONCERT & LIGHT SHOW
MOBY GRAPE
AMERICAN DREAM
NEW TWEEDY BROS.
NOV 4TH
8:30 PM
LEE MICHAELS
CALIFORNIA HALL
POLK & TURK S.F.

FLOOR ELEVATORS
MOBY GRAPE
AVALON BALLROOM
TICKET OUTLETS:

LEFT A SELECTION OF POSTERS FOR GRAPE SHOWS DURING LATE 1966 AT THE ARK AND CALIFORNIA HALL, AND WITH THE 13TH FLOOR ELEVATORS AND THE GRATEFUL DEAD AT THE AVALON BALLROOM.

ABOVE DON POSING AT STEVE PAUL'S THE SCENE, NEW YORK CITY, JUNE 1967. **LEFT** SKIP, BOB, AND PETER ONSTAGE AT THE SCENE, JUNE 1967.

LEFT MOBY GRAPE'S DEBUT ALBUM, FEATURING DON'S MIDDLE FINGER AND A MODIFIED AMERICAN FLAG. **RIGHT** SKIP LOOKING REFLECTIVE BACKSTAGE AT THE SCENE, JUNE 1967. **BELOW** MOBY GRAPE ONSTAGE AT THE VILLAGE THEATER, NEW YORK CITY, NOVEMBER 1967.

LEFT JERRY AND PETER SHARE A MOMENT BACKSTAGE AT THE SCENE, JUNE 1967.
BELOW POSTERS FOR THE GRAPE'S SHOWS WITH THE BYRDS IN MARCH/APRIL 1967, AND THEIR RETURN TO THE ARK IN NOVEMBER; A PRESS AD FOR THEIR DEBUT ALBUM.

FALL ON YOU
CHANGES
JERRY MILLER
PETER LEWIS
SKIP SPENCE
DON STEVENSON
BOB MOSLEY

SITTING BY THE WINDOW
INDIFFERENCE
JERRY MILLER
PETER LEWIS
SKIP SPENCE
DON STEVENSON
BOB MOSLEY

HEY GRANDMA
COME IN THE MORNING
JERRY MILLER
PETER LEWIS
SKIP SPENCE
DON STEVENSON
BOB MOSLEY

ABOVE JERRY RECORDING IN NEW YORK CITY, NOVEMBER 1967; DON LAYING DOWN A VOCAL TRACK; SKIP AND DON AT THE MIC.
LEFT AND RIGHT THE FIVE SINGLES, AS RELEASED IN JUNE 1967.

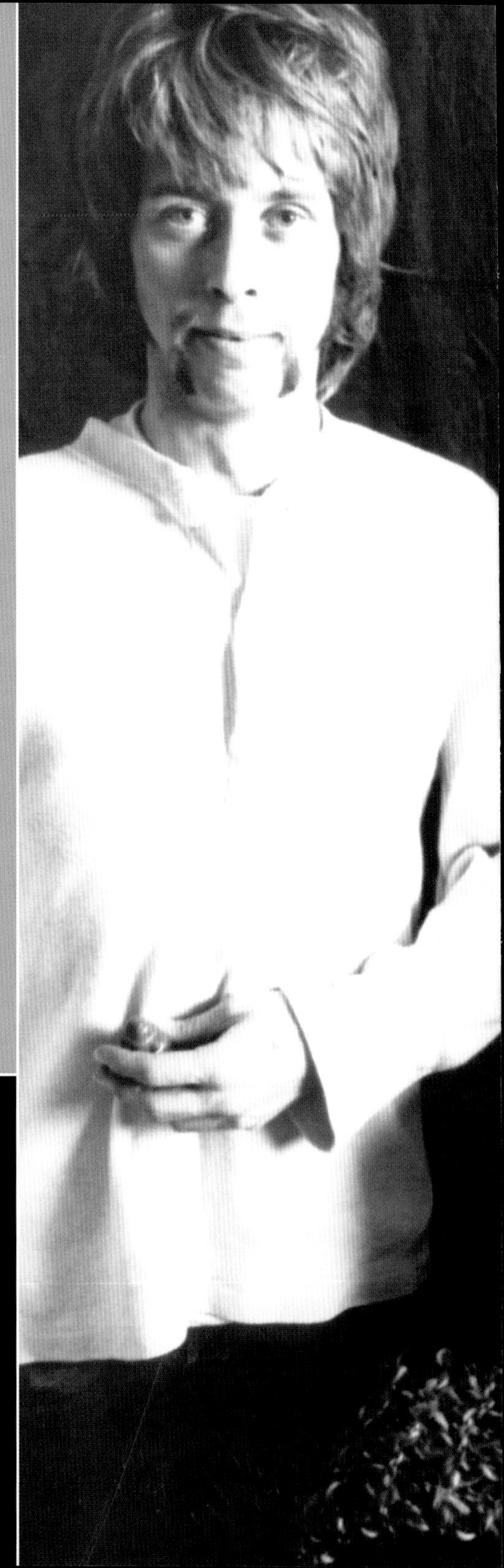

ABOVE BOB CATO'S ARTWORK FOR *WOW* AND *GRAPE JAM*, THE TWO HALVES OF MOBY GRAPE'S 'DIFFICULT' SECOND ALBUM.
RIGHT SKIP, JERRY, BOB, DON, AND PETER, LOOKING ALTERNATIVELY REFLECTIVE AND INQUISITIVE.

ABOVE SKIP AND PETER.
RIGHT DON ATOP HIS CHECKER CAB AFTER RETURNING TO WASHINGTON STATE IN THE EARLY 70s. **OPPOSITE** *MOBY GRAPE '69* AND *TRULY FINE CITIZEN*, BOTH FROM 1969, PLUS THE BACK COVER OF THE LATTER.

MOBY GRAPE '69

Truly
Fine
Citizen

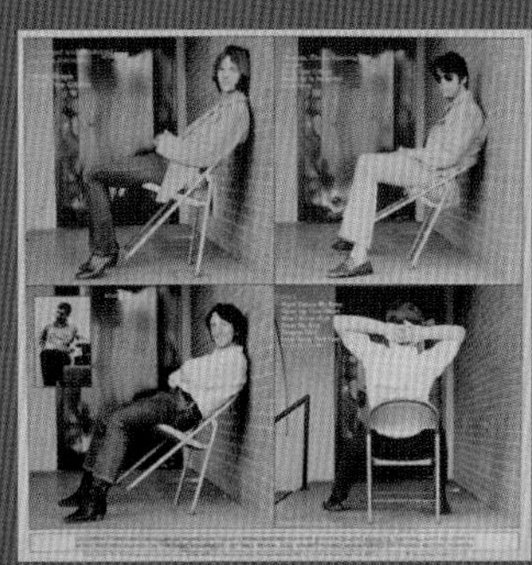

ABOVE BOB WITH HIS BAND SNAKE LEG IN HAWAII, 1971.
LEFT SKIP SPENCE ON FIRE AT THE FILLMORE EAST, JUNE 1971.
BELOW THE EXPANDED 1971 LINEUP OF MOBY GRAPE ON THE COVER OF *20 GRANITE CREEK*.

IN THE LATE 80s AND EARLY 90s, LEGAL ISSUES FORCED THE BAND TO PERFORM AS THE MELVILLES. **ABOVE** SKIP PUTS IN A RARE GUEST APPEARANCE WITH THE BAND. **LEFT** PETER AND JERRY AT THE SAME SHOW.

influenced his next film, *Juliet Of The Spirits* (1965). Simply put, LSD was pervasive—as both a destination and a route.

LSD was a part of the landscape Moby Grape inhabited—and it was a part of their *lived* experience. In his 1995 interview with Jud Cost, Peter Lewis recalled a time when Joel Scott Hill secretly gave Bob Mosley a tab of acid at a gathering in the Hollywood Hills. According to Lewis, Hill was 'a real manipulator':

> He had this way of acting like a lion tamer, and Bob was the lion. Bob started getting high and getting confused, and Joel would lead him on. That's how Bob paid the price for not driving the boat. See, Bob wasn't aware of The Byrds or any of this folk-rock stuff. He was just this guy. So, just when Bob was the most fucked-up and the dawn started breaking, I started to play this Rickenbacker twelve-string. And I saw Bob latch onto it like a log to a guy that's drowning. And he just listened to this stuff he'd never heard before. The jangling got in there, and he started to sing, and it was like The Byrds, but with the blues on it. And that was 'Bitter Wind.' And that's when we realized we had this different thing. It was happening.

Many have theorized that Skip's breakdown in New York in the middle of 1968 was caused—at least partly—by the amount, quality, and/or potency of the acid he was taking at the time.* A body of research indicates that there may be links between LSD and mental illness and other health issues.†

'Naked, If I Want To' is a beautiful melody and an absurd set of images. It's another song of contrasts. It's also a joke, or a series of jokes. Jerry and Don act as observers in a journalistic romp, capturing the things they have seen ever since they left the world of R&B nightclubs behind and started

* To read Peter's view of Skip's decline, see Jud Cost's 'Peter Lewis,' published in *Ptolemaic Terrascope* in 1996. To get Jerry's perspective, see Gene Sculatti's liner notes to *Wow*. And for David Rubinson's point of view, see Andrew Lau's 2009 *Crawdaddy* article '*Oar* After 40 Years.' See also David Fricke's liner notes to *Vintage*.

† See, for instance, Martin A. Lee and Bruce Shlain's *Acid Dreams*.

flirting with the world of hippies and the counterculture. (Don and Jerry themselves weren't hippies, but they were treading through this world—documenting what they saw and experienced along the way.)

Of course, 'Naked, If I Want To' is also a song about naturism, or nudism. Hardly new ideas, nudism and naturism have been around for millennia. In fact, we can read about their benefits in the writings of such literary giants as Henry David Thoreau and Walt Whitman. Founded in 1931, the American Association For Nude Recreation has seen continuous growth over the decades as nude resorts and beaches have sprung up across the country, most prevalently in California and Florida. By the 1960s, nudism and naturism formed a part (or, rather, portion) of America's counterculture, as both locked in with the desire for a retreat from urbanization and move back to a greener, more pastoral setting.

This brief Moby Grape song certainly isn't the only instance where nudism crops up in 60s popular culture. In a hilarious sequence of events in *A Shot In The Dark*, the second Pink Panther film, Peter Sellers and Elke Sommer find themselves stuck in a nudist retreat—and end up making a hasty retreat, still naked, in a compact car. After racing back to Paris, they promptly get stuck in a traffic jam, where they are quickly surrounded by a gaggle of shocked and rather curious pedestrians. That's when they start screaming.

A year and a half *after* 'Naked, If I Want To' appeared on the airwaves, John Lennon and Yoko Ono released their first joint album, *Unfinished Music No. 1: Two Virgins* (Apple Records 1968), its cover photo depicting the two standing together in the nude. The cover provoked outrage, confiscations, and censorship—and, in some places, it was covered up in a brown paper bag. One year after that, Jim Morrison was arrested for apparently exposing himself at a Miami concert, for which he was convicted of indecent exposure in 1970. Four years after Morrison's conviction, as David Niven was speaking at the 1974 Academy Awards ceremony, Robert Opel famously dashed across the stage, flashing a peace sign along the way—and not wearing a stitch of clothing.

With 'Naked, If I Want To,' we don't just have nudism. We have nudity with hallucinogens. As Jerry recalls, 'I just wrote that one myself right there in the studio. But the original idea—I think we were loaded on acid with the idea that we could go out on the street naked if we wanted to. It was a laugh—not much to it.'

The short song is a series of questions and images. It's a soft ballad and a fleeting, funny song. In the lyric, Jerry and Don take stock of what they see around them, superimposing LSD with nudism/naturism—two aspects of the counterculture of the 1960s. It's a delicate melody, beautifully performed; and, like 'Come In The Morning,' another song about living in the moment and being free.

After fifty-eight fleeting seconds, the song reaches its end. With its conclusion we reach the midpoint of the album. There have been so many shifts in styles, and singers, and images that it's all been dizzying.

•

Side two opens softly, with one of the oldest Moby Grape songs. Originally written by Don and Jerry for The Frantics, 'Someday' first appeared on vinyl in the early summer of 1966. Yet the song was revisited in the band's first rehearsal in the late summer, and subsequently reworked with the help of Skip. As such, alongside 'Fall On You,' it's one of only two songs that were part of the band's playing right from day one.

'Someday' is a song about longing, like '8:05.' Yet while '8.05' tries to freeze time before the narrator's love says goodbye, 'Someday' casts its eye forward, gazing longingly into the future:

Someday tomorrow will come
Though I'm not afraid of today
That's for sure.

In 'Someday'—unlike in 'Come In The Morning' or 'Naked, If I Want To'—the here and the now represents a struggle—and, the narrator needs to grasp the possibilities of future, to cope with the challenges of the present. Like so many songs on the first side of the album, 'Someday' is a performance of vocal camaraderie. Voices don't just complement one another harmonically but support one another, just as the harmonizing backup vocals support the struggling narrator of 'Mr. Blues.' Against this delicate balance, Bob Mosley belts out the haunting chorus that closes out the song:

Your mind is lost
In a world that wasn't made for you
Though I feel the same way too
I still got some things to do.

This is song about despair—and, just as in 'Mr. Blues,' the narrator is supported. In this case, he copes by looking to the future and imagining a time that will be better than what lies in the here and the now. Jerry Miller's soft, jazzy guitar solo ends the song in a way that reflects the soft lead vocals and harmonies that float throughout it. When I ask him about his solo, he says he was 'thinking of trying to get a sound for that solo that would change the idea—you know, like the guitar on the song "Apache." Remember that one? I was trying to get a sound kinda like that—completely different from the rest of the album. It worked out real good, too.'

On a predictably unpredictable album, the fragile 'Someday' is followed by the band's first foray into rollicking country-rock. From desperate longing, Moby Grape spring into the effervescent pep of 'Ain't No Use,' a song with many of its own twists and turns. It opens with a folk-country strum that's soon accompanied by a series of country hooks in the lower register of Jerry Miller's guitar.

'That's kind of a trip,' Jerry recalls. 'It goes fast and then slows down and then it does a kind of waltz. It was a kind of trip. Me and Don put that one together. It's like a roller coaster. You know, it doesn't stay on one track. And it goes all over the place. On the very end of it, I get—I can't explain it without my guitar, but it's a backward minor ninth. Then, it just lowers a whole step.'

Moby Grape race through the verses and chorus, mirroring the song's upbeat lyric, which tells the story of a love and faithfulness that is implicitly understood, and doesn't need to be mentioned. After hanging onto, and harmonizing on, the final note of the chorus, they slow things down considerably and transition into a waltz. On this brisk song, the opening instrumental totals a mere eight seconds; by the thirty-eight second mark, the band have already run through the verse twice, and by the forty-nine second mark, they have finished the verse and stepped into a nine-second waltz. Before it reaches one hundred seconds, the song is over.

From the vim of 'Ain't No Use' and the country twang of Jerry Miller, the album shift gears yet again, arriving at 'Sitting By The Window,' another quiet ballad. Soft guitars interweave chords and fingerpicked patterns, while Peter Lewis sings his lyric quietly, with some vibrato, in a manner that's slightly reminiscent of Donovan. In the song, the narrator tells his story of sitting at a window, looking out, watching for the rain, thinking about someone who he has loved, to whom he is singing. The narrator and his love are apart, yet he doesn't assign blame to one person. Blame is shared in this song:

I'm playing my game
I guess you're playing it too
Go ahead and play it on through.

Recalling his delicate solo, Jerry says, 'I took guitar lessons from Ali Akbar Khan, so I had these ideas.* Peter had that [song] all together, and I think I came up with the little solo there. That was all Peter's tune, but I just came up with the solo. Also, the tingly-tingly-tingly thing. On the guitar, I had two open strings on the end—the high end of the guitar, the E and the B string. Then, I would just descend the G-string, which is the third of the E minor, and start from there and leave the two high strings to ring while I just descended from the G. But it was an E minor, the tune's in E minor and we shifted it to D for the solo.'

* In a career that crossed continents and spanned more than seven decades, Ali Akbar Khan (1922–2009) was nominated for five Grammys. He received such honors as a MacArthur Fellowship, the National Endowment for the Arts' National Heritage Fellowship, and Padma Vighushan. His principal instrument was the sarod.

Like '8:05' and 'Someday,' this is a song about lost love, or absent love. Just like in '8:05'—where the narrator pleads for his love not to make his sunshine disappear—this is a song where the very weather outside reflects the inner state, and turmoil, of the narrator. The echoed harmonies quickly come and go, stressing that the singer is often (though not always) alone. He is neither angry nor vindictive. He's pining, in a way. In singing the song, he's describing—not venting about—his condition.

'Sitting By The Window' is a delicate, pensive song—and it contrasts sharply with the song that follows, as Don Stevenson's drums kick into a groove with Bob's rapid-fire bassline and Jerry's crunchy guitar. This ten-second opening couldn't be more different to the song that preceded it.

When I ask Jerry about this song, 'Changes,' he tells me:

> Don came up with that one. He pretty much made 'Changes' up by himself. I added some guitar parts, some ideas. Don was a natural harmony singer. He could sing perfectly parallel to me, and make my voice sound fairly okay. And Skippy would weave in and out of melodies real nice. Of course, Mosley had that strength for the strong bottom. And Pete was right there. You know, Don sang on that one while playing drums. Not just in the gigs but I think in the studio as well. And Bob, of course, was there at the height of his chops. He's all over, *boom-boom-boom*. [*Laughs excitedly.*] Oh, Bob was a hot-rod on that one! He was way up there!

'Changes' is another song of contrasts on an album that's brimming with contrasts and dualities. On one level, it's a song about despair. Here, the narrator feels helpless as he struggles to cope in a world of rapid, difficult, and unpleasant changes. It's a song of tension, where change represents something that is difficult to endure. Yet in this song, as in numerous other songs on the album (such as 'Mr. Blues'), despair is something everyone faces, and something everyone is capable of enduring and defeating. As in other songs, the narrator of 'Changes' is not alone, and the band's call-

and-response vocal delivery gives us a sense that the narrator is supported. While the narrator struggles to cope, by the end of the song, he reaches a state of contentment:

Everybody changes
But the weather's fine.

Here, again, the lyric uses weather to reflect and explain the inner state of the narrator. The pace of this song is frantic, perhaps most prominently in Bob Mosley's basslines, which sprint up and down, rapidly matching and propelling the song's tempo with confidence and strength. The entire band is on fire. While the lyric casts an air of doom and gloom, the music returns us to the joyful, breathtaking exuberance of such tracks as 'Hey Grandma,' 'Fall On You,' and 'Omaha.'

While 'Changes' is a song about coping with despair and feeling overwhelmed, the next song offers a very different take on the same theme. 'Lazy Me' is a song of questions, recalling the similar structure of 'Naked, If I Want To,' yet here the questions are posed in a state of despair and resignation. The narrator tries to find meaning, posing one set of questions after another to his love. His despair is so pervasive and potent that it even haunts him when he sees her smile. He feels a sense of despair, and yet he can't explain it.

Of his three songs on the band's debut, 'Lazy Me' is Bob's favorite. When I ask him why, he quickly replies, ''cos it tells the truth.' By posing his questions, the narrator is expressing his deepest concerns—or, rather, what he understands of those concerns. He is confused by what troubles him, and why he should even be troubled in the first place. It isn't just a matter of *being* in a state of despair—it's *the confusion of being despair*. He struggles to find a sense of purpose or explanation in a world where purpose is elusive. Describing the song to Steve Roeser, Bob likened 'Lazy Me' to 'poetic justice … you know, you think all these tremendous thoughts about what life is all about, and then you realize that there's nothing that you can do about it. So you just get: I'll just lay here and decay here.'

What Bob is describing here, and what he expresses in his lyric, are aspects of existentialism. Gaining prominence, and attention, in the 1800s and 1900s, existentialism has come to include a variety of interweaving and sometimes competing ideas, including absurdism, authenticity, and despair. We live in an unjust world where meaning—holistic meaning—can be found only in ourselves. The meaning in and of our world is that which we give it—which is a basic premise of absurdism. In terms of authenticity, everyone in the world has an individual sense of morality, and ethics, and how to act. While one may share many ideas about morality and ethics with others, in the end, everyone has his/her own individual perspective and perception of what constitutes a moral or ethical act. When we make choices according to our own perspective, within a state of freedom, we reach a level of authenticity. When we are truly aware of the absurd reality of our existence, where meaning is individually or socially constructed, and not inherent or provided, we may feel overwhelmed, and feel despair. When we understand the heavy responsibility, the weight, that accompanies the idea of authentic action, again, we may feel a sense of despair. When we feel hopeless in a world without inherent meaning, a world without answers, we may reach what is called an *existential crisis*.* This is the core of the narrator's struggle in 'Lazy Me.'

When I ask Jerry about the crosstalk between the guitars and Bob's vocals in the song, he replies, 'That was real neat, what me and Skippy did with our pieces on the guitar. I think Skippy layered his guitar on first for that one, and I came in later with my part, and that makes a few changes, too.' As 'Lazy Me' nears its end, as it rotates on its final outro, Jerry plays a variation of the 'Baa, Baa, Black Sheep' nursery rhyme, taking listeners back to their childhoods, and back to time of innocence—a time when existentialism was an unknown, and not a worry.†

Following the existential struggle of 'Lazy Me,' Spence's 'Indifference' offers us another song of musical exuberance and joyfulness. Guitar lines

* See Jean-Paul Sartre's *Existentialism And Human Emotion*, and Albert Camus's *The Stranger*.

† Interestingly, around the same time, Sly Stone was also playing with variations of nursery rhymes on songs such as 'Underdog' from *A Whole New Thing* (Epic Records, 1967).

intermingle with harmonized chanting—like the chanting of 'Fall On You' (which conveys worry) and the chanting of 'Omaha' (which expresses joy). This time, the lyric is simultaneously hopeful and cynical:

What a difference the day has made
What a difference the day has made
What a difference more of the same.

Where 'Changes' expresses worry about transition, 'Indifference' tells us that the appearance of change is only that—*appearance*. Not only do the lines of 'Indifference' contrast hope with cynicism, but in terms of vocal delivery, we have lines being traded between Bob Mosley's soul with Skip Spence's exuberance. In terms of vocal delivery, the two are miles apart. Yet while their voices differ significantly, they both convey a sense of excitement. As before, Skip delivers his lines in zestful, bubbly manner.

Closing the album, this longest track—the only one that exceeds four minutes—leaves us with what are now Moby Grape's trademarks: hooks, guitar crosstalk, sweet harmonies, contrasts, and exuberance. The last few seconds of the album offer an outro drone of Miller's descending patterned solo, finally ending on the twang of one final note.

•

Moby Grape's debut was recorded mostly live in the studio, in a matter of days, spread across two months. Studio logs indicate that the album's thirteen tracks were recorded across just five days at a cost of a paltry $11,000. By comparison, consider that Van Dyke Parks's *Song Cycle*, recorded the same year, cost around $35,000, while The Beatles' *Sgt. Pepper's Lonely Hearts Club Band* cost £25,000 (around $68,000 at the time). This was an album recorded quickly and cheaply.

CHAPTER FIFTEEN

'WE ALWAYS DID THINGS THE WRONG WAY.'

March 2017. By now, I've gotten into a routine with Jerry. Quite often, he opens our conversations by telling me about recent shows he's seen, or gigs he's performed, or lessons he's preparing. Today, I open the conversation by asking him about a song that the band chose not to include on their first album, and in fact never recorded in the studio, 'Dark Magic.'

'That was a trippy one,' he says. 'We'd get real psychedelic on that one—sometimes to the point of agnosia. As I look back on it, I would hate to hear a couple of the versions,' he laughs.

When it came to setting up recording, Jerry tells me, 'We didn't do a whole lot of isolating. We had a few isolating boards. We could sit close to each other. We could play a nice rhythm section and then come in sometimes to do the vocals afterward. But sometimes we'd do the lead vocals right then, along with the original track.'

For most of the album, Jerry played an electric Gibson L-5, but he used his acoustic L-5 on '8:05.' 'That acoustic one was beautiful,' he says. 'I would've liked to have kept that. But I guess I have too many guitars anyway,' he chuckles.

When I ask him why certain songs didn't make the cut for the album—

'Rounder,' for example—he says, 'Ah, Columbia, you know. We had too much. We had a full album and we had another few tunes out there, too—we had "Looper" and "Bitter Wind." Those were a couple of our first ones—but we could get either one on our first album. Boy, we were writing. We changed more songs—"Bitter Wind" was changed so many times, I can't believe it. It came out nice. One version came out goofy with violins and everything.'

Our thoughts then turn to the marathon portrait session for the album with photographer Jim Marshall, for which the band spent the day trekking around the Bay Area and Marin County, trying out different locations.

> We finally ended up at a place called the Junktique Store, in Fairfax. The original picture had an American Flag on it, you know. It started at an American Flag and then it got changed to different colors. I don't know why, but David said they had too many complaints. During the Vietnam War, some older people didn't like the fact that we had an American flag with us. So Columbia chicken-shitted out and changed the color of the flag. But if anybody finds an album or some of the 45s from our promotion set with the American flag on it—that's valuable stuff. There aren't many around.

The 'promotional set' Jerry mentions is the selection of five singles Columbia released from the album, all on the same day, all having to compete against one another. 'That was nuts!' he says. 'But we were always nuts. We always did things the wrong way. David said, We'll be the first band to put out five singles at once. But if we just put out "8:05" on one side with "Omaha" on the other, and just pushed those songs, they could've been hits. We could've had a few hits from that album.'

FINAL DREAM

A mid-sized conference room in an office building, second floor, Sunset Boulevard. At the center of the room is a long table, and seated around the table are ten men, all wearing suits. On the table are cups and saucers, each cup filled with coffee. There are three ashtrays on the table, and six of the men are smoking. A long rectangular series of window panels runs across the outer wall of the room. It's sunny outside, the sky virtually cloudless.

There's a piece of paper on the table by an empty chair. It has the Columbia Records logo on it. An easel stands beside the empty seat at one of the ends of the conference table, and on it a poster of Moby Grape. It's the front cover of their first album—the original one, with Don Stevenson flipping the bird over a washboard and Skip Spence holding a pole, which bears the American flag.

The presentation begins.

•

What would you say if I told you we have a hit on our hands? What would you say if I told you we've got a band that can become the next Beatles, the American Beatles? What would you say to that?

We've spent the last few weeks researching Moby Grape and preparing this marketing plan. This isn't about gimmicks. Gimmicks aren't going to sell Moby Grape. This is about conditions. Oscar Wilde once said that success is a science. If you have the right conditions, you get the result.* Well, that's why we're here today. We're here to create success. Numerous angles need to be promoted, and if we market Moby Grape the right way, we're going to have a monster on our hands.

Please save your questions for the end of the presentation. I'll be happy to answer any questions you have, but because of the cross-promotional nature of this plan, I need to give you the entire plan before we have a Q&A. Then, I'll be glad to answer all your questions.

Is everyone OK with that?

OK, let's begin. There are three parts to this marketing plan. First, we'll tap into the growing interest in San Francisco and hippie culture. Over the past few months, media outlets have been giving more and more attention to San Francisco and hippie culture. After the Human Be-In event back in January, we've seen San Francisco receive more attention in the media. Richard Goldstein, one of the most important music critics around today, recently wrote a piece for the *Village Voice* called 'San Francisco: The Flourishing Underground.' And that's what the city is: flourishing. That article came out just two months ago. In it, Goldstein sings the praises of San Francisco—a city that has two things going for it, momentum and marketing potential. On May 12, our own label will release 'San Francisco (Be Sure To Wear Flowers In Your Hair),' a new single written by John Philips and recorded by Scott McKenzie. We've listened to this track a few times, and it's a beautiful song with a beautiful message. But the best thing is that it has a lot of hit potential. This single can help to promote Moby Grape, through the San Francisco angle. There's tremendous potential here for cross-promotion. Moby Grape needs to be marketed as a band that represents and captures the vibrancy of the counterculture movement; of which San Francisco isn't just a hub, it's the symbolic capital. It's a place and it's an idea.

---

* This line is from Oscar Wilde's 1893 play, *A Woman Of No Importance*.

To stress this angle, we need to emphasize the geographic context of Moby Grape—and package the band as something that comes from the cradle of San Francisco. And they need to be edgy. You want to talk edgy, just look at the poster behind me. This is America, it's traditional and it's also edgy, and it's new. But how can we capture the vibe of San Francisco?

Imagine this. It's the day that Moby Grape's debut album is released. We're not in LA. The band isn't in LA. Imagine a community event. That's what's happening. Columbia Records has rented one of the hippest ballrooms in San Francisco—either the Avalon or the Fillmore—and we host a release party to end all parties. I mean, this will be a party that puts the Romans to shame. We throw a party and we spare no expense. Rather than taking Moby Grape to the mountain, we bring the mountain to Moby Grape—and San Francisco. Let's fly media in from LA and other places and show them a night they won't forget. Let's have Moby Grape perform at the ballroom, and perhaps have one their local friends perform—someone with a bit of hit potential. This will be an event that people talk about for years. We give out Moby Grape bottles of wine for folks to take home, so they have something special to remember the night. And we design a little package that gets distributed to guests, like a gift box with various items inside. It should be beautiful, covered in something like velvet, purple velvet. These gift boxes can have things like glossies, pins, things like that. We can make a booklet, a kind of manifesto, describes the band and their music, once again stressing Moby Grape's connection to San Francisco. With all the press the city is getting these days, it would be a mistake not to capitalize on this connection.

Understand, this isn't just another album getting released. This is a major cultural event. Because not everyone can be brought to this event, we will follow up with a series of shows on the East Coast, in New York City—right after the album is released. These events will be supplemented with print ads in major media outlets across the country, publications like *Billboard*. With this strategy, we're going to tap into the allure of San Francisco, and simultaneously hit the two capitals of Los Angeles and New York City. The print ads will ensure that Moby Grape gets additional nationwide attention.

I know what you're thinking. It's too much. It's too much to spend on a new, unproven band. But try to imagine this. Try to imagine the payoff. If you know what The Beatles have done, then you know what the potential payoff is. It's limitless. This is a plan that will use a few traditional marketing strategies, but it will also be bold. But this is just the first part of our plan.

Second, we will stress the eclectic nature of Moby Grape's style—a new wave of fusion music. As we've listened to Moby Grape's music, we've noticed that the band blends together various genres, including R&B, soul, rock'n'roll, blues, and folk. Over the past few years, some of the biggest-selling acts have made music that fuses different styles and genres. At the forefront of this are The Beatles. Just last year, on their *Revolver* album, The Beatles recorded songs that are partly classical, horns-driven with a Motown sound, pop, heavy rock, and one that can only be described as psychedelic. But what about other bands? The Rolling Stones have taken blues and rock'n'roll and fused them together in a way that's entirely different than what Elvis did ten years ago. But The Beatles and Stones aren't alone. On our own label, we've seen Bob Dylan and The Byrds take folk music and electrify it, and mix it with rock'n'roll. Also on Columbia Records, The Beach Boys have taken doo-wop and a cappella and choral music and blended it with a kind of rock'n'roll—a softer kind of rock'n'roll.

When people listen to Moby Grape, they know that they are a part of this whole movement. Moby Grape's songs on their debut LP fit neatly into this movement, and they also advance it. We will stress that Moby Grape isn't just a vanguard of San Francisco music—they're a vanguard of a whole new kind of music, a new wave of fusion music. When we issue our manifesto about Moby Grape, to be distributed with the gift boxes we give out at their release party, we're going to announce the dawn of a new age in popular music. When media outlets follow up on this, Moby Grape will become a craze. They won't just enter the hit parade, they'll climb to the Top 10, the Top 5, even the top of the charts. That's exactly where I see this band, at the top of the charts.

The third part of our marketing strategy is simple. We'll stress the fact that Moby Grape are a band with five singers and five songwriters. It's another aspect of the band's uniqueness. While Moby Grape are by no means the only band to feature multiple singers and songwriters, their dynamic is unique. There aren't too many bands that have multiple singers and songwriters. But the ones that have them are very successful. The Beatles have four singers and three songwriters. The Beach Boys have four singers and two songwriters. The Byrds have three singers and three songwriters. These are three bands that have a lot of chart action.

It will be advantageous to link Moby Grape to this elite group of bands. Never has a band had such a wide pool of talent in terms of singing and writing. Never has this happened before. When we combine this angle with the two previously outlined prongs of our marketing plan, the band's audience will grow like wildfire. But how can we stress this point? After all, Moby Grape are a new band, and America doesn't yet know who they are. Here we have something bold in mind. It's daring and its new. We've been talking to David Rubinson, Moby Grape's producer, and he's ecstatic about the band. He feels that they have an uncanny amount of hit potential, and we agree. When you listen to Moby Grape's songs, you realize they're melodic, and energetic, and infectious, and catchy. Moby Grape has an energy that no one else has. They have a whole trove of songs with hit potential. But how are hit songs usually released and promoted? We know, the traditional strategy is to release one single alongside the release of a new album. After that song starts to move down the chart, a second single's released. Then a third, and so on and so forth. Well, to be frank, Moby Grape can do better than that. Before I tell you about this plan we have, let me tell you a little story.

Back in 1963 there was this band signed to EMI Records in the UK. They offered singles to Capitol Records, their US counterpart, but Capitol declined. So a small R&B label from Chicago picked up the band's singles and put them on the market, one single in February '63 and another in May. And nothing happened. One song made the 'bubbling under' section on *Billboard*, but no hits. In August, EMI cancelled the contract for nonpayment of royalties. The next month, Swan Records, a Philadelphia-based company, released one of the band's singles, but it too went nowhere. When the band's manager arranged an appearance on a major US TV show, Capitol finally agreed to release one of the band's singles and it debuted on US radios in late December '63. Four months later, the band held down the top five spots on the *Billboard* Hot 100.

Beatlemania was only three years ago, and if we market Moby Grape properly, we can reproduce that level of excitement. All we need to do is create the right conditions. But what are those conditions? We need to fuel a level of hype. And we can do that by tapping into the growing interest in San Francisco. And we need a few traits to stress for people to grab onto. And we can do that by presenting Moby Grape as a San Francisco band—a band with a new kind of fusion music, and a band with five different singers. But how can we show five different voices with one single? We can't. It's impossible to do that with one single. Now think back to Beatlemania. The Beatles released a whole slew of singles when they broke the US market. But The Beatles had a backlog of singles. With Moby Grape, we don't have a backlog, but we can flood the singles market with Moby Grape songs with hit potential—making sure that they're known as one of those bands with a wide pool of talented voices, like The Beach Boys, The Beatles, and The Byrds. There's no rule that says you can't release multiple singles in one day. So what we're going to do is release not one but five singles on June 6. This is something that's going to be a monster hit. DJs don't have to pick just one single to play on the radio. Why should we give them just one, when Moby Grape has so many songs with hit potential?

Look, we could've played it safe with this marketing plan. We could've designed something that follows traditional strategies—and we're prepared to go back to the drawing board and do just that. But Moby Grape deserve more than *old reliable*. Columbia deserves more. Moby Grape are about breaking boundaries, and they demand a marketing plan that breaks boundaries. We know our plan is bold. We know it's pricy, but stop thinking about dollars and cents for a moment and just imagine something. When is marketing not a gamble? It's never a certainty. With this gamble, the potential payoff is limitless.

Imagine someone tells you that you have an opportunity to orchestrate a new Beatlemania. What would you say to that? Because that's what I'm telling you. What's the cost of a party in San Francisco, or a few print ads in the trades? What's the price of these things next to a second coming of Beatlemania?

Any questions?

CHAPTER SIXTEEN

THE THREE PUNCHES

It's June 1967. The Summer of Love is nearing. The Beatles release *Sgt. Pepper's Lonely Hearts Club Band* on June 1 in the UK and the following day in the US. On that same day, a race riot breaks out in Boston's Roxbury neighborhood. Others will follow throughout the summer, with Philadelphia, Tampa, Cincinnati, Dayton (Ohio), Lansing (Michigan), Atlanta, and Buffalo all seeing tension in June. Elsewhere, Israel and Egypt are locked in a six-day war. On June 12, the US Supreme Court issues its ruling in Loving vs. Virginia, declaring the criminal prohibition of interracial marriage to be unconstitutional. This decision in effect ends the outlawing of miscegenation in the sixteen states where it's still illegal. On June 12, the USSR launches Venera 4, beginning the space probe's trek to Venus. Two days later, the US launches Mariner 5, which zooms its way to the same planet. From June 16 to 19, the Monterey International Pop Music Festival attracts over 150,000 spectators, 50,000 of whom pay for tickets. On June 20, Muhammad Ali is found guilty of draft evasion by a federal jury in Texas, and receives the maximum sentence, five years in prison and a $10,000 fine (a decision the US Supreme Court will reverse three years later). And on June 27, the first automated teller machine (ATM) is unveiled in North London …

Moby Grape also dashed through the news pages throughout the month, though often not in ways they wanted. For the band, June 1967 was both climactic and anticlimactic.

On June 6, the band's debut album was released amid an avalanche of publicity. The promotion afforded to it would give new meaning to the word extravagance, with Columbia sparing no expense. The release of the album—and its accompanying five singles—was supposed to be a crowning achievement for both the band and for Columbia Records. It wasn't.

June 6 was supposed to be a special moment for Moby Grape—and it was, but not for the right reasons. The release of *Moby Grape*, and the disasters that followed it in quick succession, would profoundly impact the band's path.

June 1967 could be described as the Time of the Three Punches. Three incidents occurred during the month that would have serious consequences for the band—immediate consequences, like earthquakes, that also then sent out shockwaves that would stretch out far into the future. These three punches would precipitate so much as the band moved forward, struggling to live up to expectations, to repeat the artistic success of its first LP, to create music that scales the pop charts, to resolve their issues with their manager, to mend their relationship with Columbia (as well as the media), and to rebrand themselves as a band that's more than just a gimmick. Collectively, the *three punches* sent out waves that profoundly influenced the Grape's image, relationships, work, and psyche.

•

The first punch occurred on June 6, with *Moby Grape* released amid an over-the-top hoopla, setting impossible expectations for the band. The release had become a massive event, with media personnel flown in from out of town. The lavish Avalon Ballroom banquet that ensued included a concert with Moby Grape performing, Janis Joplin guesting, and seven hundred bottles of Moby Grape wine doled out as keepsakes, not to mention a downpour of purple orchids, flown in specially from Hawaii.

Recalling the evening's festivities, Bob Mosley told Rob Hughes, 'I remember parking the Porsche, walking in there, and there were two people at the door who handed you a five-singles boxed set and a bottle of wine with "Moby Grape" on the label. There were millions of purple orchids flying from the ceiling; they were all over the floor.'

Sparing no expense, the boxed sets were lavish. A cross between a press kit and a gift, they were covered in purple velvet, with an assortment of treats inside, including glossy photos of each member of the band, a button, the five singles, and a dossier that described the band and outlined ideas for promotion—a dossier that can only be described as a *manifesto* of sorts.

When Columbia released those five Moby Grape singles, ten of the thirteen songs on the band's debut were instantly available on 45—all at once. If there were a Guinness World Record for marketing missteps, the *open-the-floodgates-five-singles-release-plan* would surely warrant close attention. Honestly, this marketing scheme is right up there with Coca-Cola's 1985 campaign to promote 'a bolder New Coke' or 1957's 'E Day' fiasco for the Ford Edsel.

In case some folks weren't impressed with the lavish festivities at the Avalon, or the five singles themselves, the text of the Moby Grape manifesto was worded to bowl these stragglers over, with a small packet of notes tucked into each press kit proclaiming:

> Columbia Records is taking the unprecedented step of simultaneously releasing five singles by Moby Grape as part of a gigantic campaign to make the entire country Moby Grape conscious. At the same time, the label is also releasing an album by the San Francisco group, which, before signing with Columbia, was sought after by as many as seven other record companies. The kick-off date for the Moby Grape campaign is June 6, at which time Columbia executives from both coasts will fete the group at a special party and concert to be held at the famous Avalon Ballroom, the showcase of San Francisco's top rock'n'roll talent. Key West Coast press and radio representatives will be on hand, including a large contingent of magazine and

> newspaper writers and radio personalities whom Columbia is flying in from Los Angeles for the event.

For those who couldn't get their hands on one of these manifestos, strongly worded print ads plastered the trades, announcing the week of June 6 as 'the week the country went grape.' In addition to listing the names of the five singles, these print ads proclaimed, 'In one fell swoop. Just as we planned it. Moby Grape made an indelible splash in the eye, ear, and mind.'

Writing in the *Los Angeles Times*, Digby Diehl offered one of the first reports on the fiesta Columbia put on for Moby Grape: 'Hordes of happy hippies streamed into the Avalon Ballroom here last week for soul food, music and wine at the Columbia Record coming-out party for five rock debutantes ... The dance hall was crowded with long-haired youth who gyrated to psychedelic sounds. A handful of press, some teenybopper fan mag editors, and SF celebrities wandered through the hippy masses in awe, while free bottles of wine (special Moby Grape label) and elaborate gift-wrapped press kits were handed out.'

A June 17 article in *Billboard* provided further details:

> Columbia is devoting prime promotion time to the build up of a new rock'n'roll group from San Francisco called the Moby Grape. ... As part of the Moby Grape promotion, a special logo was designed and will be used promotionally on all merchandising, promotion and publicity material, as well as on the product itself. All correspondence and news releases concerning the group will be printed on special paper with the logo as a letterhead. The Moby Grape advertising campaign, concluding with the group's record debut, will feature full-page ads in all trade publications and in key teen magazines and newspapers. A Moby Grape manual containing information about the group as well as sales tips, was prepared and sent to all Columbia sales and promotion personnel in the field.

But Columbia's $100,000 strategy of bombarding DJs and record-buyers with a bevy of singles and advertisements backfired. Releasing a pile of singles in one day didn't propel Moby Grape to commandeer the *Billboard* Top 10; rather it led to confusion and choice paralysis. The singles themselves hardly sold and failed to get the sort of airplay that Columbia was expecting. Only 'Omaha' cracked the Top 100, reaching its high point of #88 in the middle of July.*

While the band's five singles failed to sell on a national level, some did become local hits, with '8:05,' for instance, reaching #9 on Santa Rosa's KPLS chart. In the Northwest, however, Moby Grape's singles received very little rotation. In an early August issue of the *Idaho Free Press*, columnist Rick Glaub noted, 'Most of the people around this area have not even heard of Moby Grape. This is because the radio stations in this area don't play the records. … Tell your local radio station you want to hear from Moby Grape.'

Further damaging the band's credibility, Columbia's marketing scheme prompted some listeners to associate the Grape with such words as 'hype' and 'sellout.' Not believing that a band could write and perform five singles so quickly, some believed the five Grape singles to be the work of other songwriters and session musicians, much like the various other prefabricated bands that were bubbling around the hit parade at the time.

As Don Stevenson recalls:

> It's well known that Columbia's marketing and publicity strategy for our first album was about the worst thing that could've been done. Nobody knew out of the five singles that were all released at the same time, which one to play, and which one not to play. And sometimes they didn't play any of them. Then people thought that we were like The Monkees—that it was just a hype job. And some thought that there were probably other musicians playing on the record and

* 'Hey Grandma' made it to #127 on *Billboard*'s 'Bubbling Under' listing that same week, July 15 1967.

> the singles. So it came off leaving a bad taste in everybody's mouth.
>
> Columbia's strategy was just not effective. It could've been a much bigger album if they would've just pushed for '8:05' or 'Fall On You'—or whatever. We could've had a big hit with one of the songs. You know, there are marketing strategies that make a difference. Columbia's marketing strategy made a big difference—just not the one we were hoping for.

Columbia's overblown promotion garnered skeptical snickers in the media. Although the Grape didn't design, plan, or execute this marketing fiasco, they became pariahs of a sort. The press coverage that followed Columbia's massive efforts would lead numerous journalists to focus on the campaign over the music itself when reporting on the new band. Within this tempest, reporters were mystified at best and skeptical or mocking at worst. Years, even decades later, most coverage of Moby Grape's music indelibly cites Columbia's promotional campaign.

•

As time passed, some at Columbia came to believe that drastic measures needed to be taken—prompting them to make a series of decisions that were rooted in short-term thinking. Yet before we unpack the aftershocks of this *first punch*, or consider the other *two punches*, there's something important we need to clear up.

Moby Grape's debut album was by no means a disaster, or even a commercial failure. This notion is a misnomer. *Moby Grape* debuted on the *Billboard* 200 on July 1 at #144. On August 3, it cracked the Top 30, and on September 2, it reached its peak position of #24. It stayed on the chart until December 30—a total of twenty-seven weeks. If this sort of chart action sounds unimpressive, it isn't. Remember, this was Moby Grape's first LP. For context, let's compare this showing to other Bay Area debuts that came before it. Jefferson Airplane's first album only made it to #128 on *Billboard* on its release in the summer of 1966, while Buffalo Springfield's first record, released that December, peaked at #80, and The Grateful Dead's first LP, issued by Warner Bros the following spring, stalled at #73.*

In terms of year-end sales, *Moby Grape* stands at #86. While that number may seem unimpressive, remember that the album only went on sale halfway into the year, so it had to complete with a great many LPs that were released far earlier. The Beatles' *Sgt. Pepper*, which was released a few days before *Moby Grape*, is only #10 on the list, and surely would stand closer to the peak position if it were released earlier in the year. So, let's compare apples with apples. Of all the albums released in the second half of 1967 included in the yearend top 100, Moby Grape's debut stands at #26. And the artists above the Grape are no slouches, including such names as The Beatles, Jefferson Airplane, Aretha Franklin, Dionne Warwick, The Doors, Bob Dylan, The Yardbirds, The Hollies, and The Rolling Stones.

So, Moby Grape's debut did quite well in terms of sales. What about the critical response?

Moby Grape initially garnered mostly positive reviews, many of them from important voices. In the June 1967 issue of *Crawdaddy*, for instance, respected rock critic Paul Williams penned the following:

> Well, it took me a long time, but I finally figured out who Moby Grape remind me of: The Everly Brothers. Also Buddy Holly, Buffalo Springfield, middle-Beatles, Byrds, New Lost City Ramblers, The Weavers, Youngbloods, Daily Flash, and everybody else. Above all, the Grape give off this very pleasant sense of *déjà vu*. Rock has become so eclectic you can't even pick out influences—you just sense their presence. I don't really know *why* the Grape remind me of The Everly Brothers. But it's a nice feeling. Moby Grape is one of those beautifully inextricable groups with four guitarists (including bass), five vocalists, five songwriters, and about twelve distinct personalities (Skip Spence alone accounts for five of them). The Grape is

* Buffalo Springfield weren't exactly a *Bay Area band*, but they were certainly a part of the scene, and they were friendly with the Grape.

> unusual for an SF group in that it does not have an overall, easily identifiable personality from song to song. Their music is always unified; it's their album as a whole that's schizoid. In fact, much as I like it, I enjoy the songs even more one at a time (for your convenience, Columbia has issued almost the entire album on singles—which is particularly nice because the mono mix is far better than the stereo, which must have been done too fast).

Reviewing the album for the *Boston Globe*, Ernie Santosuosso described the Grape's music as being 'distilled from folk, blues, country-western, rock, rhythm & blues, bluegrass and soul … instrumentally, their sound is better than many rock outfits but I think the appeal of the Moby Grape will be aimed at the dancers. Of all the selections on their LP, simply titled *Moby Grape*, the group's most ambitious selection is "Indifference" which features a pounding beat and high-voltage string work. … Columbia has a strong new entry in the rock sweepstakes with Moby Grape.'

Alongside positive reviews of the music, numerous articles made mention of the promotional efforts Columbia put on to make the band into a hit. These sorts of news stories were anticipatory, openly wondering whether the massive marketing scheme would pay off for the label—and for the band. As a review in the *Cincinnati Enquirer* put it, 'Columbia Records took an unprecedented step recently by simultaneously releasing five singles and an album by a new San Francisco group, Moby Grape. But it's the label's way of displaying confidence in the group's appeal. Columbia officials are also convinced that each of the ten sides in the initial singles has the potential of making it to the top of national charts.'

Heavy promotion and critical success can't guarantee a commercial breakthrough, however. Although the Grape's debut LP sold well, it wasn't the chart-topping hit that Columbia expected, and the label quickly grew disappointed. When June 6 failed to become *the week the country went grape*, label executives made a series of decisions they believed would elevate Moby Grape into superstardom, but which would ultimately prove disastrous for the band—on a personal, artistic, and commercial level.

After pouring so much money into its Moby Grape marketing campaign in May and June—apparently $100,000—Columbia's thinking became reactionary. While the label continued to believe the band had the potential to break through the charts, its decisions lacked a long-term vision.

Then, on the very night of their release party, Moby Grape faced their *second punch*. In the wee hours of the following morning, Jerry, Peter, and Skip were arrested and charged with contributing to the delinquency of minors (a misdemeanor), while Jerry was also charged with possession of marijuana (a felony).

The previous evening, once the release party at the Avalon began to wind down, everybody had gone their separate ways. Some headed home, others returned to their hotel rooms, and some hurried to the airport to catch a flight out of San Francisco. David Rubinson took a redeye to New York City. Peter's father, Tom Lewis, went back to his hotel, while Peter himself returned to his home in Mill Valley. A smattering of people crossed the Golden Gate Bridge and headed over to Sausalito. Jerry and Skip went over to Peter's, and the three ended up on the mountainside off Donahue Street, about a mile away from the Ark and under a mile from the Marin County Sheriff's Department. The following day, David Rubinson received a telephone call about the arrest of three members of the Grape, and Tom Lewis found himself bailing the band members out of jail.

On June 9, an article entitled 'Moby Grape Trio Posts Bail On Marin Charges,' appeared in San Rafael's *Daily Independent Journal*:

> Three of the five members of Moby Grape, a rock'n'roll combo, were charged yesterday in Marin Municipal Court with leading a trio of 'flower children' girls astray. In addition to the misdemeanor charge of contributing to the delinquency of the minors, one of them, Jerry A. Miller, 24, of 503 Pinco Avenue, Mill Valley, faces a felony charge of marijuana possession. Miller and companions Peter Lewis, 22, of 370 Sunset Way, Tamalpais Valley, and Alex Spence, 22, of 110 Redwood Avenue, Corte Madera, are to be arraigned at 1:30pm next Thursday [June

> 15]. They and three 17-year-old girls from San Mateo County were arrested by sheriff's officers on a fire trail above Marin City early yesterday. The men posted bail, then flew to New York for a television date. The girls were booked into Juvenile Hall on suspicion of marijuana possession.

Still frustrated with the whole affair, Jerry Miller told *Goldmine* in 1993, 'We caught a lot of flack for that. The party itself was the most outrageous party I've ever been to. They had bottles of Moby Grape wine and orchids all over the stage. We were slipping all over and played so nice. We were having so much good, fun energy that night at the party, we just didn't want it to stop. So we thought we'd go check out the full moon. There were probably twenty people up on that hill with us. Then the shit hit the fan.'

In the midst of this, Moby Grape flew to New York for three nights at Steve Paul's hip club the Scene, where from June 9 to 11 they shared the bill with Toronto band John Lee & The Chessmates and Tiny Tim, whom roadie Tim Dellara recalls meeting with great fondness. 'Tiny Tim was playing between sets. Some people came over and said, You've got to meet this guy! I went over, and I met him, and of course, he was the perfect human being. He was somebody who loved you from the moment he saw you and every time after. It was like Steve Paul said: He's a star, but he used to be a universe. And, at that time, he *was* a universe. He was unbelievable.'

On returning to California, Jerry, Peter, and Skip appeared at Marin Municipal Court on the morning of Thursday, June 15. All three pleaded innocent. A preliminary hearing for Jerry's felony charge was set for June 30, with a trial for the misdemeanor set for August 14. The *Daily Independent Journal* update on these proceedings opens in truly bizarre fashion, stating, 'Jerry A. Miller, 24, long-haired and bearded member of Moby Grape rock'n'roll combo, yesterday pleaded innocent in Marin Municipal Court to marijuana possession.' It remains unclear how the length of Jerry's hair was connected to the charges at hand.

While Moby Grape were in New York, they and Columbia's Clive Davis had ironed out the details for a tour with The Mamas & The Papas, and on June 16, the band's addition to an upcoming show by the latter group at the Philadelphia Civic Center Convocation Hall was announced in the city's *Daily News*. 'Incidentally,' the report added, 'Columbia Records has gone overboard promotion-wise on Moby Grape, the new combo out of San Francisco.'

Meanwhile, an advertisement in the *Los Angeles Times* suggests that the Grape were due to play at the Hullabaloo Club on Sunset Strip on June 16 and 17, but there are no subsequent reports of the first show, and they ended up elsewhere on the day of the second. That day, the *third punch* occurred at the County Fairgrounds in Monterey, California—and it was almost a knockout.

•

History doesn't tell us this, but Moby Grape played a killer set at the Monterey International Pop Music Festival.* They were on fire. Received wisdom, however, tells us that Moby Grape were an overhyped band, that their first album was a commercial dud, and that they failed at Monterey.

OK, the Grape failed to *make a splash* in the way that The Who, Jimi Hendrix, and Otis Redding did on the Sunday night. But that in itself was by no means a failure. And Moby Grape not making a huge splash wasn't the result of their performance—because it was stunning. However, by then their timeslot at the festival had been switched from a coveted Sunday evening spot to the opening slot on Saturday, June 17. On top of this frustrating shift, they would be banished from the landmark film and album that came out of the festival.

At dusk on June 17, as late afternoon gave way to early evening, excited whispers were swirling around the audience that maybe, just maybe, The Beatles would be appearing at the festival. And then comedian Tommy Smothers walked out onto the stage and began to talk in his slightly nervous, halting voice.

'The first group tonight is kind of like in a more difficult position than

* To read more about the festival, see Joel Selvin's *Monterey Pop* or Harvey Kubernik's *1967*.

another group, because everybody's getting settled, and *someone* has to start the show. And this next group, I think we're very happy that they decided to [go on first], because nobody else wanted to go first. It's a difficult position. So, let's have a warm hand—really, let's make it extra-warm—for Columbia recording artists, Moby Grape!"*

Sounding almost apologetic in tone, it was as if Smothers was buttering up the band. After what had just happened, they *needed* buttering up. But before we get into that, let's take a step back in time and consider the origins of this historic festival.

By early 1967, jazz festivals had become entrenched in American culture. The Rhode Island Newport Jazz festival started in 1954, and five years later the Newport Folk Festival was established. Jazz and folk both had long histories that stretch back decades—or, for folk, centuries—into the past. With jazz and folk festivals, music lovers were dealing with longstanding traditions.

These sorts of festivals aren't only about the live events themselves. There were other options for those who couldn't make it to the shows. In the period 1956–58 alone, Newport spawned such live albums as *Ellington At Newport* (1956), *Dave Brubeck And Jay & Kai In Newport* (1956), *Dizzy Gillespie At Newport* (1957), *Count Basie At Newport* (1957), *Eddie Costa, Mat Mathews & Don Elliott At Newport* (1957), *Ella Fitzgerald & Billie Holiday At Newport* (1958), *Duke Ellington's Newport 1958*, *Dave Brubeck's Newport 1958*, and *Miles Davis' At Newport 1958*. In all, over a dozen such albums were released in just three years. It wasn't just about audio recordings, either: the 1960 film *Jazz On A Summer's Day* captures performances from the 1958 Newport Jazz Festival.

With jazz and folk, and especially at Newport, there was a precedent for holding popular festivals *and* supplementing them with successful albums and films. New and still in their infancy in the mid 60s, rock and pop were something else entirely, a young and ever-expanding universe. There was not yet an established cadre of serious rock critics, and the pop-rock genre

* Smothers' introduction can be found on the eighth track of the album *Moby Grape—Live* (Sundazed, 2010).

itself was not yet taken seriously as a form of *art*. Bob Dylan brought rock to Newport when he famously *went electric* at the 1965 Folk Festival—a move that spawned everything from outrage to praise. At that point, though, we were still two years away from *Sgt. Pepper*, as well as the game-changing debuts of The Velvet Underground, The Doors, and Pink Floyd.

Yet times *were* changing. In late 1965, Bill Graham organized the first benefit concert for a theater group he'd been managing, the controversial and evocative San Francisco Mime Troupe. Over the next two years, the Bay Area would flourish—a part of that flourishing being the growth of the benefit event—and reach a new level of luminescence when Timothy Leary advised 30,000 hippies to 'turn on, tune in, and drop out' at the Human Be-In at Golden Gate Park on January 14 1967.

As the 60s unfolded, the San Francisco ballroom emerged as a vibrant new kind of performance space, where lights and music intermingle. The city was home to *Rolling Stone*, too, as well as a bevy of brash new rock poster artists, the Diggers (a bona-fide radical community-action group, with links to the SF Mime Troupe), LSD manufacturer Owsley Stanley, and a whole host of new bands. The Bay Area became a city-state of sorts, an artistic village where bands lived together and jammed in shared spaces like the Fillmore, the Ark, and the Heliport. By 1967, San Francisco had grabbed the attention of the media and the country itself. Like the city-states of Renaissance Italy, it had its own distinct culture and identity.

Writing for the *Village Voice* in early 1967, Richard Goldstein noted:

> That Ralph Gleason writes from San Francisco is no coincidence. The city's rapport with the source of its ferment is unique. Traveling up the coast from the ruins of the Sunset Strip to the Haight is a Dantesque ascent. It's no accident that 400 miles makes the difference between a neon wasteland and the most important underground in the nation. San Francisco has the vanguard because it works hard to keep it. Native culture is cherished as though the city's consuming passion were to produce a statement that could not possibly be duplicated in

> New York. Chauvinism in Southern California runs to rhetoric about the grandeur of nature, but up north it is all have-you-seen-the-Mime-Troupe? And Haight-Street-makes-the-Village-look-like-a-city-dump.

By 1967, we had many circumstances swirling around and leading us to Monterey: an established history of jazz and folk festivals; a precedent for recording audio tracks and documentary films at these festivals; and, in terms of the pop-rock idiom, a short history of benefit and event concerts in and around the Bay Area. Amid all this, there was also a pronounced SF/LA divide. Unlike San Francisco, Los Angeles was (with New York) one of the twin capitals of the music business. If San Fran was homey, LA was the office. While the Bay Area was hip, LA had an arsenal of vast recording studios and record company head offices—and Sunset Strip. Each city had a different feel, a different cadre of bands. Each had its own identity.

With all these circumstances all in the air, the idea for a bridge-building rock-pop festival began to take form. The Monterey Pop Festival was partly a product of the SF/LA schism, with Los Angeles–based hit-maker John Phillips and manager Lou Adler orchestrating a celebration to be held smack dab in the middle of the divide. Now was a time to celebrate, to form friendships, and build bridges.

In the months leading up to June '67, Monterey began to take form. And, as a band with buzz and momentum, Moby Grape were given a much sought-after timeslot. As the original schedule indicates, the Grape were earmarked to play on Sunday, along with The Who, the Paul McCartney–endorsed Jimi Hendrix Experience, Buffalo Springfield, The Grateful Dead, and Big Brother & The Holding Company. Somehow, though, Moby Grape's manager, Matthew Katz, and the duo of Lou Adler and John Phillips got into a conflict over the matter of filming the Grape's performance. Amid the fracas, Katz began making financial demands—some say he asked for a cool million dollars to sign the release forms—which served only to anger the cash-strapped festival organizers. And here we have the *third punch*.

While Matthew Katz was not purposefully trying to sabotage his band, his brinksmanship led the festival organizers to angrily remove the Grape from their coveted Sunday night timeslot and place them in the dubious position of opening the show on Saturday afternoon/evening. As Tim Dellara recalls:

> I went and met with John Phillips at whatever the hotel they were staying at was, and I said, 'You know, the band is willing to be filmed. It's fine with them.' And John told me, 'Well, you know, the problem is that Matthew holds the paper on these guys. So we can't do that.' I think they ended up being filmed, because there are a couple of outtakes of that, but they certainly weren't in the Pennebaker film or anything like that. They were pissed. From that point, Matthew was kind of out of the picture.

•

When Tommy Smothers took to the stage to introduce Moby Grape at Monterey, there were numerous reasons, then, why the soft-spoken comedian was trying to butter them up. The Grape then opened the Saturday evening performances with verve and energy, amid distracting rumors among the crowd that The Beatles were set to appear.

In a fiery set, Moby Grape ran through a quick succession of songs with speed and intricacy. In one of the first reviews of the festival, *Los Angeles Times* reviewer Pete Johnson wrote, 'The night-time stint opened with the Moby Grape, a polished San Francisco quintet who were well received.' Yet while the band received positive notices, they were, like everyone else, left standing in the shadow of the Sunday night trinity of Who/Hendrix/Redding. Ultimately, it would be those three acts that grabbed America's attention.

The Grape's experience at Monterey wasn't career-destroying by any means. They played impressively and consorted with some of the greatest musicians of the time. At the end of the event, Don was given the stage set of drums from the festival. But while the Grape's set was glorious, it never appeared in the film or albums associated with the historic Monterey Pop Festival—even when Criterion issued a boxed set forty-two years later. In the meantime, their last-minute program change—along with their subsequent omission from the film and album releases that grew out of the festival—would prove tremendous blows to their confidence. What happened at Monterey gave the members of Moby Grape a palpable feeling that momentum was somehow slipping through their fingers.

Following the Monterey debacle, the relationship between the Grape and Matthew Katz became more strained than ever. A few months later, Katz would be replaced by former Rolling Stones tour manager Michael Gruber; over time, his exit would lead to a variety of complications and legal entanglements, in both the near and very distant future.*

When I bring up the Monterey Pop Festival, Don is in no doubt as to how crucial a point in the band's career it proved to be.

> Our time was changed—the day and the time. We were supposed to be on Sunday, with The Who and Jimi Hendrix. We were booked for that night and time because we had a hot album at the time—it was new and it had gotten some good press. Then our time got changed. Matthew refused to let them film us. He told them that if they didn't give him *x*-amount of money, they couldn't film Moby Grape. I don't know who else was on at that [timeslot], but I guess maybe Lou Adler and Jon Phillips, well, they just said, 'If that's the way you want to do it then you can open the whole thing—you can be the first band. Nobody's gonna be there, nobody's gonna give a shit, and nobody's gonna film it—so fuck you.'
>
> That altered our career as far as I'm concerned. We might've been able to overcome the five singles [had we] been in Monterey at a good timeslot and in the film. It was a breakthrough for Jimi

* Ironically, while Monterey Pop was taking place, Matthew was entangled in a bitter legal battle with the Jefferson Airplane over payments and royalties For more on this, see Stan Soocher's 'Moby Grape Saga' at *meiea eZine*.

Hendrix and The Who and Otis Redding. I mean, he was doing fine before but it was huge. And it still gets played to this day.

Our set didn't get released [officially] until 2010. If you listen to it, you can see we're on fire—right in the sweet spot. We were just coming undone it was so good. We had no doubt about how we're gonna play those songs, and Skippy was full-blown, and so was Mos—all of us. … I've seen a clip of us playing 'Lazy Me' for a documentary that's coming out on Clive Davis. And that song has never been released on audio. So there's stuff in still in the can. Who knows when it'll come out.*

Monterey Pop was a bittersweet memory for Moby Grape. Amid the frustration, there remains great excitement. When I ask Don if he remembers some of the acts he caught, he excitedly recalls seeing Hendrix light his guitar on fire and Redding 'stomping on the stage like a lion.' And yet, at the same time, he was asking himself, 'Why aren't we up there?'

'We were down behind the stage, smoking, hanging out with everybody,' Don continues. 'It was a really beautiful event. That's what I recall about Monterey. We were upset about the schedule. There was all kinds of music there. There was the Los Angeles crowd and the San Francisco crowd, and suddenly, we're all taking to each other. It was pretty cool.'

•

Nearly a week after Monterey, on Friday, June 23, the *Detroit Free Press* reminded its readers that Moby Grape would be in town the following Monday, 'to do the Robin Seymour TV show and to perform at the Upper Deck of the Roostertail … with CKLD disk jockeys emceeing.' That night, the Grape shared the bill with The Blue Magoos and The Mamas & The Papas in Philadelphia. They were scheduled to perform two more shows

* On December 12 2017, Criterion issued an expanded Blu-ray edition of the Monterey boxed set that features Moby Grape's explosive rendition of 'Hey Grandma.' Skip stops his foot, counting everyone in. While the entire band plays with exuberance, Skip is especially animated throughout the performance—and, after more than five decades, this visual fragment is both pleasing and enticing. It leaves us wanting more.

on the short tour after that, with The Buckinghams joining the bill for the weekend performances at the Public Auditorium in Cleveland on Saturday, June 24, and the Civic Arena in Pittsburgh on Sunday, June 25.

By the night of June 24, however, the Grape and the Buckinghams were at loggerheads. According to a *Billboard* report entitled 'Buckinghams, Grape Stage Off-Stage Tiff At Concert,' a 'forty-minute hassle' between the two Columbia acts resulted in the Grape being prevented from playing.

> The Moby Grape arrived twenty minutes after the 8:30 starting time in the Public Auditorium. The Buckinghams, scheduled second, went on in their place, playing extra songs. Buckinghams' road manager Pete Shelton complained after two of the Grapes, Bob Mosley and Skippy Spence, shouted to the audience from backstage during the Buckingham sets. Matthew Katz, Moby Grape manager, said that his group had arrived about noon in Cleveland but had gone to a TV station and rehearsed. He said that he thought his group was to go on just before the Mamas & Papas. The Buckinghams' contract stated that they should immediately precede the Mamas & Papas, Shelton said. Buckinghams' manager James William Guercio backed Shelton. Mamas & Papas tour manager Louis B. Robin A/C Productions termed the hassle a 'contractual misunderstanding.' He allowed the Grape to perform after the intermission. 'Other than the obligation to the audience there was no reason to put them on,' Robin said.

Speaking to Steve Roeser about the ill-fated tour, Bob Mosley later recalled, 'The Buckinghams were supposed to go on second, and we were supposed to go on third. We didn't want to go on third. We thought The Buckinghams were kind of a jive group. So that caused some friction.'

As far as Don is concerned, there were 'probably two reasons' why Moby Grape ended up being kicked off the tour.

> One was because we bare-assed The Buckinghams—when they were performing. And the other reason was because The Mamas & The Papas were kind of like, singing 'Monday Monday' [*sings softly*], and we were kind of, like, thumping. You know, we'd come on and play 'Omaha,' and it would be like crashing this huge atom bomb on the stage, and everyone would be going crazy and they'd come out playing very soft stuff. I don't think they liked us being on—I don't think they thought we'd be a great flip, and for the venue. Probably there is some truth to that. And I think they had a little more pull with Columbia than we did. We were new artists and they were already proven. With The Buckinghams, we just thought that they did a cover of a song—'Mercy, Mercy, Mercy,' originally by Cannonball Adderley. The original was funky and cool. Then they did it and it wasn't—to us, it wasn't the same. I don't want to come off as a musical snob, but we were brash. So we bare-assed them and it didn't go over well. That's how I recall it.

For Moby Grape, leaving the tour before Sunday's final show in Pittsburgh wasn't a tremendous issue, but the bad press would prove to be toxic. As Peter Lewis later told Jud Cost, when the tour was first being organized, the original idea was the Grape and the Mamas would get equal billing—'which was weird, but we really thought we were already The Beatles'—but then the more established group heard an advance copy of *Moby Grape*. After that, Lewis recalled, 'they didn't want to come on after us, so they hired the Buckinghams to play after us. [*Laughs.*] We played two more dates and they kicked us off the tour. That's when we became troublemakers in a lot of people's eyes.'

With Matthew Katz in tow, the band then trekked to Detroit for their previously scheduled events. On the afternoon or Monday, June 26, they appeared on Robin Seymour's TV show, before playing a promotional event at the Roostertail Club in the evening. According to a report on the 'all-out promotion' for the band by Loraine Alterman in *Billboard*, the label's promotions man, Russ Yerge, had put together 'a special Moby Grape night' at the club, 'which is normally closed Mondays,' while local disc jockey Paul Drew 'provided a barrage of spot announcements about the free show' and added 'Omaha' to his 'CKLW Big 40 playlist.' The appearances in Detroit were a success, with the *Detroit Free Press* later reporting, 'Moby Grape proved Monday night at the Upper Deck that all the advance promotion wasn't wrong. They are really good. Guitarist Skip Spence told me they hope to help other good San Francisco groups happen if the Grape make it to the top.'

Recounting this trip to Detroit, Tim Dellara tells me, 'Boy, they didn't like us! The *crowd* liked us. But the people at the Roostertail didn't like us. When we showed up, they were completely dismissive. We all had long hair, and the Roostertail used to have acts like Frank Sinatra ... they were all in tuxes.' Those attitudes changed after the show, of course, 'because so many people came. That was such a strange time for a lot of people. Especially those people, who were used to the staid, regular way things go—and to see a bunch of people coming up with bare feet and stuff, to a place like the Roostertail.'

'That's where Skip went off the stage,' Don recalls. 'He fell right off the edge of the stage at the Roostertail. He was so intense!' Don breaks out laughing. 'He fell off the stage one time at the Ark also, but the stage was higher at the Roostertail. He didn't get hurt. He just bounced back up an started playing again. So, the Rooster Club was an interesting gig. It was usually a restaurant and a bar. It was right on the Detroit River. They had people who had these big hover-planes—that's why it was called the Rooster Club. It was a great gig.'

•

While Moby Grape were making their appearances in Detroit, they received some good news from home: that same Monday, June 26, Judge Peter Allen Smith dismissed Jerry Miller's felony possession charge, four days ahead of his previously scheduled preliminary hearing.

All in all, June 1967 was an up-and-down month for the band. They released a debut LP that garnered positive reviews yet somehow would take nearly a month to chart on the *Billboard* 200. In a show of overwhelming confidence, Columbia had broken the bank on record promotion and gone as far as to release five singles simultaneously, yet the ad campaign fuelled skepticism, and not one of the Grape's singles made the Top 50, let alone Top 10. In terms of high-profile gigs, the Grape put on a string of strong performances, including shows at Steve Paul's Scene in New York, and at Monterey, yet the band's spot at the latter festival was marred by a schedule change, and in the aftermath the status of their filmed recordings remained up in the air. They had also left a high-profile tour one day early on bad terms, which damaged their reputation in the media. Worse still, even though Jerry's felony charge had been dropped, the misdemeanor charges against him, Peter, and Skip remained unresolved.

By the end of June, both Columbia Records and the members of Moby Grape were left wondering what the future might hold for the band. As Peter Lewis later told Jud Cost, 'Columbia had decided not to put any more money into Moby Grape, because we weren't this neat little package, like The Buckinghams. We were hippies going crazy in public, and they didn't know how to market it.'

All in all, though they weren't aware of it at the time, the events of June 1967 would reach far into the band's future.

CHAPTER SEVENTEEN

THE SUMMER OF LOVE

In July, Moby Grape played fewer shows, perhaps partly as a result of the bad press they'd received in June. As Jerry Miller put it to *Goldmine* in 1993, the arrests 'basically cancelled the East Coast tour, which we were about to go out on.' They did however record a TV appearance during this period: a special hosted by club owner Steve Paul and called simply *The Steve Paul Scene*, for which they performed 'Hey Grandma,' 'Sitting By The Window,' and 'Omaha,' sharing the stage with The Blues Project, Aretha Franklin, and The Staple Singers, among others. The show aired locally on September 4, before being syndicated across the US later in the autumn.*

On July 14–15, the band performed two shows in Reno, Nevada, at the Reno Centennial Coliseum, sharing the bill with another Matthew Katz act, Melvyn Q Watchpocket. The following week, on July 22, they played an event at the Santa Monica Civic Auditorium, on a bill that also featured a legion of 60s icons, including The Yardbirds, Captain Beefheart, Strawberry Alarm Clock, and The West Coast Pop Art Experimental Band.

* The television special is now archived in the National Museum of Television & Radio in New York. In his memoir, Blues Project guitarist Steve Katz places this recording session in July '67. I corresponded with Steve via email in late 2016.

Despite the strong lineup, the evening was marred by technical problems, which it seems only Moby Grape and The Yardbirds were able to successfully navigate, according to a report by Pete Johnson in the *Los Angeles Times*:

> The sound system buckled against the conglomerate competition of drums and electrical instruments, leaving most of the audience unable to hear the slightest whisper from vocalists mouthing and writhing behind the microphones. … Jim Salzer, promoter of the event, periodically wandered onstage with tiresome excuses (this was his first concert in Santa Monica, he was sorry, next time he will make sure it doesn't happen) which hardly pacified the audience, who also were annoyed by long waits between the appearance of each act. … Judgments are difficult, but The Yardbirds and the Moby Grape received the most fervent applause. They were the best-known groups and each is a visual act.

Throughout July, *Moby Grape* ascended the *Billboard* 200, but the band's five singles faltered. Perhaps the negative media attention the band had been receiving prompted Columbia to have second thoughts about the album's cover, which showed Don Stevenson 'flipping the bird' and Skip holding a poll bearing the American flag. Panicking, Columbia airbrushed out Stevenson's offending digit and recolored the American flag orangey-red. But with the Cold War in effect, and the USA embroiled in the controversial Vietnam War, that reddish flag would soon garner a different sort of negative attention. These changes to the album cover led Columbia to incur additional costs, precipitating further feelings of disdain.

•

August was a hectic month. On August 2, the band played a show at the Eagle Auditorium in Seattle, which for Don (and Jerry) was a homecoming of sorts:

I remember I used to go to the Eagles Auditorium when I was like fifteen years old. The bill would be like Little Richard and Fats Domino and The Platters. I saw Hank Ballard & The Midnighters there. And they got kicked out of Seattle. Remember, this was when I was like fourteen, fifteen, sixteen years old. They had really good songs like 'Annie Had A Baby' and 'Work With Me, Annie,' and there was 'Thrill On The Hill.'* They were pretty loud for the time. It was the late 50s, so they actually shut them down one time at the Eagles. Those guys were great. They had some amazing shows with people like Lavern Baker and shows with amazing talent. It was really fun to go back to the Eagle. I remember the local bands that played with us. There were a lot of great local bands around at the time. I remember a band called The Daily Flash. That Seattle scene that we came out of was an amazing scene. Dave Lewis, The Frantics, The Playboys. I played with The Playboys and a band called The Continentals. And then later, I played with The Frantics. You could not go to a high school dance and not see a live band. There were so many bands! And a lot of them turned out to be excellent. The guy who played bass in the Continentals, Butch Nordal, he's a top composer and arranger and pianist. He's got a beautiful home in Washington. He's an academic and he's also a performer. He plays like nobody else. He played with Larry Coreal and these guys are jazz legends. When I played with The Playboys as a B-3 trio with Lee Parker and Mike Mandal, we played over at the Black & Tan.† I'd played at a tavern and then pack my stuff up and then head over across town to the Black & Tan afterhours. It was amazing, with amazing musicians. And it's generational,

* R&B singer/songwriter Hank Ballard was inducted into the Rock and Roll Hall of Fame in 1990. Twenty-two years later, The Midnighters were also voted into the Hall. In 1958, Hank wrote and recorded 'The Twist,' which was famously covered by Chubby Checker two years later.

† Operating from 1922 to 1966, the Black & Tan was a leading jazz club in Seattle. The history and sound of Northwest rock is captured in Peter Blecha's award-winning book *Sonic Boom*.

> too. You get all these bands popping out of Seattle over the years, like The Sonics, and Soundgarden—so many of them.

On August 3, the jury trial for Jerry, Peter, and Skip was granted a continuance from August 14 to September 21. According to a report in the *Daily Independent Journal*, attorney Terrance Hallinan appeared at the Marin Municipal Court on behalf of the defendants, explaining that they were unable to attend due to being in Montreal, Canada, at the time.

After returning to California, the band played two nights each at the Fillmore (August 8 and 9) and the Avalon (August 10 and 13). After that, without a firm plan for the band, Columbia flew them down to Malibu to live as sojourners and hurriedly write and record a follow-up album. Yes, that's correct: Moby Grape were back in the studio recording their *second* album in mid-August, barely two months after the release of their debut, and less than four months after they finished laying down tracks for that album.

As a first step, Moby Grape took part in a movie that was due for release the following May. *The Sweet Ride* was a biker exploitation film directed by Joe Pasternak and starring Tony Franciosca and Jacqueline Bisset. After quickly writing a song for the film, 'Sweet Ride (Never Again),' the band whisked into the studio to record it on August 14. 'We wrote that when we were in the studio,' Don recalls of the song. 'I remember sitting in a stairwell with Peter and writing some of that. And Skippy—we all got into it. I think we all took credit for it because nobody wanted to take the blame for it,' he laughs. 'So we just blamed everybody. For what it was, it was good.' When I ask Bob about the song, he replies, 'I don't remember writing it. I remember singing it. I just sang what they wrote down.'

Later in the month, the band spent a day filming a large set piece at the Tarantula, which had been dressed to look like a hip club on Sunset Strip. A report on the filming appeared in the *Philadelphia Daily News* on September 1, noting how 'The Moby Grape, one of the fastest-rising new rock'n'roll groups in the music business, will make their motion-picture debut in 20th Century Fox's *The Sweet Ride*, which is now before the cameras on location in Malibu. For a key sequence set in a psychedelic nightclub, the long-haired quintet of singers and instrumentalists will perform their own original material. In addition, the group has also written and arranged another song to be used in the Joseph Pasternak production, which concerns young people and their contemporary morals.'

Casting his mind back, Don tells me, 'I think Steven Stills and Neil Young were down in Malibu at the same time. We got together with them a couple of times when we were there. We went to the leading actor's house from *The Sweet Ride*, a little starlet party—Tony Franciosca, that's who I'm thinking of. Most of the people were there. We smoked a lot, got really stoned. We met Joe Pasternak [the director]—he was on site when we did that scene. We did the scene in one day, I believe: *Hey, let's go up to the shack, Moby Grape's playing—come on kids!*' he laughs.

•

Five days after recording 'Sweet Ride (Never Again),' Moby Grape played a show at the Earl Warren Showgrounds in Santa Barbara, with The Jimi Hendrix Experience opening. Over the next few days, they also made a guest appearance on the TV show *Boss City* in Los Angeles, then played a run of gigs at the Whisky A Go Go from August 21 to 23. On August 28, they returned to Columbia Studios on Sunset Boulevard to record 'Bitter Wind,' a song Bob Mosley wrote about his first LSD experience.* Then, in the final two days of August, they recorded 'He' (written by Peter) and 'The Place And The Time' (written by Don and Jerry as a snapshot of the times).

Although the band had produced four songs in as many studio days throughout August—along with playing numerous shows—Columbia was unsatisfied. The company had wanted the band's debut LP to sell better, and now wanted a new product for the market. In frustration, the label put the band's recording sessions on hold.

Meanwhile, to boost sales of *Moby Grape*, the label's marketing executives organized a 'poetry-writing contest' in collaboration with the radio station KRFC, with the promise that the band would select a winning

* Peter Lewis speaks to the origins of 'Bitter Wind' in interviews with Jud Cost and Craig Morrison.

poem and then transform it into a song for their second album. At the end of September, *Billboard* announced the winner of the contest as Michael Heyworth of Point Richmond, California. The result was one of the band's least-liked songs, 'The Lake,' as featured on the following year's *Wow/Grape Jam*. As Don recalls, 'We *really* picked a song called "Hairy Mary" … and the suits at Columbia found it very scary. They put the kibosh on the song we picked.'*

On September 15 and 16, the Grape played the Continental in Santa Clara; further gigs were scheduled in Long Island and Greenwich Village the following weekend, but it is unclear whether they took place. Certainly, in October, the band were forced to cancel performance a series of shows at the Trauma in Philadelphia and the Grande Ballroom in Detroit. According to a report in the *Philadelphia Daily News*, the first set of shows was canceled 'because of illness,' with The Fugs brought in to replace the Grape. These shows would eventually be rescheduled for November and December, by which time the band were suffering from another complaint: *Pepper-itis*.

* While Moby Grape found the whole lyric-writing contest both disheartening and frustrating, they weren't unique in this experience. During the Summer of Love, Los Angeles radio station 93-KHJ Boss Radio also beckoned listeners to send in their poems to compete for the prize of writing a lyric for the Buffalo Springfield's next album. The winner—one Micki Callen—received $1,000 in cash, plus royalties, with her lyric becoming 'The Hour Of Not Quite Rain' on Buffalo Springfield's third and final album, *Last Time Around* (ATCO 1968). For the full story behind this episode, see Richie Unterberger's *Jingle Jangle Morning*.

CHAPTER EIGHTEEN

PEPPER-ITIS/JAM

Throughout October and into early November, Moby Grape played sporadic gigs in California, including shows at the Ark (October 7, 13, and 14, and November 4), at McNear Beach in Marin County (over the weekend of October 28–29), and in Concord (November 3–4). It's possible in fact that they played twice on November 4, as Concord wasn't far from Marin County, and the Ark show may have ended up turning into a late-night affair.

With Columbia maintaining a short-term mindset, the label then uprooted everyone again, dispatching them to New York for two weeks of recording sessions and numerous shows followed by weeks of touring. The change of location would do little to help matters, however. As Bob Mosley put it in an interview with Rob Hughes for *Classic Rock* magazine, 'Going to New York just brought the trouble to New York.'

On November 6, Moby Grape stepped into Columbia's New York recording studio to cut six demos. When I ask Don about one of these, 'Loosely Remembered,' he pauses for a moment before telling me that he doesn't remember the song at all.

> We were getting fragmented at that time. You know, Peter and

> Mos were tight, and Jerry and I were tight. That was how it worked out. So, 'Skip's Song'—we all were there and recorded it together. I'm not sure if we're all on 'What's To Choose' and 'Looper.' A lot of the work that was done on those songs was done with just Bob and Peter—if you notice the vocals, I think with 'Bitter Wind,' I was in on the loop at the very end.
>
> By that point it was kind of ... we would do basic tracks and then people would come up and do their own parts. With the first album, everybody was always there. We did it live in the studio. With our second album, it was different. You'd lay down the track, and you'd just have Peter and Bob come up and add the vocal or something.

Over the next two weeks, the band continued to make progress on their second album, cutting three more songs across five studio days (November 8, 10, 14, 15, and 20): a re-recording of 'Bitter Wind'; a forceful new track, 'Can't Be So Bad'; and the catchy song that had been held over from their first album, 'Murder In My Heart For The Judge.' (Of the latter song, Jerry says, 'We had a little contest because Don and Bob both wanted to sing it. And Bob ended up getting to sing it.')

Discussing 'Can't Be So Bad' with Peter 'Tab' Walker in 2007, Jerry recalled writing the song with Don in a New York hotel room the day before they recorded it, and then humming the idea for the brass parts to an arranger, who 'sat with me and wrote it all down on a chart.' The vocal harmonies, he added, also came together easily: 'Don's harmony with me was a parallel on a third and sometimes a fifth, [and] Peter was a good harmony singer and just fitted his on real quickly without much discussion.'

Jerry's favorite part of the song, meanwhile, was 'the most amazing shuffle drum part,' played by Don, who also has fond memories of recording it:

> That was probably the most fun I had, playing drums on that. Because it was maybe a twenty-seven- or twenty-eight-piece band. It was like playing with Johnny Carson's band. We had

> these heavyweight musicians and they got their charts, and they came in and they just played. The shuffle was like a train going down the track. It was really up-tempo, and, suddenly, I'm sitting there and I'm pushing twenty-eight pieces and playing, and it's just like that—it was like heaven. It was the best thing. You know, you take the break and the horn would be playing and then you come back in—it was like smashing watermelons off the top of a roof. And it was very much like a train going down the railroad track, and you couldn't get it of the track—and that was fun. It was fun singing it too! It was on Letterman, you know, that's what it reminded me of—remember when they used to smash pumpkins from the top of a roof? [*Laughs.*]

During another of our conversations, when I ask Jerry about recording 'He' in Malibu, he clarifies that the band worked on that one in New York, too.

> It was a real bear to try to figure out what the hell to play on that thing. I was the last guy putting guitar on it. We kind of stacked them up with the orchestra and everything. And I was just getting as frustrated as I could be. And Paul Simon came in and said, 'Relax. Forget it. Let's go downstairs and watch Miles [Davis].' [*Laughs.*] So that was a nice break. But I was pretty frustrated, 'cos it already had two guitars on it, as well as the goddamned New York Symphony players.
>
> Peter put in his original guitar part, you know: *be-da-bap-dap-dap-bap-ba*. Then Skippy put some on there, I believe, if I remember correctly. I know I was the last. And I was sitting in a little control booth thinking, *what the heck can I do to this song to make it any better? It's already beautiful.* I finally put a couple of *dilly-dallies* in there, and, got away with it. [*Laughs.*]

Around the time of these sessions, the Grape played a series of gigs in the city, first at the Village Theatre (on November 11), and then the Café Au

Go-Go (November 17–19), with the newly formed Blood Sweat & Tears making their own New York City live debut as the opening act on each night.* Also round this time, Moby Grape transitioned to a new manager, Michael Gruber, with Matthew Katz now exiting the band's story for the moment. Katz had been instrumental in forming the group, establishing them at the Ark, and generating interest among record companies while they showcased their skills at the ferryboat-club, but when Jud Cost reminded Peter Lewis of Katz's 'good side' during their 1996 interview, Lewis noted, 'The ambience he created, that you were already a star, because he had a couple of Jaguars, himself ... Matthew's main function at first was just as a way to get from LA to San Francisco.'

Katz was a key variable in Moby Grape's formation and initial development, yet his role in their career soon became ... *complicated.* Over time, the band's relationship with him soured, with issues regarding the band's freedom to make their own decisions and questions over income and royalties leading to conflicts. Although the debacle at Monterey had not immediately prompted Matthew's departure, the link between Moby Grape and their manager soon reached a breaking point, with his departure from the role confirmed a few months later.

The band's change of managers received its first print mention in the November 23 edition of the *Courier-Post*, with Earl Wilson's 'It Happened Last Night' column noting the appointment of 'Mike Gruber, who recently left The Rolling Stones.' All was not as it seemed, however. Recalling this time, Don tells me, 'When he interviewed us, or when we interviewed him, he rented out a place. I believe it was overlooking Central Park. It was certainly impressive. When we went to his office to talk to him, one of his buddies was enthusiastically assuring us, You know, this is the first day of

* Situated in a long narrow basement without windows, its tiny stage placed to the left-hand side of the end wall, the Café Au Go-Go was located at 152 Bleecker Street from 1964 to '69. In those five short years, during which time the stage lightning because a key part of the club's atmosphere, it was visited by a glittering array of rock, folk, and blues stars, including Jimi Hendrix, Van Morrison, Tim Harden, Tim Buckley, Joni Mitchell, Howlin' Wolf, and Muddy Waters. John Lee Hooker and the Blues Project recorded live albums there, while in 1964 comedian Lenny Bruce and owner Howard Solomon were arrested on obscenity charges after two undercover officers watched Bruce's show there

the rest of your life! Gruber had some pretty cool credentials, because he'd been with the Stones. We were impressed. But it turns out that the office he had was a shell. It disappeared after we had our interview with him and signed our agreement.'

•

After stepping out of the recording studio on November 20, Moby Grape would not resume work on their second album for nearly two months, yet the intervening period would be a hectic one. On November 23 and 24, they returned to the Village Theater for four more performances, before journeying to Salt Lake City for a show at the Terrace the following day, sharing the bill with Country Joe & The Fish and Spirit.

The Grape put on a dozen shows in December, playing at the Second Fret in Philadelphia (5 and 7), the Grande Ballroom in Detroit (8 and 9), and the Shrine Auditorium in Los Angeles (15, 16, 18, 19, 21, and 23). In early January they made the trek to the East Coast, for an appearance on *The Mike Douglas Show* in Philadelphia ('He was really nice,' Don laughs, despite introducing the band as 'The Moby Grapes') and a pair of performances at the Psychedelic Supermarket in Boston. Then, after the band flew back to the Bay Area, it was finally time for Jerry, Peter, and Skip's jury trial—a trial that had been brewing for seven months.

The looming trial had been an ongoing source of stress for the band, especially the three who faced the charges. The whole affair had also done nothing to endear Moby Grape to the folks at Columbia, who remained unhappy with the band's record sales. Before moving forward in time, however, let's take stock of what led up to the trial.

Initially, Jerry, Peter, and Skip were arrested for the misdemeanor charge of contributing to the delinquency of minors on June 7 1967. On top of this, Jerry had been arrested for possession of marijuana—a felony charge. Later in the day, the three members of the band posted bail. Eight days after that, on June 15, Jerry, Peter, and Skip pleaded innocent to the misdemeanor charge, and Jerry pleaded innocent to the felony charge. Jerry's preliminary hearing was then set for June 30, with the misdemeanor trial scheduled for August 14. Eleven days later, Jerry's felony charge was dropped, and on August 3 the misdemeanor trial was moved from August 14 to September 21. Then, the day before the September trial was set to begin, a further continuance was issued, this time to November 16. Finally, on January 13 1968, the three members of the band were acquitted after a two-day trial and ninety-minute jury deliberation.

Recalling the sequence of events, Peter Lewis told Jud Cost:

> The thing that really fucked us up was that we weren't really a show-business thing. It was more like a gang of juvenile delinquents. Somebody once said, 'At its best Moby Grape was more like a gang fight than a rock band.' We behaved like what we sounded like. We didn't give a shit about the cops. We got busted at our press party, being with under-aged chicks and smoking dope in a car. That could have been good press, but it freaked Columbia out. We had a jury trial over it. On the last day I took my toothbrush, because I thought we were going to jail.

Clearly still frustrated with the whole fiasco, Jerry Miller told Rob Hughes that the whole thing was 'bullshit':

> The way it came out was that it was just the Grape involved, but it wasn't. There was a whole bunch of people out there on the mountain looking at the stars. Then everybody scrambled when the police came. I had one of the roadies' Mustangs at the time. The police ploughed through the ashtray until they found what they thought was an empty marijuana paper. But there was nothing there. And the stuff about the girls was bullshit too. So we spent the night in a holding facility and the papers are full of 'Moby Grape busted on drug charges!' They really made it look ugly.

Although the band members were all exonerated, the memory of the affair would linger for decades, becoming a part of the Moby Grape mythos. Unfortunately, while details of the *arrests* are nearly always included in stories about the Grape, the *outcome* of the trial is sometimes left out. Immaterial of the dropped possession charge and eventual acquittal, the Grape would never shake this *cause célèbre*.

•

When Moby Grape left California again in mid-January 1968, they were finally free of the looming trial and ready to finish their second album. Yet they were tired, too. Since August, they had been constantly on the move, touring or relocating their home base time and time again.

On January 15—just two days after the acquittal in Marin County—the band returned to Columbia Studios in New York City. Over the next month, they'd race to finish their sophomore album, all the while playing shows in New York City and along the East Coast. In a whirlwind of activity, the band recorded one demo, ten songs, and six extended jams over twelve studio days (January 15, 16, 21, 22, 25, 29, and 31, and February 1, 3, 5, 12, and 13).

Recalling Bob's ballad 'Three-Four,' which they recorded on January 22, Jerry notes that it features Patti Bowen on piano, while Jerry himself played 'a Fender Jazzmaster with a twanger bar on it … which I'll very rarely ever use. But I thought I'd give it a try. You know, that's another beautiful song, and Bob did a little off-time thing: he'd go, *Don't worry about me and I'll take care of thee*. I kinda wanted him to straighten it out and make it all straight—but I'm glad he didn't, 'cos it came out real nice.' When I ask Bob about the song, he says, 'I played it on the guitar without singing it. I sang it in my head while I played the melody. Then I put the words to it and sang it, and it was a whole song.'

That same day, Bob took lead vocals on Jerry's 'Miller's Blues.' 'That was just a vehicle for guitar,' Jerry says, 'and we had to do a little blues in there, because the people at the Fillmore and the Avalon, and all those places, they all liked it when we played a little bit of blues. We wanted to get some blues in there.' The turnaround chords, he notes, are from an old tune of his called 'Gonzo': 'It goes from a G to A B-flat 13 to an E-flat major-7 to a D-9. A little jazzy.' Even today, he adds, 'I teach those chords and those kinds of changes. I've been teaching, "*All of me, why not take all of me.*" And I've been teaching "Round Midnight" and "When Sunny Gets Blue."'

Three days later, the Grape cut a new song by Skip, 'Funky-Tunk.' 'God! We laughed so hard!' Jerry bursts out. 'That was just Skippy having a laugh. Then there was that duck sound we made up. Like Donald Duck,' he adds, before singing the first lines of the song:

> *Oh, my dove, where are ya goin'?*
> *Where are ya goin' down the road?*

'It gave me a chance to play a couple of little country licks in there,' Jerry chuckles. 'We had fun with that.'

Later the same day, the band also recorded 'Rose Colored Eyes,' a soft ballad by Bob. 'When I met Bob in San Francisco, his girlfriend was Rose,' Jerry recalls. 'He always thought a lot about her. So that [song] had a lot to do with it.'

Incidentally, January 25 1968 marked the one-year anniversary of the day the Grape first stepped into Columbia Records in LA to record their first demos. For the band, it was a hectic time. On all the moving around the band did during the final sessions in January and February 1968, Jerry recalls:

> We did Stonybrook, and we ended up in Augusta, Maine, one time. Then, we had to drive back through a snowstorm to get back to the Fillmore, and I remember we were just putting along because it was all ice with snow on top of that. We were coming down through Boston and stuff. And it was so slick we had to go really slow. Then here comes Skippy at the wheel, going something like 100mph past us. [*Laughs.*] And I think to myself, 'Man, I'm glad I'm not riding with him.' We got there first and Bill Graham was really pissed off with us because some of the

> guys were late. And those were the guys that passed us. So, I don't know what happened exactly, but Bill was not pleased.

I wonder if this might've been the show the band played at the Anderson Theater in February '68, with Procol Harum also on the bill, the month before Bill Graham renamed the venue the Fillmore East.

'That was in the wintertime,' Jerry tells me.

> But I get timetables mixed up sometimes. I don't know how we could've done what we did in such a short amount of time. You know, like me going down to Texas and then coming back up here and then going somewhere else.
>
> You know, I didn't appreciate a lot of what I should've appreciated. Even old Matthew Katz. As much of a pain in the ass as he was, he had knack to get things started. Then it just got a little out of hand. You know, not helping us stay at a creature comfort level. So then people go haywire. You need the creature comforts when you're out on the road. You have to take time and get sleep instead of running around and burning out. But those were the days when everybody did that. Some things were a lot of fun on the East Coast, because we'd always bump into, you know, The Turtles at a certain place and The 5th Dimension, all our old friends, 'cos we'd all do the same tours. We'd all stop in a restaurant somewhere on the East Coast and there would be another band and we'd shoot the shit. That was always kind of fun.

•

By February, the LP had grown into a double album. In all, Moby Grape's sophomore effort, a seventy-five-minute giant, was recorded in a mere twenty-two studio days. But those days stretched from August 1967 to February 1968.

For a double album, twenty-two studio days is a brisk pace—and it's a far cry from the 700 hours that went into the recording of *Sgt. Pepper*. However, when compared to the mere five studio days it took the Grape to record their debut, the pace for *Wow/Grape Jam* may have appeared sluggish. If anyone at Columbia thought the band was being sluggish, though, they were failing to consider *the percolation factor*. Moby Grape's debut percolated for months before the band ever stepped into the studio. For their second album, they were sent to Malibu without a reservoir of songs on hand—*and* they were being asked to create hit songs on the spot. In addition, the band's sophomore LP was recorded under a stop-start-stop-start regimen, with everyone constantly on the move throughout.

Not including tour dates, over a seven-month period Moby Grape were uprooted no less than six times, switching their home base from San Francisco to Malibu in mid-August, back to the Bay Area in mid-September, to New York in early-November, to the Bay Area (again) in late-December, to New York (again) in mid-January, and finally to the Bay Area (again) in March. The pressure to write new material while constantly moving about took a heavy toll on everyone. Over time, this pressure proved to be damaging to band morale, and catastrophic to their career. Of this period, Peter Lewis told Jud Cost in exasperation, 'We had to do it [the second album] in New York because the producer [Rubinson] wanted to be with his family. So we had to leave our families and spend months in hotel rooms in New York City.'

All the while, Columbia's decisions, despite having a certain logic to them, were rooted in short-term thinking. For instance, in shuffling the five members of the band from city to city and studio to studio—as though they were chess pieces on a board—Columbia believed its strategies would prompt Moby Grape to produce a hit. On top of this, Columbia, David Rubinson, and the band took two more gambles. Somehow, along the way, it was decided that more production-oriented effects were needed enrich Moby Grape's music—and boost sales. It was also decided that the band would record an album's-worth of improvised numbers to be released alongside their second LP.

These two strategies produced mixed results.

First, there's the 'bells-and-whistles' production angle. If you listen to *Wow* right after listening to Moby Grape's debut, you soon realize the band were up to something *completely* different. Some love it, others don't. Robert Christgau would famously call it 'pepper-itis' in his (otherwise upbeat) *Village Voice* review of the album. But what is *pepper-itis*?

To understand *pepper-itis*, we need to consider the context of *Sgt. Pepper* itself. Released in the first week of June 1967, *Sgt. Pepper's Lonely Hearts Club Band* was a cultural landmark. It took 700 studio hours to create between November 1966 and April 1967, the results exploring new possibilities in terms of words and music, as well as technology and production. While The Beatles' previous LP, *Revolver*, expanded the rock-pop universe and brought on (or synthesized) new paradigms—baroque pop, Motown rock, psychedelic rock, raga rock, and so on—*Sgt. Pepper* thrust pop into the terrain of symphonic music, art rock, tempo rubato, and more. It pushed popular music into a new space, its lyrical sketches overlapping Edwardian nostalgia with the contemporary psychedelic social milieu, blending them with fresh soundscapes of studio wizardry (or trickery, depending on your point of view).

In the *Revolver–Pepper* period, The Beatles—in collaboration with producer George Martin and engineer Geoff Emerick—made an assortment of technological leaps, including work with vari-speeding, automatic double tracking (ADT), reverse taping, pitch control, dynamic range compression, and so on. Following the band's use of full orchestra, a string nonet (with harp), mixed-media application, a tabla and swarmandal with tamburas, and other combinations, instrumentation and arrangement within the rock-pop idiom were changed forever.*

The impact of *Pepper* began with the release of the 'Strawberry Fields Forever' / 'Penny Lane' single in February '67. Then, a few months later, came the highly anticipated LP. There had not previously been an album like

* To read more about the creation and influence of *Pepper*, see Mark Lewisohn's *The Beatles Recording Sessions*, Ian MacDonald's *Revolution In The Head*, George Martin and William Pearson's *Summer Of Love*, and Geoff Emerick and Howard Massey's *Here, There And Everywhere*. For a nimble album-by-album survey of the music landscape, see Richard Morton Jack's *Psychedelia*.

it, and the entire pop world shifted on its release. Of course, no matter how you feel about the album itself—whether you love, like, dislike, or even hate it—the impact of its release would be pervasive and undeniable. Simply put, there's a line between what came before *Pepper* and what came after it.

Before *Sgt. Pepper*, The Rolling Stones produced *Between The Buttons*; after *Pepper*, they come out with the production-heavy *Their Satanic Majesties Request*. After *Pepper*, The Who produced their first full concept-album, *The Who Sell Out*. After *Pepper*, The Pretty Things, The Zombies, and The Small Faces would all tread further away from their previous R&B-heavy fare, each producing a concept album (either musical or lyrical) in the form of *S.F. Sorrow*, *Odyssey & Oracle*, and *Ogden's Nut Gone Flake*, respectively. Even the blues-influenced Cream and jazz-bluesy Doors immersed themselves in the new terrain of production and strings, resulting in *Disraeli Gears* and *The Soft Parade*.

Some of the many *Pepper*-influenced albums were great successes (*Odyssey & Oracle*, *Ogden's Nut Gone Flake*), others intriguing misses (*Their Satanic Majesties Request*, *The Soft Parade*). After *Pepper*, however, *serious* music critics could no longer ignore pop music. After *Pepper*, the pop album, as a canvas, would be understood differently.

Like so many other musicians, Moby Grape stood not under the shadow but in the sunrays of The Beatles. Like so many others, they were inspired by *Pepper*. They couldn't help but be inspired by it—just as The Rolling Stones, The Who, The Small Faces, and so many others couldn't help it. Why shouldn't they? After all, as a trailblazing work, *Pepper* pushed musicians to consider new possibilities, in terms of composition, lyrics, instrumentation, technology, and production.

When Columbia ushered Moby Grape back into the studio—two months after their debut, and before the band was even a year old—*Sgt. Pepper* was in the air—the radio waves and the very atmosphere. Before long, under David Rubinson's guidance, Moby Grape found themselves reaching for *Pepper*-like possibilities as the members of the band strive to write, arrange, record, and produce songs that ventured into new terrain.

Were the executives at Columbia rushing the band? Were they putting too much pressure on the Grape to produce a hit? Or was David Rubinson too enamored with the sort of production that worked so well on *Pepper*? Was he too keen to add different effects to songs—like strings, horns, or technological modifications? Perhaps the members of Moby Grape themselves were too keen to abandon the approach that worked so well on their first album? Was the band too easily swayed by Columbia and Rubinson?

It wasn't any one of these things. Perhaps it was all of them.

Ultimately, none of these things made *Wow* a *bad* album—because it isn't. It's a misunderstood album, and perhaps not on the same level as *Moby Grape*, but then few albums are.* And while some *moments* on *Wow* could be described as ill-conceived, the album itself isn't ill-conceived at all—and, over the years, retrospective reviews have often pointed this out.

•

Perhaps tellingly, in the case of two of the songs from *Wow*, 'The Place And The Time' and 'Bitter Wind,' earlier, alternate takes (since included on reissues and compilation albums) are now commonly regarded as superior to the versions on the original release.

Don calls the first of these 'a pretty strange song. There are a couple of hooks in there that I think are good. I didn't like when … Rubinson went off on kind of a Beatles strange thing. You know, there's one recording that we did that goes into this alternate song, space. Maybe he thought it was necessary because the song was kind of unique or strange. But I liked it better without those effects. The original version [recorded in August 1967] is the better version. It's kind of pure. It's not commercial. It's interesting.'

When I ask Don about 'Bitter Wind,' he says:

> The unadjusted version is *way* better. The version on the album—with all those backward vocals and masking—it's

* It isn't a one-star album, either—not by any stretch of the imagination—yet somehow that's how it's rated in *The Rolling Stone Record Guide*. As a reminder, according to the *Guide*, a one-star album is 'Poor: A record where even technical competence is at question or it was remarkably ill-conceived.'

> like trying to cash in on what The Beatles were doing. It had nothing to do with—you know, Rubinson, bless his heart, he was the adult in the room and a very creative guy, and he'd always try to get the best out of you. But that was bullshit. That wasn't a great addition. But I think it was more—that whole album was made … almost under duress. All the charts were all done and the [session players] were all there and all the stuff was already happening, and we really didn't have a whole hell of a lot to say. We didn't say a lot. We probably could've, but as it was, by the time we got there [to Columbia's New York studios], Dave knew most of the songs, and he had people writing charts. Some of that stuff is cool, like 'He.' That's beautiful. 'Can't Be So Bad' was great. But when you add all these effects …

According to Jerry, when the band finished work on 'Bitter Wind,' it 'didn't have all that stuff on it—all that backward violin and stuff. And then when the album came out I said, What the hell? Some of that stuff is pretty strange.' A further complication, he adds, was that a mixing session with the band could become a 'nightmare' for Rubinson, as he tried to manage the various band members' competing agendas. 'They're all saying to David Rubinson, Turn me up, turn the guitar louder,' Jerry laughs, 'and Bob would say, Get that bass up there … get that drum up there. So all David would do is just turn the whole damn thing up to make them all happy!'

'When you look at David's history with us,' Don concludes, 'by and large he was an amazing, amazing producer. And it was great that we had him working with us.'

•

The path from Moby Grape's concise, thirty-one-minute debut to their sprawling seventy-five-minute second album—which includes nearly forty minutes of extended jams and improvisations—is an interesting one. It reminds me of Orson Welles's path from *Citizen Kane* to *The Magnificent Ambersons.** *Moby Grape* is a *Citizen Kane* of sorts. I'm not claiming that it's the greatest album ever made, as some argue *Kane* is the greatest film ever made, but both are stunning debuts. Moreover, they were both stunning debuts that weren't commercial smashes, yet, over time, both have endured. Like *Kane*, *Moby Grape* has weathered endless shifts in criticism and styles—including the epochs of progressive rock, disco, punk, synth pop, grunge, and so on. Just as RKO was enamored with the youthful Welles, Columbia was enamored with Moby Grape when they signed their recording contracts in February '67. Just as RKO had tremendous hope and faith in Welles while he was developing *Kane*, Columbia was gleefully expectant as Moby Grape was developing its own debut with David Rubinson. Just as RKO was disappointed with *Kane*'s box office showing as well as Welles's media hiccups, Columbia was disappointed with Moby Grape's sales as well as their own media missteps. And unfortunately, just as RKO made poor decisions in response to that disappointment, so did Columbia.

---

* From the instant Orson Welles burst into Hollywood in 1939, he was a sparkling young star—a brilliant twenty-four-year-old *enfant terrible*, young, bold, and brilliant. RKO Productions put a lot of faith and trust into this charming rebel, and by 1941, in return, this precocious actor-writer-director-producer had developed the groundbreaking *Citizen Kane*, which garnered critical praise but a mixed reception at box office (partly due to the livid response of media tycoon William Randolph Hearst). Somehow, in just one year, everything went topsy-turvy. By the time postproduction began on Welles's follow-up film, *The Magnificent Ambersons*, the *enfant terrible* was no longer seen as endearing—partly because *Citizen Kane* wasn't the box office smash RKO had expected it to be. Then, in one of the most upsetting disasters in cinematic history, RKO panicked, and its flustered, studio executives made a series of decisions that coalesced into some of the biggest Hollywood blunders ever. While Welles was making a propaganda film in Brazil (to promote pan-Americanism during WWII), RKO decided to modify his cut of *Ambersons*. The studio wanted things happier and less ambiguous, so had new material shot and a large portion of the film recut, drastically changing its tone, rhythm, tempo, message, and ending. Worse, the material excised from Welles's cut of the film—totaling over forty minutes—somehow got lost. Welles's original vision of the film was gone forever. While *The Magnificent Ambersons* is by no means a weak film, it wasn't on the same level as *Citizen Kane*. And with the RKO recut fiasco—now a well-known disaster story—*Ambersons* is now seen more in terms of *what might have been* rather than what is. Had the circumstances been different, *Ambersons* might've been something greater. To read about Welles's challenges in Hollywood, see Welles and Peter Bogdanovich's *This Is Orson Welles*, Robert L. Carringer's *The Magnificent Ambersons*, V.F. Perkins's *The Magnificent Ambersons*, Clinton Heylin's *Despite The System*, and Joseph McBride's *What Ever Happened To Orson Welles?*

Like *Ambersons*, *Wow/Grape Jam* is a sophomore effort that's often seen in terms of *what might have been*. From this perspective, the album is regarded as an uneven work, a misstep, and a disappointment. Over the years, various alternate versions of tracks have been liberated, which in turn has only intensified *Wow/Grape Jam*'s reputation as a *what might have been* album.

Wow/Grape Jam wasn't rock's first double album. In May 1966, Bob Dylan released the seventy-three-minute *Blonde On Blonde*, which was followed in June by The Mothers Of Invention's sixty-one-minute *Freak Out!*. Even so, in 1968, the double album was still a relatively new format in rock music. It wasn't even two years old yet. With *Wow/Grape Jam*, Moby Grape and Columbia Records put a whole new spin on things, since it isn't exactly a double album; rather, it's two single albums released together.

Wow is a twelve-song sequence of material Moby Grape recorded in between August '67 and February '68. The songs have great variety, ranging from hook-driven psychedelic-pop ('Murder In My Heart For The Judge') to horn/orchestra-driven blues ('Can't Be So Bad' and 'Miller's Blues') to baroque pop ('He') to big and small ballads ('Three-Four' and 'Rose Colored Eyes') to music hall ('Just Like Gene Autry (A Foxtrot)') to pop songs rooted in more experimental fare ('The Place And The Time' and 'Bitter Wind') to songs that feature both sound effects and comedy ('Motorcycle Iren' and 'Funky-Tunk'). All three of Skip Spence's compositions are parodies of one sort or another, treading into music hall, motorcycle songs, and country music.

Grape Jam, on the other hand, consists of five extended studio improvisations with guests including Al Kooper (who plays guitar on the seven-minute 'Black Current Jam') and Michael Bloomfield (who guests on keyboards on the fourteen-minute 'Marmalade'), recorded across four studio days in New York in January and February 1968. The latter disc also includes 'The Lake,' a song that pulls from the poetry contest Columbia put on in the late summer and treads into the realms of avant-garde and *musique concrète*. *Grape Jam* was an innovative idea that would later be duplicated by such releases as *Super Session* by Mike Bloomfield, Al Kooper, and Stephen Stills, the *Apple Jam* disc of George Harrison's *All Things Must Pass*, and parts of the Derek & The Dominoes' double album *Layla and Other Assorted Love Songs*. While *Grape Jam* may not be strongest LP of its type, it's unquestionably a trailblazer.*

Fondly recalling 'Motorcycle Irene,' Jerry says, 'That was pure genius! It's poetry, really good poetry.' He sings the first lines of the song:

There she sits a smokin'
Reefer in her mouth
Her hair blowin' northward
As she travels south.

After pausing for a moment, he adds, 'Yeah, I remember doing that one. I think I played a little piano on that. I can't remember if it was me or Pete who played the piano. We would trade back and forth because we could both play a little bit of piano—but not a whole heck of a lot.'

Interestingly, in early October 1968, nine months after Moby Grape recorded 'Just Like Gene Autry (A Foxtrot),' The Beatles began work on 'Honey Pie,' which revisits the same music hall idiom—right down to the crackling sound effects that give the results the feel of an old 78.

When I ask about Skip's old-timey track, Don begins to laugh. 'Arthur Godfrey was down the hall, and Skip went down the hall and got him. And he did that whole introduction. It was just so funny!' Don pauses. For 'Motorcycle Irene,' he adds, 'I remember Skippy being there in the studio, and he was cracking up! And at the end he was making motorcycle noises. It was just with his lips. And it sounded like farts!' Don laughs. 'He thought it was hysterical. And I listen to that demo, and it sounds organic, and cool. Then they go and put the motorcycle with all those crash sounds. That was just so unnecessary, you know. It had it. Then you just go and screw around with it.'

* Interestingly, by February 18—just five days after the band finished recording the album—the *Honolulu Star-Advertiser* had somehow already got the scoop that the album will be 'a twin LP set for Columbia with long jam session tracks with a host of guest performers including guitarist Mike Bloomfield and organist Al Kooper.'

Recalling 'Just Like Gene Autry (A Foxtrot),' Jerry chuckles:

> That was funnier than hell. That one had Lou Waxman and his orchestra. And Lou was a really fun guy. All of those old guys from the old days—all of the guys who just missed vaudeville.' [*Laughs.*] That was great, getting to know 'em. Arthur Godfrey was wonderful. Him and Skippy would go walking down Fifth Avenue, arm-in-arm. Him and Skippy. [*Chuckles.*] Now, Arthur Godfrey thought most of our stuff was like that. He didn't know about 'Can't Be So Bad' and things like that. That's one of my favorites. It had a nice shuffle. Like I was saying, Don Stevenson is a great shuffler. Great drummer, period.

Listening to the full orchestra on 'Can't Be So Bad,' or the horns on 'Miller's Blues,' or the strings on 'He,' I'm reminded that charts were written up for top session players in New York City to come in and guest on the record. Although I prefer the other versions of 'Bitter Wind' and 'The Place And The Time,' I realize that a reasonable chunk of studio time was given to the record's production. With *Wow/Grape Jam*, Columbia was still ready to invest in Moby Grape—and still had faith in the band's potential to create a hit.

'I think that Skip had the right idea for our second album,' Don reflects.

> I thought it was brilliant, but Columbia wouldn't go for it. He thought, every time we recorded an album, we could change our name. He wanted to have green-and-white outfits, so we'd be environmental. So we'd have green over here [on one side of his jacket], and white over here [on the other side of his jacket]. And every time we'd do an album we'd change our name, and next time it would've just been all our favorite rock'n'roll songs. It would've been the best thing in the world for us. We would've gone back to Little Richard and Fats Domino and Jerry Lee Lewis and Chuck Berry—to

> the songs that we loved to play. So that was the whole idea. And I'm sure that Skip was at the forefront of that idea. But it wasn't *all* his idea, and we were enthusiastic about it. The suits [at Columbia] kind of just said, 'No. We want more creativity and more new music.' It probably had to do with publishing money—there wouldn't have been any publishing money to distribute if we did an album of all covers—other than the fact that it would've been insanely popular, and the next time we would've created something we would've created something special! So I think, you know, you look at it and there's kind of path that we could've gone down but we didn't, or we chose not to. That was one of the ones where I think we should've taken the path we didn't take. It would've been a brilliant move. We were all so familiar with those old songs. We could've just got together and knocked them out in two or three days. And we would've done it. You know, there were five of us, so we each taken two songs and then played with each other. We needed a manager to say to Columbia, 'This is what we're doing.'

Summing up the *Wow* album, Jerry sighs:

> That album got doctored up so much. Like 'Bitter Wind.' You know, with all of that monkey business on there. We did one version of that—and that was in New York too—that was acoustic. And it was real, real clean. Then Bob changed his mind. He wanted to do it another way. That sort of thing would happen lots of times. We'd have something that I'd really like, and sometimes the writer—Bob, or even me—would say, 'No. You know, the other version is much better.' If I could relive those days I'd change a few things. I'd be livin' up on the hill with a driver. [*Chuckles.*] Well, I live up on a hill with a driver anyways. The only thing is, the driver's driving a Ford.

•

The folks at Columbia—*and* David Rubinson, *and* Moby Grape themselves—made some poor decisions when developing *Wow/Grape Jam*. Yet as I said before, there's a kind of logic to these decisions. Columbia wanted a hit. Rubinson wanted to try something new and innovative. The band—facing pressure from Columbia and excitement from Rubinson, a trial, and a transition of managers, not to mention an itinerant life of sojourning—got swept away. Whether they wanted to or not, the five members of Moby Grape acquiesced, allowing their songs to be reworked during the production and postproduction phases of the *Wow/Grape Jam* sessions. Skip even *wrote* differently between the band's second and third batch of recording sessions—shifting from the rock-pop of 'Seeing' and 'You Can Do Anything' to the novelties of 'Motorcycle Irene' and 'Funky-Tunk' and 'Just Like Gene Autry (A Foxtrot).'

Discussing the album with Don on a crisp spring day in April 2017, I suggest that *Wow* could've been a much stronger record if the material had been sequenced differently, with the 'non-spacy' versions of songs such as 'Bitter Wind' and 'The Place And The Time'—plus unreleased cuts like 'Looper,' 'Seeing,' and 'You Can Do Anything'—included.

'I don't think *Wow* was received that well,' he says. 'I didn't really read reviews—I wasn't interested in them. I knew when we were shitty and I knew when we were good. I didn't want to feel worse about the bad shows. I'm sure we got some terrible reviews along the way.'

Listening to all thirty-four subsequently released songs from the *Wow/Grape Jam* sessions—recorded in bursts between August 1967 and February '68—in chronological order, I imagine how I might sequence them into one single album of forty or fifty minutes. In my perfect *Wow* mix, part one opens with the infectious, epic pop of 'Murder In My Heart For The Judge,' perhaps the catchiest song the Grape recorded during these sessions. Things then speed up with the driving, wall-of-horns power of 'Can't Be So Bad,' wherein the Grape transform into a kind of psychedelic big band. Slowing down, we move to the meditative 'He,' and when its final notes fade into silence, the pace quickens again with the rollicking

'Sweet Ride (Never Again).' The next two songs continue to draw from the Malibu sessions, moving from Bob's folky, poetic 'Bitter Wind' to the multi-sectioned snapshot of 'The Place And The Time.' For another sharp turn, we shift to a forceful blues workout showcasing Jerry Miller's liquid lead guitar-work, the appropriately titled 'Miller's Blues,' before we close part one with at the haunting, prophetic demo of 'Skip's Song.

Part two is more light-hearted, with a few humorous numbers and more demos. Opening with Skip's old-time 'Just Like Gene Autry (A Foxtrot)' tells us we're on a different path. To remind ourselves that the Grape haven't *completely* left seriousness behind, we switch to Bob's pining ballad, 'Rose Colored Eyes,' its melodic bassline reminiscent of the soft bounciness of McCartney's 'Penny Lane.'* Then we speed things up with the November '67 demo recording of Peter's 'Looper,' before returning to humor on 'Motorcycle Irene,' a unique biker story that could perhaps only have come out of the imagination of Skip Spence. The three songs that follow offer more variety, with the electric reworking of 'Naked, If I Want To,' the Donald Duck country & western of 'Funky-Tunk,' and a reflection on free love, 'What's To Choose.' Then, taking a final unexpected curve, part two closes with Skip's wacky, infectious rough demo of 'You Can Do Anything.'

This two-part, sixteen-song sequence runs to forty-eight minutes. It shows the Grape on top of their game, exploring new terrain while still writing tightly constructed songs. No matter what sorts of complications were unfolding in their lives, they were pushing forward, even if they were now a less unified entity than before. Like the band's debut, it reaches levels of exuberance and alchemy few can match.

Even with this, I know I've made some omissions, including three of Bob's: the power-ballad 'Three-Four,' the soulful demo of 'Loosely Remembered,' and the bluesy 'Never,' which Led Zeppelin would later draw on for 'Since I've Been Loving You.' And while Moby Grape's extended studio jams offer many interesting moments, they're too different to include in my two-part

* Bob would not yet have heard McCartney's song when the Grape track was recorded. Speaking about the song to Steve Roeser in 1999, he recalled, 'I wrote it in New York at the Albert Hotel. It was a song about how we had, you know, started to fall from grace … we were doing real well and then all of a sudden everything kind of got to a bummer.'

mix. Perhaps if a third part were added, it could kick off with the thirteen-minute Milt Jackson number, 'Bags' Groove,' then the seven-minute sway of 'Black Current Jam,' followed by the fourteen-minute bluesy waters of 'Marmalade' and the six-minute rocking tension of 'Boysenberry Jam.' That's a total of forty minutes of blues-jazz, or, alongside the other selections, a three-part, a twenty-track, eighty-eighty-minute canvas. (That still leaves 'The Lake,' which, while certainly an inventive piece of music, is not one I am compelled to revisit.*)

While it may not be a *perfect* album, *Wow/Grape Jam* is, in either configuration, a strong collection of songs that are sometimes powerful, sometimes thoughtful, and sometimes downright silly. Two questions linger: why am I compelled to make different mixes of *Wow/Grape Jam*, and why have I never felt bound to the original version of the album? Perhaps it's because I originally experienced the double album in pieces. In the early 90s, I first encountered most of the songs from *Wow*, along with alternate versions of others, on the *Vintage* collection. For years, that was all I knew of the album. Then, in 1997, I picked up a CD of *Wow* (without *Grape Jam*) in Japan. Ten years after that, Sundazed finally put out a reissue of the entire double album. Because I had waited about fifteen years to listen to the proper album, however, my understanding of it has been a slow process of expansion. Throughout that time, I've been on a journey of continually making and remaking my own *Wow/Grape Jam*, which is why I don't feel bound to the original release. For me, *Wow/Grape Jam* has been an ongoing experience of reinterpretation—and becoming.

* Interestingly, one month after 'The Lake' appeared on record shelves, The Beatles (primarily John Lennon) recorded their own venture into the avant-garde, 'Revolution 9,' at EMI Studios.

CHAPTER NINETEEN

FROM THE ALBERT TO BELLEVIEW

June 15 1968. Exactly one week ago, James Earl Ray was detained at Heathrow Airport in London, before being arrested for the assassination of Martin Luther King Jr. sixty-nine days earlier. The previous weekend, *Rosemary's Baby* premiered in the US, receiving mixed-to-positive reviews—and a touch of controversy. Earlier today, jazz guitarist Wes Montgomery passed away at the age of forty-five in Indianapolis, Indiana, shortly after returning home from a tour, while on the other side of the Atlantic Ocean, John Lennon and Yoko Ono are planting acorn seeds at St. Michael's Cathedral, Coventry, that will quickly be stolen by fans …

June 15 1968 was also the date that Moby Grape reached the commercial zenith of their career. After entering the *Billboard* 200 at #114 on May 4 1968, *Wow/Grape Jam* quickly sprang to #91 in its second week on the chart, then jumped an astonishing 51 spots the following week. On May 25, it rose to #27 and then skipped five more spots up to #22, remaining there for a second week on June 8. The following week, it climbed two more spots to #20—a respectable showing by any standard.

Chart action of this sort would please most record company executives, but the executives at Columbia were still not impressed. Having spent a small fortune marketing Moby Grape's debut album the previous summer, they wanted something more than #20—something in the top ten, perhaps, or even the top five. They *expected* more, too. While Columbia may not have funneled as much money into promoting Moby Grape's sophomore album as they did the first, the label had spent a lot on the recording sessions and print ads, and on the discounted 'bonus LP' strategy of the *Grape Jam* disc.

Partly because of Columbia's levels of expectation, Moby Grape's first two albums are often touted as flops, both in terms of record sales and chart action. Yet this is a myth—one that arose out of the haze of folklore. Folklore, like talent and bad luck, is something Moby Grape had in spades. What's often forgotten is that *Wow/Grape Jam* and *Moby Grape* were both solid sellers, each album spending six months on the *Billboard* 200.

In terms of chart action, then, June 15 1968 was Moby Grape's pinnacle. At this moment, the band and their label still held hope for the album to climb even higher. After all, the coveted top ten was now within their grasp. Yet over the weeks that followed, the dream quickly faded. Worse still, and with painful irony, this commercial high-water mark for Moby Grape arrived just days after Skip Spence was arrested and committed in dire circumstances.

What could've led to this?

•

After finishing off the recording sessions for their second album, Moby Grape played two nights at the Anderson Theater in lower Manhattan, on February 10 and 11, with Procol Harum opening. In a mostly positive recap for the *New York Times*, Robert Shelton reported that the band had 'been in better form, but still engendered considerable interest. A solid phalanx of four electric guitars and drums set up quite a wall of sound, and the Grape's four voices at shriek volume are additional excitement-builders.'

The following week, on February 17, they played at the Tempo Dance City in Brooklyn, before stopping off on their way home to California to play two quick dates at the Cheetah in Chicago on the 23rd and 24th.

Reviewing the band's second album two months later for the *Chicago Tribune*, columnist Robb Baker noted that he had been 'kind of down on' the Grape ever since seeing the first of these shows. 'Admittedly, they had just gotten off a plane that night and it was late and one of them was sick and unable to perform—but they were still lifeless, rude to the audience (though that's understandable at times at Cheetah), and not nearly so good as their album which was being played on the stereo in the downstairs entranceway.'

As *Wow/Grape Jam* was being mixed, marketing executives at Columbia began to map out a plan to promote the album. Unsurprisingly, no one was talking about putting out five singles to coincide with the album's release this time, but the label executives had other ideas. The *Wow* disc offered a whole new sound, with production that differed greatly from the Grape's debut, which could be pointed out in the print ads. And then there was the bonus disc. While *Grape Jam* wouldn't exactly be *free*, the double album would be sold at a discounted price—a common practice for two-LP releases.

March 1968 was a time of anticipation for Moby Grape. But things were about to get complicated, with the band's former manager, Matthew Katz, about to return to—or, more accurately, reinsert himself into—the Moby Grape narrative. It was a strange time.

As mixing and marketing plans continued to move forward, Moby Grape returned home to the Bay Area for a long-awaited rest. Then, on March 15, the Ides of March, they played Legion Hall in Merced, California. Mysteriously, and simultaneously, Moby Grape were also playing a show up in Seattle, where they had been booked to play two nights, March 15 and 16, at the San Francisco Sound, a new ballroom a newly opened ballroom in a building formerly known as the Encore. Sharing the bill for these shows were two small bands from the Northwest, West Coast Natural Gas and Indian Pudding & Pipe.

While the band had played two shows in one night before, those rarities always occurred when the venues were geographically close together. Short of the availability of transporter technology, playing in Merced and Seattle on the same night was an impossibility. How could Moby Grape be in two places at once? Thus begins the Mystery of the Second Grape.

The following Friday, March 22, Moby Grape (or, rather, one of the Moby Grapes) played a rather unique venue at a private show for an international group of downhill skiers competing in a tournament in Sun Valley. Writing from Bear Valley, California, for the *Reno Gazette-Journal*, was columnist Dick Dorworth, who noted, 'San Francisco did its bit for skiing this week [when] a Pacific Heights lady from the upper spheres of finance and society gave a party where Moby Grape provided the sound, Cutty Sark added lubricant, and a wide range of cultures, attitudes and backgrounds merged to provide character. Those uninitiated to hard rock found the thirty-by-sixty-foot dancing room a bit too small for Moby Grape's amplifications. But the Germans solved the problem, stole the show, and gusted the mind by dancing like crazy with white cotton sticking from their ears.'*

Back in San Francisco, the band played strong shows at the Fillmore on March 21 and Winterland on March 22–23, with Traffic, Spirit, and the Lemon Pipers appearing alongside them. Three numbers from the Grape's March 22 show—'Rounder,' 'Miller's Blues,' and 'Changes'—would eventually be released on the band's *Vintage* compilation in 1993. They offer a sparkling example of the band's live act in early '68—they were on fire—while with 'Rounder,' we get to hear a song that never made it onto an album, with Skip delivering his lyric with verve.

On March 29 and 30, Moby Grape played the Cheetah Club, a small discotheque on the Santa Monica Pier in Los Angeles, with Spirit and Genesis supporting. But which Moby Grape was it? The Grape that played in Merced, or the one that played up in Seattle on the Ides of March? The question would be answered in a couple of days.

Fittingly, the first newspaper account of a *fake Moby Grape* band appeared on April Fool's Day 1968. Somehow, in shadowy circumstances, a *second Moby Grape* seemed to have solidified in mists of the rock-pop landscape. A partial explanation of this perplexing mystery would slowly emerge over the next few weeks, yet as far as media coverage is concerned, the story began

---

* Playing private parties was not uncommon among rock/pop bands in the 60s. These sorts of small shows offered a way of earning some much-needed extra money in between the larger gigs.

here, with Pete Johnson's report on this strange turn of events in the April 1 edition of the *Los Angeles Times*.

> If you saw Moby Grape at the Cheetah this weekend, you did not see the Moby Grape. The San Francisco group, due to release a double album in the next few weeks, fragmented just before the Cheetah booked them. Their ex-manager offered the club a group he called the Moby Grape, and his offer was accepted. Meanwhile, the real Moby Grape got back together. Three members of the real Grape stopped in Friday to hiss the artificial Grape.

Who started the rumor that the Grape was splitting up? The real Grape were actively recording into the middle of February, and played gigs throughout January, February, and March. Their sophomore album was due out in April. Yet somehow, amid all of this activity, a story that Moby Grape were breaking up sprung up in the media.

Whatever the source of this rumor might have been, what we do know is that a second Moby Grape performed at the Cheetah in March '68—just as the original band were on the verge of releasing their second album.

•

Moby Grape—the real Moby Grape—returned to the Winterland on Wednesday, April 3, sharing the bill with The Grateful Dead, Electric Flag, It's A Beautiful Day, Mother Earth, and The Youngbloods at a 'Strike Benefit' for the San Francisco FM radio station KMPX.* Three days later, the Grape headed to Fresno for a show at the Selland Arena, and a week

* Like the poster art, the light shows, the Diggers, the jams, and everything else, KMPX—an underground radio station of sorts—was in the oxygen of counterculture San Francisco. DJ Tom Donahue was the most famous figure associated with the station, having hosted, since April '67, a show that helped to spearhead the station's transition into playing more full albums, more local talent, and fewer *hits*. Unsurprisingly, this switch led to heavy rotation of Bay Area acts such as Jefferson Airplane, The Grateful Dead, and Moby Grape, along with names like The Beatles and the up-and-coming Jimi Hendrix Experience. A whole new stable of DJs would be corralled, and would at one point include the future Dr. Johnny Fever, Howard Hesseman.

after that, they played two nights at the Carousel Ballroom in San Francisco, sharing the bill with It's A Beautiful Day and Sweet Rush on April 12–13.* Yet the Mystery of the Second Grape persists.

By now, it had become clear that the *original* Moby Grape—the Columbia-Recording-artist Moby Grape, the we-just-finished-recording-a-double-album Moby Grape—weren't the only Moby Grape around. The other Grape—the second Grape, the fake Grape—were still touring and popping up in the press. On Saturday, April 13, the mystery of the bogus Grape reappeared in the media, with Dave Donnelly of the *Honolulu-Star-Bulletin* adding intrigue to the unfolding narrative:

> The latest issue of what is probably the finest pop music magazine in the world, *Rolling Stone* (out of San Francisco) tells of the jam created by two 'Grapes,' or Moby Grapes to be more specific. One Grape is the real San Francisco group which has recently released a two-record set, one containing more or less

---

In a report for *Crawdaddy* in June 1967, Paul Williams described how KMPX 'totally ignores the top 20 ... and just plays what it feels like playing. KMPX is run something like a college radio station; the people in charge know much more about rock and roll than they do about radio programming, how to talk jock, how to sell an audience, or any of that other crap. They make mistakes—records go on the turntable at the wrong speed, careless comments go out over the air—and everyone loves them. There are no mistakes, because they can do no wrong. They're human, and they love the music—and that's what's been missing in radio till now.'

When tensions arose between Donahue and station owner Leon Crosby in early '68, the owner implemented a dress code along with other new directives, prompting Donahue to resign. Shortly afterward, on March 18, the rest of the staff walked out. Unfortunately, the *Strike Benefit* failed to break the impasse, and, when the strike ended on May 3, there would be no resolution between Leon and his former employees, many of whom would be hired by Metromedia and go on to work at KSAN in San Francisco and KMET in Los Angeles. Tom Donahue went on to manage acts such as Blue Cheer guitarist, Leigh Stephens and work as a DJ in LA before tragically succumbing to a heart attack in 1975. In 1996, he was inducted into the Rock and Roll Hall of Fame as a non-performer. For an articulate snapshot of the events surrounding the strike, see Sarah Hill's *San Francisco & The Long 60s*.

* Located at Market and Van Ness, the Carousel was formerly the El Patio Ballroom. To challenge Bill Graham and Chet Helm's lock on the major performance spaces in the Bay Area, The Grateful Dead and some other San Francisco bands got the Carousel up and running. By the summertime, though, Graham had taken over the lease and renamed it the Fillmore West, which would become a landmark in the city until its closure in June 1971. For more, I again encourage you to peruse Sarah Hill's thoughtful book *San Francisco & The Long 60s*.

> commercial appeal numbers, and the other lengthy jam sessions. We'll deal with the album more fully in another column. But now another group clandestinely calling themselves 'Moby Grape' has surfaced in Seattle. One Moby Grape we'll believe, but two? Perhaps lawsuits are the only way to settle the pilfering of an established name.

The following day, Sunday, April 14, the first advertisements for *Wow/Grape Jam* appeared in the *Los Angeles Times*. Then, a week later, the story of the fake Grape resurfaced in a report for the *Arizona Republic* by Jon Sargent, who was able to add important details to the narrative.

> Many people walked away from last weekend's Moby Grape concert with not only a song in their hearts, but an ache in their pocketbooks. The pain seemed to stem from the rather disgruntling rumor that they were not only led like sheep to a slaughter at the state fairground exhibition hall, but that someone was pulling the wool over their eyes. The Moby Grape onstage definitely weren't the same group of recording fame. But never fear for the answer's now here. According to reliable sources, the confusion tends to revolve around the Grape's manager Matthew Witt [sic] from San Francisco. He owns the name of the group lock, stock, and barrel and when the original fivesome had their parting of ways several months back he formed another group and christened them Moby Grape.

Though he got the name of the band's ex-manager wrong, Sargent was able to shed new light on the mystery, noting both Matthew Katz's involvement in the tale and also the confusion over who *owned* the name 'Moby Grape.' Conflicts and entanglements with Katz, as well as wrangling over the right to use the Moby Grape name, are two issues that would linger in the lives of Jerry Miller, Don Stevenson, Peter Lewis, Bob Mosley, and Skip Spencer for decades, and would only be resolved in 2007—a full four decades after

Moby Grape's original parting of the ways with Katz, and eight years after Skip's death, by which time the original members of Moby Grape would have intermittently appeared under the cover of a variety of other names, including The Melvilles.

•

Meanwhile, back in 1968 … on April 22, Bob Mosley returned to the studio to record a solo acoustic demo of his new song, 'It's A Beautiful Day.' Two days later, on April 24, Moby Grape reconvened to rework Skip's track 'Seeing,' which was first demoed five-and-a-half months earlier, when the *Wow* sessions were reactivated in New York. With Bob's newly added vocals, the song promised to become one of the highlights of the band's next album. Sadly, by then, Skip would have left the band in traumatic circumstances.

On April 26, the band played a show in Santa Rosa with The Nitty Gritty Dirt Band and Morning Glory.* Moby Grape's set received poor notices, with an unnamed reporter's sketch for the April 28 edition of the *Press Democrat* detailing a dramatic scene of missing and faulty equipment, flaring tempers, and a good performance gone awry:

> The Moby Grape was storming Friday night and it was the bad scene that ended in an angry clatter of flying drums and microphones at center stage. The famed Bay Area rock group was scheduled to play two forty-five-minute sets in a concert at the Sonoma County Fairgrounds, but only played for forty-five minutes before stomping violently off the platform and out of Santa Rosa. For the Grape, it was a story of a wayward drummer and wayward equipment and finally a poorly functioning microphone system that finally quit operating altogether. It was eleven o'clock before drummer Don Stevenson showed up for the performance, and the equipment never did arrive. Finally,

* Years later, Bob Mosley recorded three demos with Chris Darrow of The Nitty Gritty Dirt Band. The pair shopped them around to various record labels before their eventual release as a vinyl EP, *Desert Rain*, credited to The Darrow Mosley Band (Shagrat Records, 2010).

> the five young men agreed to use the equipment of two other bands on the bill: The Nitty Gritty Dirt Band's mics and the drums and amplifiers of the Morning Glory. The mics never did work right, and the audience of 1,400 wasn't particularly receptive to the band's Fillmore Auditorium sound. But the Grape was good, and they looked like they'd play at least an hour before the midnight close of the concert. Then a mic quit during a Bob Mosley solo. He shoved it angrily off the stage and onto the concrete floor below before jumping to the next mic to complete the last lines of the song. The lyrics of frustration were revised a little bit—'G—damned—,' he yelled, just before cutting the last word off—just in time. Drummer Stevenson stood up and left. The Grape's leader Skip [switches from] guitar to the drums for an abbreviated version of the group's big hit song—'Omaha.' The mics still weren't working right, but the drum work was beautiful—if violent. ... In the last bars, the drums started to come apart as stage hands worked frantically to keep them together. But it was too late. With the last drum roll, Spence started kicking wildly and drums flew in all directions. He grabbed a hand mic and threw it angrily onto the wooden platform. It took one big bounce on the stage, and landed 100 feet into the teenage crowd. And the Grape was gone.

During one of our conversations, Jerry speaks about the volume at Moby Grape shows, recalling situations like this:

> Nobody shuffles like Don on the drums. He's the best there is on that. When things got super-loud, he didn't enjoy that as much. During our day, we weren't quite *that* loud. I mean, it sounded loud—we had plenty of volume—but it wasn't, you know, Rage Against The Machine loud. We didn't have thirty-five mics on the drums [*laughs*] and, we just had a couple of small sets when we used to play together. We were louder than Jerry Lee Lewis,

> and louder than a lot of those—but still nothing like what was coming up.
>
> Don liked it when it was sane, but when it got real loud and some guy started putting up plastic in front of the drummers, it got real loud. They did that so they could make it even louder. Then I got a whole stack of Marshalls, because we saw that at Monterey with Hendrix. Then we did the Earl Warrens Showgrounds in Santa Barbara [on August 19 1967] and, we had exactly the same stacks of Marshalls, and Don got so frustrated, he kicked over his drums it was just so damn loud. It was pretty frustrating for Don. We were still rookies, you know, and we didn't know how to act. We weren't strictly business, you know? We were, as Bill Graham called us, 'adult delinquents.' And he wasn't far off the beam either.

On the final day of April, the band returned to the studio to record a demo of 'Cockatoo Blues,' a song penned by Skip and Jerry. The band would revisit the song in May '69, by which time they were on their last legs. Renamed 'Tongue Tied,' the song appears on the band's final album for Columbia, *Truly Fine Citizen*.

•

By May 1968, *Wow/Grape Jam* was beginning to receive reviews, and they were mostly positive. History tells us that the album was a bomb, critically and commercially, but that isn't how it happened. While Jim Miller gave the band a poor review in the May 25 issue of *Rolling Stone*, we can balance that with a rather different one in the June issue of the respected magazine *Esquire* by Robert Christgau, who offered a much sunnier view. 'The only follow-up record that makes it completely is Moby Grape's *Wow*,' he wrote. 'The group's first record, overpromoted and underproduced, was dismissed as a hype by people who should have been listening. Hopefully this one, which includes a free disc of improvisations called *Grape Jam*, will make up for it. The Grape can jam but on records tries to maintain a tight sound.'

With *Rolling Stone* and *Esquire* canceling one another out, most other reviews tended to fall in the mixed-to-positive spectrum. Writing in the April 24 edition of the *Honolulu Star-Bulletin*, Dave Donnelly concluded that the album 'features some better than average songs, interesting arrangements, but no unified group sound and no particular musical point of view.' The following day, Wayne Harada's review for the same paper called it 'an intriguing assembly of contemporary melodies.' Robb Baker's glowing review for the *Chicago Tribune*, published on April 30, maintained that Moby Grape were 'clearly still among the best of the west coast groups, and their strong suit is versatility.' In May, further positive responses appeared from Dave Wagner in the *Green Bay Press-Gazette*, Bill Yaryan in the Pasadena's *Independent Star-News*, and Holly Spence in the Lincoln Journal Star, while in June, Pete Johnson of the *Los Angeles Times* was more mixed, deciding that the album's strengths were marred by 'some childish hokery' and 'unnecessary sound effects.' Conversely, *Arizona Republic* journalist Scott G. Campbell preferred the *Grape Jam* half of the release to the *Wow* disc. By no means, however, was *Wow/Grape Jam* seen as a flunkey in the eyes of contemporary music critics, the notion that it was a critical flop being yet another Grape myth.

•

With *Wow/Grape Jam* out in stores and ascending the *Billboard* 200, Moby Grape performed at the Fillmore West from Thursday, May 2, to Saturday, May 4, with The Hour Glass (featuring Duane and Gregg Allman) and The United States Of America opening. Simultaneously to their Friday and Saturday shows at the Fillmore, it seems, the band played two nights at the Merchandise Mart at the Old State Fairgrounds in Sacramento. For the Sacramento shows, they shared the bill with Buffalo Springfield, Quicksilver Messenger Service, HP Lovecraft, and the Troggs.*

On the last day of the Grape's Fillmore run, an unknown writer for the

* As I look over the poster for these overlapping shows at the Fillmore and Sacramento, I realize these may be the overlapping shows Jerry Miller once told me about—and that Jerry might have gotten The Turtles mixed up with The Troggs.

Freemont *Argus* seemed to be gazing backward rather than forward, noting in an announcement for the show that Moby Grape 'last appeared at the Fillmore in March amid rumors that the group was on the verge of its demise.' But where did the damaging rumor of the band breaking up—or teetering on the verge of breakup—begin?

Three days after their Saturday show at the Fillmore West, the band began a run of shows in New York. Between Thursday, May 7, and Sunday, May 12, they played six nights at the Generation on West 8th Street (the club that would soon be bought by Jimi Hendrix and his manager, Michael Jeffrey, and transformed over the next two years into Electric Lady Studios). On May 15, Peter went into the studio on his own to demo a new song, 'If You Can't Learn From My Mistakes,' its melancholy lyric and soft, vibrato-filled vocal delivery reflecting his disappointment and bitterness about his troubled marriage.

Two days later, Moby Grape were back in Los Angeles, playing two nights at the Kaleidoscope with The Hour Glass and Mt. Rushmore opening. In a brief but positive review of the shows for the *Los Angeles Times*, Pete Johnson again made mention of the *other* Moby Grape. 'The Moby Grape, the real Moby Grape, as the ads said, since the San Francisco quintet had recently been impersonated at another club, attracted a sizable audience for a weekend appearance at the Kaleidoscope,' he wrote. 'They are fun to watch, fun to listen to and danceable. Some of their songs—"Sitting By The Window," "8:05," and "Omaha"—are among the best products of San Francisco combos. The Moby Grape projects a vigorous sound through four synchronized guitars and a vocal flexibility matched by few groups.'

After that, the band journeyed to Cleveland to play four shows over two nights at the LaCave on May 22–23. According to Larry Bruner, who was the manager at LaCave in 1968 and 1969, the venue had a Day-Glo 'Feed Your Head' mural on one wall and was known as 'Cleveland's House of Folk Music,' often featuring acoustic solo acts such as Buffy Sainte-Marie and Neil Young.

During our correspondence, which took place in January 2017, Larry sent me an expense report for Moby Grape's shows at LaCave, which reads as follows:

Moby Grape at LaCave, **The Tiny Alice Jug Band** opened
paid flat $500 2 nights, 4 shows tickets $3:50 gross gate $1281

Wednesday, May 22 1968	#	$
Advance	171	598.50
Advance	025	87.50
Door refunds	-25	-87.50
Thursday, May 23 1968	**#**	**$**
Advance	72	252.50
Advance	30	105.00
Door	93	325.50
Total Ticket Sales	366	1281.00
Other Moby Grape Expenses		
Balloons, helium		80.00
Airport limo		34.00
Speaker rental		20.00
Signs		7.50
Tiny Alice		100
½ week payroll		248.40
Total / other		489.90
Net		+291.10

According to Larry, the refunds were given out on the first night because one of the band members was unable to make the shows, but he can't recall who was absent. (It might have been Peter Lewis, who flew to California around this time, or Skip Spence, who would part ways with the band shortly afterward.)

Right after the shows in Cleveland, Moby Grape whisked down to Texas, where on Friday, May 24, they played at the Vulcan Gas Company in Austin, followed by two nights at the Catacombs Club in Houston. While in Texas, Jerry and Don wrote 'Big' as a way of expressing their frustration with a grueling tour schedule, a competing fake Grape, and a host of other complications, as Don recalls:

> We liked Texas. We went and listened to a couple of blues bands there. But if you listen to 'Big' you can see that we were just disgusted with our situation. We were disgusted *about* our schedule. Just tired. [*Sings*] 'I get tired of being treated this way / I've been used, abused, I'll be long gone / Don't try to find me / Just look for the stage I'll be on.' You know, there's that line, '*my best friend's a cow*.' Jerry and I were pissed off when we wrote that. We didn't even want to play.

Following their shows in Texas, Moby Grape returned to New York—essentially the band's de facto headquarters since they were sent there in November.

On Sunday, May 26, a mysterious advertisement appeared in the *St. Louis Post-Dispatch*. The artwork resembled another advertisement for an upcoming show at the Fillmore East, yet this one was not presented by Bill Graham, and it wasn't in New York, either. This advertisement indicated that Moby Grape would be playing on June 7 and 8 at the National Guard Armory at 3676 Market alongside West Coast Natural Gas and Black Swan. The shows was to be 'A Velvet Plastic Production.' Interestingly, back in March, West Coast Natural Gas had appeared with the fake Grape. Could this be the same fake Grape as before?

On May 28, a part of Moby Grape—the *real* Moby Grape, that is—went into the studio to record an instrumental track for 'Soul Stew,' a new composition by Bob Mosley. By now, it had become common practice for the band to enter the studio in contingents, rather than working as a quintet. Around this time, worried about his marriage, Peter flew back to California. With Peter gone, the rest of the band prepared for four shows over two nights at the newly inaugurated Fillmore East. Of this difficult time, Lewis later told Jud Cost, 'Finally I just quit and went back to California. I got a phone call after a couple of days. They'd played a Fillmore East gig without me, and Skippy took off with some black witch afterward who fed him full of acid.'

•

On Friday, May 31 1968—the day before Simon & Garfunkel's 'Mrs. Robinson,' as featured in *The Graduate*, hit #1 on *Billboard*—Moby Grape made their debut at the Fillmore East, playing the first of four shows across two nights. Their debut at the Fillmore East, that is, but not their first appearance at the venue itself, which had been an East Village landmark for decades, most recently as the Village Theater, where Moby Grape last performed in November 1967, in the midst of recording their second album. Now, however, November 1967 seemed a long way away.

With Peter away, Jerry, Don, Bob, and Skip considered postponing their Fillmore East debut, but decided it was far too prominent a venue to cancel—and, besides, dynamic promoter Bill Graham famously would not tolerate late performances or cancelations. So the band soldiered on, ready to appear as a quartet. Now more than ever, they felt uncertain about their future, yet with two memorable nights and four killer shows in prospect, perhaps they might still find their footing.

Sharing the bill with the Grape on these two nights were the comic and lewd Fugs and The Gary Burton Quartet, led by the Indiana-born jazz vibraphonist. The Fugs recorded their performances, releasing them a year later as *Golden Filth: Live At The Fillmore East*. As with every show during this period, the concert featured liquid lighting by the Joshua Light Show, who had been the resident artists at the Fillmore since it opened in March. Vibrantly describing their work in a piece for the *New York Times*, Barbara Bell noted, 'The Fillmore's screen has blazed with Mondrian-esque checkerboards, strawberry fields, orchards of lime, antique jewels, galaxies of light over a pure black void and, often abstract, erotic, totally absorbing shapes and colors for the joy of it—each a vision of an instant, wrapped in and around great weaves of sound and, with the sound, in constant motion. From impressionistic raindrops blowing across a windshield, the Light Show shifts, in the blink of an eye, to the cosmic intensity of solar flares.'

Even the light show could not revitalize Moby Grape, however. Though the they continued to push forward, their audience (and their critics) were not aware of their troubles. Richard Kostelanetz included a scathing review of the Grape's June 1 show in his 1995 book *The Fillmore East*, describing how the band 'came on with not two or three but *four* guitars, only one of which is manned by a particularly good fingerman; such superfluous instrumentation perhaps accounts for why their arrangements tend to be chaotic. Even worse, their songs are not only all but unintelligible, but they are invariably sung in monotone. Poor for listening, they aren't much good for dancing either. Perhaps because they weren't too enthusiastic about doing encores before an audience that expects them to, the Moby Grape struck me as, can I resist, mopy.'

While Moby Grape may not have put on a great—or perhaps even good—show at the Fillmore East on Saturday, June 1 1968, it's perplexing that Kostelanetz should criticize the band for what had often been regarded among their strengths: interwoven guitar crosstalk, intricate arrangements, and complex harmonies. Yet what's more perplexing, and concerning, is his assertion that the group performed as a five-piece. By the time of their Fillmore East debut, Moby Grape had been reduced to a quartet. Writing a negative review of a band's performance is fair game, and is a part of a critic's job—but detailing the failings of a quintet when there are only four people standing on the stage is baffling.

•

On Sunday, June 2 1968, an interesting announcement appeared in the *St. Louis Post-Dispatch* beneath the headline 'Announcement From Velvet Plastic Promotions Re Moby Grape':

> We are very sorry to announce that due to circumstances beyond

our control we will be unable to present MOBY GRAPE as we had planned on June 7 and 8. This seems to be a case of mistaken identity. It has come to our attention that there are two MOBY GRAPE bands. The one we are all familiar with headed by Bob Mosley that records on Columbia Records is the MOBY GRAPE we thought we were going to be presenting. We learned that their ex-manager owns the name MOBY GRAPE and, since his separation from the original group, has formed a second group and is presently booking them as MOBY GRAPE. Fortunately, we learned of this before it was too late BUT hope to be able to present at some later time the original MOBY GRAPE. It will be our policy to always present exactly what we advertise. We realize that we could have brought the other band in and many people would not have been the wiser; but we do not wish to be a party to what we feel would be unfair to the original MOBY GRAPE, and to you, our audience. Anyone who has purchased advance tickets for this engagement may bring them by our office anytime between 12 noon and 6pm for a full refund.

•

The following day, Moby Grape—or at least *some* members of the band—returned to Columbia Studio B to record 'Soul Stew,' a new song written by Bob Mosley. The band had demoed an instrumental version of the song just six days earlier, and as Bob would later tell Steve Roeser, 'That's just a title, the title of a tune that I had that was a mishmash of different kinds of soul, and made a stew out of it.' Even so, the bluesy track pounds forward, featuring Jerry's multilayered guitar lines, sometimes duplicating and other times harmonically complimenting one another. According to Matthew Greenwald's review of the track for allmusic.com, it 'weds Jimi Hendrix–inspired funk with a powerful rock base, sort of like a psychedelic Otis Redding. Lyrically, it's a kiss-off to an old girlfriend and has some stream-of-consciousness lines about performing music and the artistic process.'

Surprisingly, 'Soul Stew' will be passed over when the band came to select tracks for their third album in the autumn. It eventually emerged on the well-received forty-eight-track compilation *Vintage*. Although the band was pleased with the new recording, they had bigger concerns. Peter Lewis was in California; *Wow/Grape Jam* was selling well but was not a blockbuster; and there was a second Grape floating around. With Skip Spence now temporarily gone, the remaining members of the band were scheduled to perform at the Café Au Go-Go in Greenwich Village on Thursday, June 6, and at the Limit in Howard Beach on Friday, June 7.

As these shows approached, the band were entering troubled waters. Skip Spence was edging closer to his confrontation at the Albert Hotel. While no one can be certain of Spence's actions between his departure and his eventual breakdown, his condition dramatically changed for the worse in a matter of days. When he returned to his bandmates, he was delusional, paranoid, and violent.

•

'There was a lot of pressure on us, and it showed,' Bob Mosley later told Steve Roeser. 'You know, we had that falling out with Skip Spence, who tried to take over the band and started fighting and causing trouble. And ended up going to some kind of—either go to jail or go to a rehab place or something. You know, and so they took him in for a little while, and then let him go. And he went and did his solo album.'

'I didn't like it when we were staying at the Albert,' Jerry reflects, thinking back on the band's time in New York. 'We should never have been there. That's where Skippy met these people who led him astray. It sure wasn't a nice place. It was full of cockroaches with mattresses on the floor. People said we'd save money. You know, we never should have listened to shit like that. 'Cos we didn't save any money. We never got any goddamned money.'

Of this time, and the period that followed, Jerry tells me, 'It came apart pretty fast. And then we went on. We did some stuff with just me and Pete and Don and Bob. That was OK, but we had a lot of cancellations because they wanted the full band—the original five people, and we just didn't have it. That was the start of the slide. It was a big slide, because we just had something magic with the five of us. When it was the four of us it wasn't the same. Although it was still fun, and we were still making up tunes. You know, we did what we could—but, when Skippy slipped out, that was about it.'

•

While the original Moby Grape—the *real* Moby Grape—were in the middle of a crisis, the *fake* Moby Grape were still flagrantly active. Following the assassination of presidential hopeful Robert Kennedy, Matthew Katz redubbed his act the *New Moby Grape* and booked them to perform at a memorial concert honoring the fallen politician (arranged as a coproduction between Velvet Plastic Productions and Katz, the producer of the San Francisco Sound). As reported in the Sunday, June 8, issue of the *St. Louis Post-Dispatch*, 'A memorial jazz concert from noon to 3pm in Forest Park near Union and Lindell boulevards will feature speakers and four pop music groups—The New Moby Grape, West Coast Natural Gas, Black Swan, and The Fifth Pipedream.'

Rereading the three pieces from the *St. Louis Post-Dispatch* dated May 26, June 2, and June 8, I'm mystified. First a *fake Grape* materializes in the Missouri city, advertising two shows. Then an ashamed promotion company cancels the shows, publishing an apology in the newspaper. Then, after Robert Kennedy is assassinated, the *fake Grape* schedules a memorial concert on the day of one of their previously canceled shows. It's baffling. Yet as bizarre as the St. Louis fiasco was, what was brewing in New York was even more disconcerting.

•

In early June 1968, a young man was escorted by police officers to Manhattan's House of Detention. Located in Lower Manhattan, the building, commonly known as the Tombs, was becoming more and more overcrowded. It would see rioting in 1970; and, amid litigation and the lens of the media, it would close for good in 1974.

The young man who was being escorted by the officers had just had a violent episode. After being booked in, he was transferred from the Tombs to the psychiatric ward of Belleview Hospital, where he would stay for the next five months. The young man was Skip Spence, Moby Grape's lively, offbeat guitarist.

•

June 2017. Sitting down in the same midtown café where I first met Don Stevenson back in January, I open our latest conversation by recapping the aftermath of *Wow/Grape Jam*'s release, with the band going on a whirlwind tour that saw them zigzagging from California to New York to California to Cleveland to Texas and back to New York, like some sort of scavenger hunt spanning the entire continent.

'I believe that Michael Gruber was the genius behind that schedule,' Don says. 'That tour he put together for May '68 was the worst schedule possible.' Don takes another look at the May itinerary, then adds:

> This is the time that Skip probably tried to kill me.
>
> Jerry and I were up in the studio, recording 'Big.' It was just the two us with a guitar. When we got done recording, we headed back to the Albert Hotel, and we noticed that there was a huge, gaping hole in the door. So we said, 'What the hell's that?' And somebody said, 'Well, Skip was looking for you.' And I go, 'Oh, shit.'
>
> Skip had been acting kind of strange. He had this woman he was staying with, and there was this old man living with them. He wasn't related to her but it was strange. She was into some sort of metaphysical stuff. She was like an oracle, and she was into acid and some crazy shit. Skip had been taking quite a bit of LSD at that time, and she kind of had him on a short string.
>
> After they knocked down the door at the Albert, they headed up to the studio to see if I was there—to see if Jerry

> and I were there. And when they got to the studio, she had him standing on his head and doing all these strange things. She was saying stuff like, 'Skip, show him what we've got here. Go ahead, show 'em, stand on your head.' So he was doing her bidding, in a way.
>
> At that point, David [Rubinson] was basically the adult in the room in the whole situation, and he somehow managed to talk them down and get the axe and try to get Skip some help. I think they called for help, and I think it was then that NYPD picked him up. I can't verify exactly what happened there because I wasn't there. But that's how I remember it.

After this, of course, Skip was sent to the Tombs in New York.

Looking back on the incident nearly five decades later, Don remains unclear on what Skip had in mind.

> To think that … I don't know if he wanted to kill Jerry, but he did want to introduce me to Mr. Axe. It was scary. David said to me, 'Maybe you want to go check into another hotel.' So I checked into another hotel, I can't remember where exactly. At that point, I called this woman—I called my Indian Mama. She was the grandmother of Paula, who was my wife at the time. I spent some time with her and her husband. They had a ranch in the middle of California, and I spent some time there. She was cool. She and her husband were independent. They did their own farming, had their own chickens. She was always very cool. When I took off with Moby Grape for the first time, she made me … it's not a charm, it's a necklace for protection. It *was* protection. It was almost like a rosary with many beads. It formed a circle and then came down together in a line with a little cross at the end of it. It was kind of an amulet.
>
> At various times, something weird would happen. You know, I'd do some shitty things, I'd do something I wasn't too proud

of, and it would break. And I'd have to get out little pliers and put it back together again. It continued to break until it was almost like a choker. [*Laughs.*]

So I called my Indian Mama, and I said, 'I'm in New York, and I thought I'd call you because it seems like one of the guys in my band, he kind of chopped a hole through my door—I was supposed to be there. I think he was trying to ...'

She said, 'Get on your knees.'

I said, 'What?'

She said, 'Get on your knees.'

So I got on my knees, and she said, 'I'm going to tell you what to say, and you say it.'

I said, 'Sure,' and she said, 'Plead the blood of Jesus Christ. Plead the blood of Jesus Christ, for yourself, and for Jerry, and plead it over that situation, and plead it over Skippy. Skippy is—he did what he thought he had to do, have no resentment, have no hate, have no fear, have love for Skippy, have love for yourself, have love for the situation. And the blood of Jesus Christ will keep you safe from harm and free.'

That freaked me out, almost more than seeing the hole in the door. But it was true. The truth of it was, I never did hate Skippy, or fear him, or consider it personal. I just thought he went off the rails—and he saw things that were so real to him, he just couldn't compromise with whatever reality he saw. It was like he went into another dimension. So, under those circumstances ... anytime I look at it, he was following the path that he thought was right. And I was protected by whatever—by angels.

Even before the axe incident, Don adds, the spring tour had taken a toll. Skip had been behaving in a way that was 'very strange' to his bandmates, including at the band's shows at the Fillmore East on May 31 and June 1. 'The Fillmore gig was kind of like a precursor,' he notes. 'It was a crazy gig, right at the time when it was all getting kind of crazy.'

By now, Skip had become involved with the aforementioned woman, named Joanna, who would be described by others as a 'white witch':

> I went down to the Village and visited Skip, who was staying with Joanna at the time. She had a kind of influence on him. They were both—kind of like they were in somewhat altered states, you know. Having been in an altered state myself for a lot of the time back then, I hardly noticed, but when I got there it *was* kind of strange. It was down in a basement. It was almost like a one-room flat, a cold-water flat.
>
> There was a couch there and a guy laying on the couch. A really old guy. I think he was a street person, and they were kind of feeding him and helping him along, you know, giving him the proper amount of medication. It probably wasn't prescribed medication. [*Laughs.*] He was like their oracle, and they would ask him questions, I guess you'd call them cosmic questions. Having cosmic conversations. I asked Skip, 'What are you doing, man? This is really fucked up, you know. What's going on?' And he goes, 'No. This is great. This is like—Joanna is, you know, is like brilliant, and I'm crazy about her, and we're having this great time together. Paul is like our oracle over here, and we're like—we're just doing fine.'
>
> That was kind of ... well, I had a little cup of tea, we sat and talked, and a few days later he came looking for me with a fire axe. I think that maybe my fate was sealed. Maybe the old guy said, 'Watch out for that guy.'

Don's thoughts return to what his 'Indian Mama' had said to him after the axe incident. 'She also asked me pray for Skip,' he recalls. 'That was comforting in a way, because it's true, you know? He was in a bad situation. Even Joanna and the old man—the three of them were really in a bad situation. It's just by the grace of God that something worse didn't happen, and all our lives—Jerry's, too—weren't altered forever—more than what happened.' The whole situation, Don adds, was indicative of the mood of the time. 'Charles Manson had his following right around that same time … and that horrible spirit of murder was in the air. It was like this war of good and evil.'

•

Roadie Tim Dellara describes the circumstances of Skip's breakdown:

> It was just after Bobby Kennedy got killed. I think [Don and Jerry] were doing vocals at the time. I got a knock at my door. I think this was at the Albert [Hotel]. They had these doors that you could open from the inside and open from the outside—a kind of a double door. You could put your clothes in the door and then close your door, so people could come along, open the outside door, take your clothes, and get them cleaned.
>
> I got a knock at my door. By that point, I hadn't seen Skippy since the [Bob] Cato incident. Skippy was standing there, and he had this little Boy Scout axe and leather pants and stuff, and no shirt. He said, 'Where's Don and Jerry?' I said, 'Well, they're down in their room.' I knew that they were still at the studio. And he said, 'OK.' He was sweating and acting strange. When he left, I called the studio and said, 'Let me talk to Don and Jerry.' And they said, 'Oh, they already left.' I thought, *oh fuck*. So I ran down two floors, and I went to their room, and he had chopped through the door—through that outside door, *and* the inside door. It was just a thin plate of tin, really. I can remember to this day that I thought that I was going to walk into a bloodbath. And I walked in, and of course, there was no bloodbath, because they went someplace else.
>
> Then I called … I don't know if I called Gruber or Rubinson, and then we all met—Rubinson, Gruber, and the band and I—and they convinced the band that the best thing to do was to file a complaint so that he'd get picked up, and not get shot.

> That was their take on the thing. And, you know, the guys in the band were not all into that. They didn't really want to go that way. They didn't want to treat Skippy that way. But none of them wanted him to get hurt either. So then Skippy was picked up, and he was put in the Tombs, and then Belleview for six months, or however long. That was a terrible thing to happen to him—and for the band. And I think it broke him. Skippy was a great guy. He was the sparkplug.

With the others members of the Grape still wondering when Skip will be released, a call was made to Peter to break the news of Skip's breakdown and committal. In the midst of this, Jerry, Don, Bob, and Peter decided to take some time off and consider their future. For Moby Grape, this respite had been a long time coming.

CHAPTER TWENTY

SKETCHES OF SKIP

Whenever people speak to me about Skip—those who knew him before his time in Belleview—they often describe him as a lively, impish, energetic, beautiful person. When they talk about Skip's antics, they speak with affection, humor, and love. Sometimes, they speak with a sense of sadness and loss. For everything Skip realized, which is impressive in itself, there's more he could have achieved—and not just artistically. Reflecting on the time Skip seemed to lose his sense of reality, I feel a sense of sadness. Perhaps it's because of what I've heard from people who were close to him.

I've been listening to Skip Spence's music for over half my life. Yet I never knew him. From what I've read, and what I've been told, it's as though a bright light got dimmed—not extinguished, not put out, but dimmed—when Skip spent his time in Belleview. He was never the same afterward. He still had his brilliance, his playfulness, his unique way of looking at the world, his genius (as Jerry likes to say). We can see this in the songs he recorded over a smattering of days in early December 1968. Yet the light that emanated from Skip's smile, and his cheer, and his energy, never fully returned. After Belleview, Skip still wrote introspective, witty, haunting, funny songs. He still produced inspiring music. But ultimately, the man who left Belleview in November 1968 was a different man than the one who entered the hospital in June. Whenever I think about this, although I never knew Skip, I understand why so many of his friends speak about him with a mixture of excitement and wistfulness.

What was it like to be in the band, on their journey? What was it like to be at the center of the marketing firecracker that Columbia set ablaze in June 1967? What was it like to wait seven months for a trial, with updates appearing in newspapers? What was it like to jump from one home base to another in a seemingly never-ending time of sojourning? What was it like to be short of money while playing sellout ballrooms and with albums reading #24 and #20 on the *Billboard* 200? What was it like to see a dream appear on the horizon and then slowly disappear as the weeks and months pass by? What was it like to see what happened to Skip? The answers to these questions can only be understood by the five members of Moby Grape, their families, and those who were close to the band.

Speaking about Moby Grape with Ted Burke in 1976, Bob Mosley described Skip as 'the main focus point of the group. He was exceptionally talented in the songs he wrote, and the way he played his guitar, he was real flashy to watch. The Grape went on the road for two years without him. The whole feeling the band originally had was dead, and eventually everyone went their own way.'

Recalling Spence's treatment at Bellevue, Peter Lewis told Jud Cost, 'He thought he was the antichrist. He tried to chop down the hotel room door with a fire axe to kill Don to save him from himself. He went up to the fifty-second floor of the CBS building, where they had to wrestle him to the ground. And Rubinson pressed charges against him. They took him to the Tombs, and that's where he wrote *Oar*. When he got out of there, he cut that album in Nashville. And that was the end of his career. They shot him full of Thorazine for six months. They just take you out of the game.'

With Skip gone, the Grape had reached a point of no return. From this moment on, the chain of events, and time itself, seemed to speed up, as though the Grape's endpoint, which once existed as a blurred possibility, had solidified into a fixed point in time, stretching from distant future into the present, reaching ever closer and closer …

CHAPTER TWENTY-ONE

THE END IS BECOMING A FIXED POINT

On June 25 1968, Moby Grape were scheduled to play the Commodore in Lowell, Massachusetts. It's unclear if the performance—which would have been the band's first in front of an audience for nearly a month—went ahead, but either way, according to press announcements, the band due to perform was not simply Moby Grape but 'Moby Grape Columbia Album Recording Sensations,' the wordy billing perhaps a strategy to indicate that this wasn't the fake Grape.

Four days later, on a warm day in New York City, Moby Grape performed at the Schaefer Music Festival, an annual event held between 1967 and 1976 at the 5,000-seat Wollman Rink in the southeast corner of Central Park and sponsored by the F. & M. Schaefer Brewing Company. With guitarist and vocalist Peter Lewis having returned from California, the festival set represented an opportunity for the struggling band to mount a comeback—or, at the very least, a return.

On this, the third day of the '68 festival, Moby Grape shared the bill with Chicago blues icon Muddy Waters. For the young band, once the darlings of the rock media and executives at Columbia Records, however, it was an uneven concert. Reviewing the group's up-and-down performance in the *Fond Du Lac Commonwealth Reporter*, Richard Robertson described how they 'sauntered onto the stage at the Central Park Music Festival last week without their rhythm guitarist, Skip Spence. Skip is reported to be resting and unable to play with the group, although no official statement has been made. The rest of the group performed a set that was a combination of polish and complete sloppiness.' Little did the audience (or reviewer) realize, Moby Grape were by now desperately struggling to survive, while Skip would not return to the band until their fleeting '71 reunion.

As the summer gave way to autumn, Moby Grape toured America and Canada, trying—with some hiccups along the way—to establish a new identity as a quartet, and to figure out how or even *if* they could continue. After performing at the Sanctuary in Lake Tahoe in July 1, they played two nights at the Fillmore West with Jeff Beck and Mint Tattoo (July 23–24) before heading north for two nights at the Eagle Auditorium in Seattle (August 2–3). Advertisements for the latter shows identified the band as 'The Original Moby Grape,' again to differentiate them from the fake Grape.

On August 9, the band made their way to Canada for two nights at the Cave, a dinner club-turned-performance space in Vancouver. Casting his mind back to this show, Don recalls, 'It was a small dinner club, and it was so crowded. There were so many people there. It was so confined on the stage. There was an added ceiling over the bandstand, like a little bit of a fake ceiling, and while we were playing I noticed that I was getting wet. I mean, I sweat like a dog anyway, but I looked up and all that was coming from the sweat from everybody in the room. It was really gross!'

In the middle of August, the band performed in Toronto at Time Being, a special youth-oriented event at the 1968 Canadian National Exhibition. There, in a preshow interview with *Globe & Mail* journalist Ritchie Yorke, conducted during a drive from the airport to the venue, Peter Lewis expressed his disappointment with the band's second album. 'Our current album, *Wow*, was thoughtless. It was like putting together a jigsaw puzzle. We never had time to get it together, and the result was a thoughtless album. Man, there's just no way that I'd ever play the record.' Disagreeing with Peter's assessment, Bob Mosley retorted, 'It's a masterpiece.' Then, after noting that they were 'going nuts with the paranoia on the West Coast,' Peter explained to Yorke that the band were 'playing it by ear' with regard to a third album. 'We'll go back to Los Angeles after this gig and work some more on it. But unless we get our own thing together, there isn't going to be another album. Nobody is going to release anything until we've decided that it represents us properly.'

Unfortunately, the band's performance, which was attended by some 12,000 people, was hindered by technical difficulties with the sound system and a lackluster performance, prompting Yorke to pen a scathing review. Worse still, according to his report, the band members were then 'arrested for possession of narcotics when they returned to the States,' although when I ask Don about this, he says he can't recall ever being busted on the Canada–US border.

The following week, from August 23 to 25, the Grape returned to the Kaleidoscope in Los Angeles, with support acts including another Michael Gruber act, Group Therapy; Genesis, a new band from the UK; and The McCoys, who would go on to become the '&' behind Johnny Winter on a pair of Columbia albums. Penning a mostly negative review of the performance for the *Los Angeles Times*, Pete Johnson noted how the Grape 'has become a quartet with the departure of Skip Spence, who sang, played rhythm guitar, and mugged and danced frenetically during their appearances. Spence left because of ill health. His absence does not seem to have thinned the group's musical ability, but their Saturday night performance was rather dull, except for Jerry Miller's work on lead guitar.'

According to studio logs, on Thursday, August 29, Don and Jerry returned to Columbia to work on 'Big,' a cutting song they wrote about their life on tour back in May. Thinking back to that time, Jerry tells me that it was written primarily about 'a place called the Cellar, in Houston. It was … well, we'd see some strange shit. Pistols are going off, people just wild crazy,' he laughs.

The following weekend, on September 6–7, the Grape played the Bank in Torrance, California, with Fair Befall supporting. During this quiet period for the band, a fleeting, cryptic note appeared in Ralph Gleason's

'Rhythm Section' column in the *Honolulu Star-Advertiser*: 'Moby Grape's star figure Skip Spence has left the group and there's now a possibility that it's all over for them.' While his prediction was somewhat rash, the band's days *were* numbered.

•

After a period of inactivity, the quartet once again made the trek to the East Coast for a month-long tour. During their time in Boston, while playing the Psychedelic Supermarket, Don and Jerry found themselves wandering into a sort of metaphysical, new age bookshop. Six months later, they would sketch a picture of the owner, a sort of oracle and car mechanic known as the Great Kamoo, in their lyric for the song 'Truly Fine Citizen,' as Don recalls:

> I remember that Jerry and I went down into the old town of Boston, while we were playing there. It was in the gaslight district. That's where we met Kamoo. He had a place that was like a Chinese herbal shop, and he had all kinds of weird stuff—jars filled with liquids in various colors. It was pretty freaky. But he also had some cool clothes in there, so Jerry and I went in. He was a very impressive-looking man with a nice beard, well trimmed. He got into a conversation with us, and we told him we were playing in Boston. He asked us what kind of music we were playing, and then he told us about his fight for truth and justice. He said, 'You have to have one hand with thunder, and the other hand holding lightening—to beat down the forces of evil.' So he started preaching this. Some of this made its way into the song lyric, 'Truly Fine Citizen.'

On October 4 and 5, Moby Grape played the Electric Factory in Philadelphia, sharing the bill with Chrysallis and Woody's Truck Stop, a relatively new venue, set in a converted tire warehouse, that had become the biggest draw in the city since opening in February.

Then, after taking the train back to New York, they played a six-night stand at the Café Au Go-Go, with The Moke-Eaters opening. The shows ran from Saturday, October 12, to Thursday, October 17, with *Billboard* publishing a positive review of the October 16 show:

> Moby Grape had a powerful set at the Café Au Go-Go on Wednesday (16) … Now a four-man unit, the Columbia Records artists faced each other during most of the set, positioned in another diamond formation. An exception was lead guitarist Jerry Miller, who occasionally turned to face the audience. But the quartet was all business as they blasted their way through much of their set. Miller's guitar playing was first grade, while Peter Lewis, usually handling rhythm, and bass guitarist Bob Mosley supplied heavy support. Steady work was also turned in by drummer Don Stevenson. While all four participated in the vocals, it generally was the strong bluesy voice of Mosley or the combination of Lewis and Stevenson who carried the lead. Much of the material was from their first Columbia album, 'Hey, Grandma' and '8:05,' which Lewis and Stevenson led, and 'Mr. Blues,' a good number for Mosley. 'Omaha,' also from the first album concluded the set in top fashion as Mosley, Miller, Stevenson and Lewis participated in the vocal. 'Sitting By The Window' was another good selection.

On Friday, October 18, the band headed to Long Island to play the Action House, and the following day they journeyed back to Philadelphia for a performance at the Quaker City Rock Festival. For the latter show, held at the Philadelphia Spectrum, they shared a large bill with Big Brother & The Holding Company, Vanilla Fudge, Buddy Guy, and The Chambers Brothers. Writing for the *Courier-Post,* Hoag Levins gave a negative assessment of the 'Sour Grape,' who in his view 'chalked up a repeat of their miserable performance last week at the Electric Factory.' When I mention this review to Don, however, he's baffled. Though he's open about the band's up-and-down performances, from his perspective, the one at the Spectrum was memorably great, and reminded him of gigs he'd been to in years past at the Eagles Auditorium in Seattle.

> It was jam-packed. Janis was there, and maybe Vanilla Fudge was there, and maybe The Chambers Brothers. Buddy Guy. It was a heck of a headline, and one of the first big gigs we did without Skip. The stage was like this table—it was round. It was the first time I got to look at anybody singing. So I'm playing drums and singing, and I'm looking across, straight at Jerry, and Bob's looking straight across at Peter. [It was like] when you're in the studio, and you're singing with someone, you're really looking at him, and you've got this simpatico thing going on—and, you understand what the next part is by facial expressions, and by everything else. You really know where you're at.
>
> At the Spectrum, from the first note to the last note, it was amazing. We could hear our vocals and we could see each other, we could sing, and when we were done it was like twenty or twenty-five thousand people—there was this huge, huge ovation. And when we got off the stage we thought, 'God, that was a great set!' I remember we got off the stage and Janis said, 'You guys are the best performers in the world.' It was *that* kind of set. Then we were able to sit and play with everybody backstage after the concert. After they shut the place down, we were all playing with sticks on the tables. It was a phenomenal experience.
>
> It was a sad time, too, because we didn't have Skip with us. So it was kind of difficult. But Skip was probably there, in a way, because it soared. We got that response from the crowd. Then we got that response from our peers. And then we had the chance to just sit down and play. They came to kick us out so they could close the place.

Another highlight, Don adds, was getting the train from New York to Philadelphia and back again. 'That was one of the great train rides of my life. Everybody just sat and played and sang and smoked. It was a great way to relax after the gig. I can't remember everyone who was there but it was just a great time.'*

•

According to studio logs, Moby Grape were back in the studio on Sunday, October 20, recording a rough demo of 'Hoochie,' a new song by Bob. That night and the following evening they were scheduled to appear at Steve Paul's club the Scene, before playing at SUNY, Stony Brook University, on October 22. The latter show was famously bootlegged as a part of *Dark Magic* before receiving a formal release on Keyhole Records in 2014 as *Moby Grape—Live At Stony Book University, NY, October 22 1968.*† The band's mixed set featured twelve songs (the last one a medley), but during the penultimate song, a disagreement erupted when Bob and the band stepped into the opening out of sequence. In his review of the album for the *Attic*, Scott D. Wilkinson gave it three stars out of five, summing up the band and the performance as follows:

> Moby Grape in its quartet incarnation was a band that remained capable of greatness. … While there are glimmers of such grandeur on this album, one cannot help but notice a general feeling of ennui that pervades the performances. Jerry Miller, Peter Lewis, Bob Mosley, and Don Stevenson were simply too talented to play badly, but it often sounds like they were just going through the motions at this gig. … While it has been edited out here, the onstage banter that precedes 'It's

* It's possible that the members of Vanilla Fudge would have been on that train, too, as they were basically the house band at the Action House at the time, and Moby Grape would have been heading to Philadelphia straight from their show there.

† The liner notes to the album reproduce a 1972 piece that appeared in *Fusion* magazine. A time capsule of sorts, the article offers an interesting perspective of the band shortly after the Granite Creek reunion, and right around the time of Bob Mosley's debut solo release.

> A Beautiful Day Today' (which can be heard on *Dark Magic*) features a very cranky Mosley arguing with his bandmates about the arrangements (*'What's this 'hey, man' jive? I counted the song—one, two, three, four—and I went halfway through it.'*) Yes, hearing a band disintegrate onstage is something that should be considered more depressing than entertaining, but I kinda wish they had left that bit on this disc for the sake of historical completeness.

Around this time, the band also recorded an appearance for *The Jerry Lewis Show* that first aired on Tuesday, October 29 1968. Other guests at the taping included singer Bobby Darin and Paul Lynde, then staring in *Bewitched*. When Moby Grape took the stage to mime 'It's A Beautiful Day Today,' Bob looked studious, with tidy hair and a cardigan, but his performance appeared reticent. If the four members of the Grape were having a difficult time bringing verve into their performances in the autumn of 1968, however, it's unsurprising. According to David Fricke's liner notes for *Vintage*, the band's difficult relationship with former manager Matthew Katz had 'continued to deteriorate,' leading, by the end of the year, to Katz filing 'a million dollar lawsuit against the Grape.'

If that was the case, then Jerry, Don, Peter, and Bob may well have seen their band's endpoint edging closer and closer. This isn't merely fatalism but the process of events transpiring, choices made and paths influencing one another; and, over time, the unfolding narrative solidifying from many possible future points to a single fixed event …

Let's imagine ourselves at Moby Grape's first rehearsal. From this perspective, the disintegration of the Grape is always a *possible* future event. It's more than that—because no one's immortal, it's *always* an eventuality. But as time passes, and events unfold, the Grape's endpoint gradually becomes less of a distant possibility and more of a close reality. Columbia's overhyping of the band's debut, the lingering trial, the mishap at Monterey, the move to New York City, the fractured *Wow/Grape Jam* sessions, the fake Grape fiasco, Skip's breakdown, the legal complications with Matthew

Katz ... all of these things, over time, blend together to bring Moby Grape's endpoint closer to the present. Of course, an *eternalist* would argue that *all* these events *always* existed, immaterial of past, present, and future, but I much prefer the idea of *indeterminism*. No single event caused the end of the band. It was a long process with many ever-changing variables.

•

On November 1 and 2, the Grape played shows at Aaron Russo's Kinetic Playground in Chicago. A few days later, Robb Baker—one of the journalists who'd been most intrigued by the band over the past few years—expressed his disappointment in his review for the *Chicago Tribune*:

> Most guitarists, at least those we've seen, play best with both hands. And most vocalists sing best when they don't have anything in their mouths. Furthermore, a forty-five-minute set isn't such a long time. It doesn't seem really unfair to expect a musician to get through one without having to light up a cigarette and then stop twice in the middle of a number to take a drag. So it sounds like a picky little thing. But Jerry Miller's action Saturday night at the Kinetic Playground was indicative of the whole attitude that Moby Grape seemed to have about performing, and—even sadder—of the don't-give-a-damn attitude toward the audience that many groups in rock seem to have today. We have seen the Grape earlier this year at Cheetah and the night before as well at the Playground, when they arrived for their first set over three hours late. In both cases, their performances were even more lackadaisical and low-key than Saturday. They didn't announce numbers and they wandered around onstage. The really unfortunate thing is that, on record, the group is one of the best around. And at least Saturday things worked pretty well musically, particularly the vocals and Miller's guitar (when he opted to play instead of smoke). But the live performance situation demands stage presence as well. ... The

> second night the Grape were into their country bag, which, like The Byrds, they do extremely well. Skip Spence is missed (he did have stage presence), and I'd be willing to bet there's a new bass player as well. The voice sounds like Bob Mosley, but that early Elvis hairstyle and sullenness just can't be the blond former sex symbol of the group.

On Saturday, November 9, after two previous cancellations, Moby Grape were finally set play at *Super Scene '68* at the Rose Bowl in Pasadena, sharing the bill with The Grass Roots and The Look. Then, between Monday, November 11, and Sunday, November 24, they spent nine days hunkered down in a studio in Malibu, laying down ten tracks for their third album, *Moby Grape '69.**

'We got down to business,' Jerry reminisces. 'We didn't take forever to do anything. We'd get up in the morning and get off at night. We were at Malibu Colony. It was a pretty swanky place, right on the beach—the big kahunas!' he laughs heartily.

On the first day, Moby Grape recorded Bob Mosley's thumping new number, 'Trucking Man.' Describing the song to journalist Steve Roeser, Bob said he wrote it 'to keep awake when I was driving from San Francisco to San Diego to visit my folks'—an 'actual true story,' according to Jerry. 'Bob was broke down on the highway, and a trucker came and helped him out. So he wanted to pay tribute. So that's how that one came about.'

Jerry energetically sings a line from the song:

> *Truck drivin' man, he's man's best friend*
> *He's the backbone of the fatherland.*

Jerry pauses, lost in thought. 'Once in a while, I'd get the guitar solo all wrong. There's a little change in there that I would miss from time to time, then I'd get the stinky eye from Bob,' he chuckles. 'Yeah, we'd pass around the stinky eye if somebody played a shitty chord.'

* For session dates, see Gene Sculatti's liner notes to the 2007 Sundazed reissue of the album.

Over the next three days, the Grape returned to the studio to lay down three more tracks: Peter's 'If You Can't Learn From My Mistakes' 'I Am Not Willing,' and 'Ain't That A Shame.' The first two were ballads, the third a country-rock song of frustration. Of the first, Jerry later told David Fricke, 'That was one of those things. I think it had to do with [Peter's] ex, Diana.' When I ask Jerry about 'Ain't That A Shame,' he adds, 'Well, I kinda felt that way at the time. Just expressing my feelings.'

Thinking back to these sessions, Don recalls how, during their time in Malibu, the band were 'trying to rediscover that creative place. We were having a hard time communicating, so we went on a word strike. There was a period of, like, a day or so when we did not talk. We thought, if we can't communicate, then we better *not* communicate.'

The band's working methods had become 'compartmentalized,' he says:

> Bob and Peter were close, musically, and Jerry and I were creatively close together. So it became a little more difficult to include all of us—to collaborate with all the creativity we had the first time. We found spots, we found things that were really good, but … it wasn't the same as the first album. We were trying to find something, and it was difficult to find. When we recorded the first album, we had just come out of the Ark and out of rehearsals and we were practicing, and we had all of this creative stuff happening—and then you perform, and it isn't the same thing. It's the *performance phase* of what you do, and not the creative phase of what you do.

Bob also remembers hooking up with some of the other musicians who were based in Malibu during this period, including David Crosby and Graham Nash. 'It was a pretty creative time,' he says. 'We got together, and we were writing and playing and getting something out of it. We were also, again—it's like a marriage, you know. It wasn't always fun. Sometimes things would happen, and you'd just think, *what am I doing here?* But the music was always working. The music was really, really good.'

The second week of recordings opened on November 18 with the taping of 'Ooh Mama Ooh,' a 50s-tinged number with Jerry filling in for Bob on bass and David Rubinson providing some vocals. Thinking back to the song, Jerry begins to mimic David's deep, deep bass—'*mama-mama, ma-ma-ma-ooh, ma-ma-ma-ooh*'—before adding, 'He had a good little voice. I liked David.' Pausing, he adds, with some regret, 'I wish we weren't such punks at the time—that we couldn't get along with anybody. You know what I mean; we tried. But we just didn't have the maturity that we should've had.'

Two days later, they cut the punkish, 122-second 'Going Nowhere,' a song that Jerry tells me 'didn't make any sense at all! I would call that almost a filler. We never liked to do fillers, but sometimes we'd get caught up and just couldn't agree on what we wanted to do.' After reflecting on this for a moment, he add, 'But it was fun for the guitar. I liked that part. I have a 1956 Explorer amplifier that I used on that. It had a cool little sound. I enjoyed that part of it. The words are kind of evil.'

On November 21 and 22, Moby Grape lay down three more tracks: Bob's storming 'Hoochie,' Peter's pensive 'What's To Choose,' and Bob's meditative 'It's A Beautiful Day Today.' Reflecting on the latter song, Jerry tells me, 'I still do that song [in my shows]. It's a beautiful sentiment.'

On Sunday, November 24, during their final studio session for the album, the band recorded the swirling 'Captain Nemo.' Running to just over one hundred seconds, the song has a guitar pattern that just goes around and around, giving the effect of a boat that's rocking in the water. 'That is just a crazy song,' Jerry sighs. 'That is just a bunch of lunacy.'

Apart from mixing sessions, this would be the last time Moby Grape worked with producer David Rubinson until their 1971 reunion.

In finalizing the album, the Grape would also reach back into the past to one of Skip's old songs, 'Seeing.' 'That was another of Skip's genius songs,' Jerry recalls fondly. 'But Skippy didn't do much that wasn't genius. He was … what can you say, almost crazy genius.' Jerry sighs. 'I sure liked the guy. He was a good friend.'

While the Grape had managed to put together a strong set of songs in a very short amount of time, all their struggles have taken a toll. Recalling this period, Peter Lewis would later tell Jud Cost, 'At that point I was under the care of a psychiatrist, taking all this Librium so I could stay with the band. We kept drifting along as a quartet. We made *Moby Grape '69* in an attempt to rebound from the *Wow* album, which was over-produced. And it's a cool album. Although we could have rehearsed it a little more, we still believed in it. But I think we were waiting for Skippy to come back.'

•

Sometime in November, Skip Spence was released from Belleview Hospital. In a 2009 interview with *Crawdaddy* journalist Andrew Lau, producer David Rubinson offered his recollections of the circumstances surrounding Skip's breakdown, his release, and the recording of his solo album. When Skip stepped out the doors of Belleview, David picked him up and took him uptown to buy some clothing and have some lunch at a hotel. 'I asked, What do you want to do? He said he wanted a Harley-Davidson and he wanted to go to Nashville and wanted to record; he'd written a lot of songs while in the hospital. Then he wanted to get on his motorcycle and drive home to his wife. I said, Fine.'

Meanwhile, in the midst of a five-night stand at the Whisky A Go Go (November 27–December 1), Moby Grape were simultaneously scheduled to play the Commodore Ballroom in Lowell, Massachusetts, on Sunday, November 30, with The What Group supporting. Again, to differentiate the show from those put on by the fake Grape act, the ad for the latter show identified the band as 'The Moby Grape Columbia Recording Stars.' The following week, on Friday, December 6, they were booked to play a show at the New Place in Algonquin, near Chicago, with the Illusions supporting. By now, however, identifying which gigs the *real* Moby Grape played during this period poses a challenge.

Elsewhere, between December 3 and 12, Skip spent a smattering of days in a makeshift Columbia studio in Nashville, recording a variety of songs he'd written in Belleview. No longer working in a group setting, he was now a completely solo artist, playing everything on the resulting album, *Oar*, from bass to piano to drums to guitar to vocals. It was, says Don, 'the first album that I know of where one person plays everything':

> He played all the instruments and did all the vocals. Nowadays that's common thing. There's a lot of people doing that now. But at that point he was the first person to do it. He had the engineer record one track at a time. So, you know, he would lay down the bass, and then he would lay down the guitar, and then he would lay down the drums, and then he would lay down the piano, and then he would lay down the vocals, and everybody would go, 'This is really weird.' And it was weird and wonderful.

Twelve months later, Paul McCartney would take the same approach when he began to lay tracks for his own debut solo album.

I've listened to *Oar* many times over the past two decades. It's an experience that's haunting and ethereal—and at times fun. The album is painful, witty, catchy, thoughtful, silly, simple, ghostly, complicated, and so many other things. It's hard to put to words. Like the Grape story itself, capturing *Oar* on paper is like trying to grab smoke as it wisps through the air. It's an album you need to be in the mood for. But when I *am* in the mood, and when I *do* play the album, it moves me. It may be impossible to explain. Possibly. You need to experience this album for yourself, without my influence. You need to hike that path alone. It's a nighttime album—not a record to play in a restaurant, or in a café. It's music for solitude.

•

While Skip was busy recording, Moby Grape remained inactive. For Jerry, Don, Peter, and Bob, it was time for a rest. Their next gigs were set for December 27–28, at the Felt Forum in New York. Following these shows, they were scheduled to play a New Year's Eve Bash at the Fillmore, sharing the bill with Vanilla Fudge, Richie Havens, and Cold Blood.

CHAPTER TWENTY-TWO

MOBY GRAPE'S LAST STAND

You may wonder: what has become of the fake Grape? By the turn of the year, The mysterious *alternative* Moby Grape were still merrily touring the Midwest, playing the Cellar in Arlington Heights, Illinois, with The Nova Express opening on Friday, January 17, and Saturday, January 18. On the latter date, The mystery of the second Grape took an unexpected turn with a *third* Moby Grape performing at the same time at the Valley View YAK in Frankfort, Ohio.

For the real Moby Grape, January '69 marked a Bay Area last stand, of sorts. They played their final shows at the Ark with Steve Miller on January 17–18, followed by their last shows at the Winterland, on January 24–25, sharing the bill with It's A Beautiful Day, The Other Half, and Tim Hardin. Shortly afterward, they traveled to London for a short European tour, first playing venues in England and Scotland, then flying to the continent for a tour that ran for just under three weeks.

'Was that all?' Don asks when I mention this timeline to him. 'I thought we played something like seventeen nights in twenty-five days. It was a lot. And Gruber … we were supposed to be paying our rent, and taking care of our bills, and all that stuff—and I got back home and my lights were out. They were not paying attention. Management. So that was not good.'

Jerry mentions the same mishap when we chat about the tour, pointing out that Gruber was only with the band 'for a very short time. All he did basically was set up that English tour and bounce some checks on us. There was some sort of mix up, and Gruber bounced a big check—not a *big* check, but big enough for those days. Big enough to pay the rent. That's when we were living around Santa Cruz, but we had to find out about it when we were in Scotland, and we had to try to get the rent paid and everything with bounced checks and our wives were out of sorts—*that* was a real drag.' He pauses, chuckling to himself. 'But we did have a hell of a good time on that tour—especially in Amsterdam.'

Casting his mind back to the start of the tour, Don continues:

> There were a couple of things in London. We played a gig, we did a radio show … and we stayed in some kind of—it was a house with a bunch of different rooms in it. It was almost like a bed and breakfast.
>
> Management gave us a kind of bodyguard. His name was Alfie. I think it was due to some kind of criminal activity that they were involved in. They were watching the band and taking care of us, moving equipment and helping [Tim] Dellara do all that stuff.
>
> At one point, Alfie hung a guy out of a hotel room window by the ankles! It didn't have anything to do with the band. But the guy was up in our area, and they brought him up there and they just said, 'You know, you're gonna' … they just hung him out there, and they asked him a few questions, and they said, 'You answer these questions and I'll let you go.' Alfie and these guys were just with us when we were in London They just took care of us while we were there.

According to UPI press reports from the time, Group Therapy, the Grape's backing band, had arrived in London on Thursday, January 23, with Moby Grape following shortly thereafter. Then, on January 26, a gang of hooligans attacked two members of Group Therapy, along with a booking agent, as they entered the Roundhouse Auditorium. In one of these reports, which appeared in the *Philadelphia Inquirer*, manager Michael Gruber was quoted as saying, 'Our agent Ian Tilbury has been taken into the hospital. He was blinded when he was smashed in the eyes with a plank of wood … Tommy [Burns] had a broken bottle in his face and Ray [Kennedy] had three cracked ribs from the kicking he received when he fell to the floor.' It's unsurprising, then, that security became a concern for the bands on this tour.

Things would get worse for Group Therapy as the tour continued. Just three days after the attack outside the Roundhouse, members of the band were arrested at their cold-water hotel in Chelsea for possession of marijuana. According to an Associated Press report from the time, the upshot was that 'four members of a California rock group called Group Therapy were fined $60 each at London's Marlborough Street Magistrates Court Wednesday for possessing marijuana. The four, who pleaded guilty were Thomas Burns, 22, Michael Gruber, 31, Patrick Nolan, 22, and Larry Martin, 21. Police say they found the drugs in the group's London hotel rooms.'*

After a Saturday show in London, on February 1, the Grape made their way to Bath to play a gig on February 3. Then, on February 4, they were back in London, recording a set at the BBC Playhouse that was broadcast the following month. They then played with The Nice in Newcastle on February 6, but after that the schedule details get a bit hazy: dates in Edinburgh and Birmingham followed, but the order of the shows is unclear. By February 9, they were on the continent for the start of a weeklong run of shows in Denmark, Sweden, and the Netherlands.

Going over this itinerary, Don admits, 'I was in Europe, but I could've

* When I ask Don what he remembers of Group Therapy, he first recalls the 'great version' they did of The Chambers Brothers' 'People Get Ready,' before adding, 'They were more East Coast–sounding, you know—Vanilla Fudge-y. We were a little more … edgy. They misbehaved themselves very well when we were in England.' Jerry, meanwhile, remembers the band being 'friends of Gruber.' The band's vocalist, Ray Kennedy, later co-wrote 'Sail On, Sailor,' as recorded by The Beach Boys.

been in Tacoma, except for a few little differences.' One thing that sticks out in his recollections is playing an old theater in Edinburgh with a screen in front of the proscenium:

> We got to the venue and did our sound check, and there was a long presidium and a theater in the balcony, and all that. It's an old theater. So the stage manager says [*dons Scottish accent*], 'It sounds good. But you better play well tonight.' And we said, 'Why, what's going on?' And he says, 'Well you see that proscenium, where the lights come up?' There was also kind of a little gutter and inside it there's a chain-link fence. So the stage manager says, 'If they don't like you, they'll throw bottles, they'll throw fruit, dirty old underwear.' [*Laughs.*] 'If you don't play well, the stagehands have to pull the chain-link fence up so people can't throw stuff at you and hit you.'

Fortunately, Don adds with a laugh, 'We played really well!'

Thinking back, Jerry notes that Fleetwood Mac (with Peter Green) had accompanied the band for one of the shows on the tour, too. The following day, he adds, he and Don traveled down to Birmingham on the train, 'which was just beautiful, looking out the window and seeing all the sheep and the English countryside. We got nice seats with clean windows and we had dinner, and I remember it was, I believe, a lamb dinner. We asked if they had any Coke or RC Cola, and they did! It was real nice on that train. Then, when we got to Birmingham, we got into this pub with these guys and started shooting darts, and singin', and, I tell ya, I've never been that screwed up in my life! And then we had to play! I swore I'd never get that tuned up again, before I'd have to play. And I never have!'

During another of our conversations about that jaunt, Don bursts out laughing, then sighs, when his mind turns to the tour's stop in Amsterdam:

> We were still … we were popular in Amsterdam. We played a concert, and I remember we did a television show, and we did

a couple of radio shows. And we went to a club there. That was the first time I ever saw such a thing as—where—and I guess it's commonplace now, but they had a place where you go and check your coat and you could go buy some hash and go buy some weed or whatever.

So I was dancing with this great-looking woman all night. I was stoned, and I'd had a little bit of Irish whiskey, and a little hash and the whole band was sitting there. And I had no idea. This is how naïve I am. I was dancing with this girl, and I remember [road manager] Tim Dellara saying, 'Hey, Don, isn't this kind of a drag?' And I still didn't get it. [*Chuckles to himself.*] Finally, Jerry says, 'Hey, man, that's a dude.' And I looked at him and said, 'You're kidding. I'm only going to dance with him one more time and that's it!'

When I ask Jerry about his favorite show on the tour, he replies, 'Well, the one in Amsterdam,' although he admits that his memories don't quite tally with the recording of it, released by Sundazed in 2010 as part of the well-received collection *Moby Grape Live*. 'When I hear that, it sounds like we were a little slow,' he says. 'I don't know if it was the recording quality—I don't know what it was.' Of the show itself, he adds, 'It was fun because with security here, you just step on the stage and they just take you away, and knock you down and everything, but over there, we'd be playing, and here comes some guy in front of us on a unicycle, and then some clown coming by, and then some jugglers in front of us … then some guy on stilts! So they were a lot looser. You never noticed security unless it was really necessary.'

•

While the Grape were in Europe, their third album, *Moby Grape '69*, was released. Since the hoopla of their debut, each subsequent release had received less and less attention, both from Columbia Records and from the media. In a ten-week run on *Billboard*, the album reached only #113, yet the reviews were good. If *Wow* received mixed-to-positive reviews, *Moby Grape '69* did better all around.

In a sparse three-line review in the February 8 issue of the *Honolulu-Star-Bulletin*, Dave Donnelly wrote that the album 'features the reconstructed group in a new light, sans gimmickry. Here they shine better than at any time since their first releases. Maybe they'll have a big future after all.' Five days later, in his review for the same paper, Wayne Harada offered the same positivity, stating that the album 'just might be [the] LP that will put Moby into the Grape bunch.' One week later, on Thursday, February 20, *Chicago Tribune* journalist Robb Baker admitted that he didn't yet like it as much as *Wow* but left room for that to change, adding, 'Both of the previous albums were of the it-grows-on-you variety.'

The first negative words on the album appeared in the *Albuquerque Journal* on March 12, with Bill Hume stating that the songs on *Moby Grape '69* 'are all run-of-the mill pop efforts with nothing in particular to distinguish or condemn them.' For Gary Jobson of the *Ashbury Park Press*, the album 'marks the rejuvenation of Moby Grape' in 'an honest attempt to get away from the music in *Grape Jam*,' while *Los Angeles Times* critic Pete Johnson called attention to the taut arrangements and production on the album, which he felt was the band's 'first which seems to have had as much thought put into what to leave out as what to include.'

Writing for the *Cincinnati Enquirer*, Jim Knippenberg declared, 'Almost all the tracks are good, but particularly good are "Hoochie" and "Ooh Mama Ooh." The album is one to listen to and enjoy immensely—but don't expect a mystical experience as a result.' Dave Wagner of the *Green Bay Press-Gazette* was more measured concluding, 'This is a good album, but not perhaps the one that all that all that searching could have inspired.'

In a retrospective review for allmusic.com, Mark Deming notes that 'the high points come close to recapturing the electric magic of the group's nearly flawless debut, especially the gritty groove of "Hoochie," the doo-wop-influenced boogie of "Ooh Mama Ooh," the beatific joy of "It's A Beautiful Day Today," the raucous celebration of one "Trucking Man," and the folk-tinged wisdom of "If You Can't Learn From My Mistakes."' Yet on the down side, 'the absence of Skip Spence ... robs *Moby Grape '69* of a significant share of the energy and drive that was the hallmark of their finest studio work.'

Looking over the track list for the album, Don reflects, 'It was back to our roots a little bit. Because after *Wow*, this was getting back to what we'd done before. I always thought this was a good album. I like everyone's contribution.' Of the cover, which features a photograph of the band at the beach, he adds, 'That was at sunset, in Malibu. It was something we'd always do ... go relax on a rock.' Don pauses for a few seconds then bursts out laughing. 'We'd never do that!'

•

On their return from Europe, the Grape had a smattering of shows lined up, but of their scheduled performances at the Avalon (March 7–9), the Silverbell Hideout in Clarkston, Michigan (March 14–15), and the Palm Springs Drive-In (April 1, with John Mayall, The Paul Butterfield Blues Band, Lee Michaels, Jeff Beck, and Hard Luck Boy sharing the bill), only the first shows took place. Pondering this last stint to the Avalon, Don reflects, 'I think we were falling apart at that point.'

It was at this moment that Bob Mosley left the band.

As a quartet, Moby Grape had scaled great heights. Yet as they soldiered on, Jerry, Don, Peter, and Bob struggled with internal and external disagreements, trying to find a new balance, trying to recapture their momentum, treading through up-and-down performances and mishaps, and coping with a growing disinterest from Columbia. On top of everything, they were struggling financially in the face of the disruptions of the fake Moby Grape and a tightening legal knot.

During one of our conversations, I ask Don if he had any inkling that Bob was going to leave the band when they were returning from their European tour. 'Well, no, I didn't,' he replies. 'I had no notion that he was gonna leave. And then he went into the marines. I was surprised.' After pausing for a moment, he adds, 'Next thing you know, we were in Nashville doing [another] album, with just Jerry and myself and Peter ...'

•

March 12 1969. Though the month is not yet halfway over, it's already been hectic. On March 1, Jim Morrison exposed himself while performing at the Dinner Key Auditorium in Miami, Florida—or, at least, he *apparently* did. The following day, in a Los Angeles courtroom, Sirhan Sirhan admitted to killing US presidential candidate, Robert F. Kennedy. On March 4, three days after the boisterous Miami concert, Jim Morrison was arrested after a whopping six warrants were issued by the Dade County Police Department. On March 5, a new rock magazine, *Creem*, made its debut. Five days after that, James Earl Ray pleaded guilty to killing Martin Luther King Jr. in Memphis, Tennessee. And on that same day, Mario Puzo's novel *The Godfather* was released ...

Wednesday, March 12, was also an up-and-down day for The Beatles. On the day Paul McCartney married Linda Eastman at Marylebone Registry Office, officers from the drugs squad raided the home of George and Patti Harrison. The Harrisons were arrested on various charges and taken to the Esher police station for processing and fingerprinting. (Detective Sergeant Pilcher, who orchestrated the bust, would later be convicted of conspiracy to prevent the course of justice, receiving a four-year prison sentence in 1973.)

That night, the eleventh annual Grammy Awards were held in various locations, including New York, Nashville, Chicago, and Los Angeles. Initially, the Grammys were the brainchild of the organizers of the Hollywood Walk of Fame, as a way to reward those in the music industry who might qualify for a star on Hollywood Boulevard but never receive one. As awards day unfolded, nominees' emotions might range from nervousness to ambivalence to unawareness.

Those nominees were not just musicians, either. Some were artists and designers. And why not? After all, as celebrated artists Storm Thorgerson and Aubrey Powell write in *100 Best Album Covers*, 'These designs are the visual signposts, the flags, symbols, the awning, the camouflage, the "skin" of these much loved records.'

One 'Best Album Cover' Grammy hopeful in 1969 was the vice president of creative services at Columbia Records. Now forty-five, Bob

Cato initially 'studied art in Mexico with José Clemente Orozco and David Alfaro Siqueiros, and then at Chicago School of Design with Moholy-Nagy,' according to author Nick de Ville. He had already shared a Grammy twice, most recently for his work on the cover of Bob Dylan's *Greatest Hits*. This year, his nomination—or, rather *one* of his nominations—was for a San Francisco band's sophomore release. Yet by now said band was on the verge of disintegration.

Moby Grape weren't the only collapsing band to be nominated for a Grammy in 1969. Up for 'Best New Artist,' ironically, were Cream—a band who had been around for two years and were rapidly approaching their own breakup. Of course, Bob Cato likely wasn't thinking about the folly of nominating the Cream for 'Best New Artist.' No, he would more likely be wondering who would walk away with the Grammy for 'Best Album Cover.' His competition included albums by Thelonious Monk (*Underground*), Rhinoceros (*Rhinoceros*), and Wes Montgomery (*Road Song*), as well as one he himself co-designed: Leonard Bernstein conducting the New York Philharmonic on *Ives: Holiday Symphony*.

Before we consider the artwork for Moby Grape's *Wow* album, however, let's look back at its predecessor.

In the spring of 1967, Moby Grape recorded their debut over a smattering of days spread through March and April on Sunset Boulevard, all the while hopping back and forth between Los Angeles and San Fran for sessions and shows. In the midst of all this, photographer Jim Marshall led the five members of the band on an odyssey around Marin County, seeking out the *perfect shot*—the one true shot to mark the front cover of the band's first LP. When we speak about that album cover, Bob recalls a long day of trekking around Mill Valley and Larkspur and driving down back roads with the thirty-one-year-old Marshall, who would go on to snap numerous seminal photos, creating historic images of the era in the weeks, months, and years ahead, at Monterey and Woodstock, and of musicians of such renown that only surnames are needed (Hendrix, Coltrane, Joplin, Allman, Redding). Although he might still have been 'up-and-coming' at that point, he was indomitable.

Jim Marshall, Matthew Katz, David Rubinson, and the members of Moby Grape would all have been familiar with the idiom, 'You only get one chance to make a first impression.' But the question remained: what first impression would Moby Grape make with their debut album cover?

As the Grape contingent flitted from site to site, the band members grew more and more tired. In nearly every shot, Don Stevenson is seen to be naughtily slipping the finger, silently voicing his frustration with the whole affair—an endless afternoon of setups and takedowns. Exhausted, worn-out, verging on revolution, the travelers eventually wound up in front of an antique shop called Junktique, in Fairfax. It was here that Jim captured the image he'd been searching for.

The photograph—a combination of Bay Area hipness and the days of yore—shows the five members of Moby Grape looking ambivalent as they stand and sit in front of the old shop, holding such objects as a rifle, a washboard, a ladle, an old frying pan, and a poll bearing an American flag. It's an image of Americana, change, youth, and psychedelia, and—with Don slipping the finger over the washboard—in-your-face rebellion. Dressed in the fashions of the day—blending the old with the new—and steeped in objects of the past, the five musicians on the cover of *Moby Grape* are like a contemporary band of traveling minstrels. Like Odysseus, they'll journey far and wide, encountering iterations of the Lotus-Eaters, the Cyclops, Circe, the Sirens, and many others. Like Odysseus and his leather bag containing three of the winds, Moby Grape had a bag filled with exuberance, alchemy, and possibility—the past, present, and future all twisted up. It's alchemy, and a kind of folk art. And with the Grape logo tucked in the top-left corner, it also shows the commercial dimension of popular music. As Nick de Ville notes, 'During the twentieth century, design for music was the closest thing the design world of the West had to a living folk art. Which is to say that, as an art form, it was clannish, heterogeneous, disposable, generated from "beneath," amateur, faddish on the surface (although in many ways rooted in symbolic continuity), and firmly part of popular culture.'

This album cover displays these five modern minstrels, these travelers, as they announced their presence to the world. This image—censored after the record's release—shows us just how quickly the past can be rewritten, with the gentle stroke of an airbrush. Abracadabra, and Don's middle finger disappears, while the American Flag transforms itself into an orangey apparition. Moby Grape would become a myth, stuck between fact and fiction, between what's real and unreal. We know this all too well. The very building that stands behind the quintet—Junktique—doesn't even exist anymore. This album cover isn't only a picture from long ago; it's an image of five young men on the verge of fame, near an old structure that's no longer standing. It isn't just a photograph of a lost moment; it's a photograph of a place that's disappeared—not figuratively but literally, physically. Distributed as a poster within the LP, this album cover stands up as a frozen portrait of psychedelic Americana. When Jim Marshall snapped this photograph, the Summer of Love was just on the other side of a threshold, a matter of future possibility. Like the best record covers, Moby Grape's debut was, as Thorgerson and Powell put it, 'a barometer of the times.'

When Bob Cato came to design the Grape's *next* album cover, the times would already have changed. By then, Summer of Love was no longer a matter of future possibility but a thing of the past.

In early 1968, while meandering through the sporadic sessions for their second LP, the Grape began to discuss possible names for the album. Over time, they would home in on one idea—and with the album provisionally titled *Hot Mom And Apple Pie*, a photo shoot was arranged. In the company of an elderly granny, the members of the band dressed up in a variety of costumes, including a mechanic, a spaceman, and Superman. As shot after shot was taken, the six figures posed with such props as a motorcycle, an old gramophone, a dishwasher, and a giant crate bearing the words 'Napalm Prop. US Army.'

Eventually, this idea was set aside and the album retitled *Wow/Grape Jam*. The artwork was completed by Bob Cato, with whom Peter Lewis and his bandmates were evidently taken, as Lewis explained to Jud Cost. 'CBS wasn't as cool as the smaller labels, but Bob Cato stuck out from the rest. Even though he wore a suit, he was still hip. We liked him and we wanted him for the cover, as we felt he was the only one at CBS who understood us.' Trusting Bob, the band took a hands-off approach as the designer zeroed in on a vision and crafted the foldout cover of the LP. 'It was all Bob's deal,' Lewis added. 'We just saw the finished product and that was it.' And what a finished product it is.

Wow is a striking album cover for any age—and completely unlike its predecessor. It blends realistic drawings with something wholly unrealistic and mysterious. It shows us something of the olden days, something familiar, and something fantastical. It looks like a moment in history—a memorable event—but it's an impossibility, too. Inviting us to step into this mystery, the colorful drawing is at once elusive and alluring. Describing the design in *100 Best Album Covers*, Thorgerson and Powell write:

> WHOA, WHAT HAVE WE HERE? A humongous bunch of grapes on the seashore, big as a house, that's what. Grapes as big as a whale. Moby Grape. And who are those people coming ashore to look and marvel, and say 'WOW, what's that?' Giant Dali-esque grapes propped up on a seashore, but not a Dali-esque seashore, more like one from an old etching (although, in fact, newly drawn from Victorian woodcuts by designer Bob Cato). The onlookers come perhaps from an older world, peering up at this strange arrival from a newer age. No band name or record title, just a massive bunch of grapes. Excessive, noisy, enormous, out-of-place grapes, but strangely fitting, gravely sitting, inexorable on the sand, in the bay of plenty. Sands of time, grapes of wrath.

In the event, as the evening of March 12 1969 unfolded, John Berg and Richard Mantell would walk away the 'Best Album Cover' Grammy for their work on Thelonious Monk's *Underground*. Although he was nominated twice over, Bob Cato would not take home his third Grammy on this occasion. But though *Wow* may not have garnered a Grammy in March 1969, the album endures, half a century after its release.

One last note about March 12. That day, a foreboding sentence appeared in Kathy Orloff's 'Record World News' column in the *Indianapolis News*. Describing the band's legal predicament, she wrote, 'There is still a court battle raging as to who owns the name and can record and perform as Moby Grape.' Over time, this conflict intensified—and would not be resolved until the early years of the next century.

•

By late March 1969, Bob Mosley was gone. Moby Grape would be no more, yet somehow the band continued. Their recording contract called for one more album, so, with some reluctance, Columbia Records booked three days in late May for the band to quickly and quietly record one final album with Bob Johnston, who had recently worked with such artists as Bob Dylan, Leonard Cohen, Johnny Cash, and The Byrds.

When Jerry, Don, and Peter agreed to head to Nashville, Peter telephoned Bob to see if he'd join them. Recalling this period in his 1999 interview with Steve Roeser, Bob clarified one of the many myths about the band—that he had left to join the marines.

> I didn't actually leave them. I got a call from Peter and he said that they were going to do an album in Nashville, which turned out to be *Truly Fine Citizen*. It was he and Jerry and Don, and he wanted me to go along, [but] I was in [my] third year at state college, and I was just kind of having a hard time … I had lost my driver's license, for speeding tickets, so I had to take the bus to school. And it was getting kind of tough, trying to do my homework, and get up at 5:30 and go to school, and then come back at 3:30 in the afternoon, and still get everything done. And I wasn't making any money, so that was a hardship. So I volunteered my draft.
>
> I got drafted into the army … and then I went to the induction center and volunteered for the marine corps, and went in the marine corps. … On both sides [of my family

> home] were retired gunnery sergeants … so they were down there when I was going to boot camp …

Bob spent around nine months in the marines, for most of which he was stationed at Twentynine Palms, out in the Mojave Desert. 'I got through boot camp,' he continued, 'and finally when I went to my first duty station, it was just—you know, I was a cook, and it was just, nothing to do. And so you get into trouble. I got in a bunch of fights and ended up in the hospital.'

Unable to convince Bob to return, Jerry, Don, and Peter—the last three members of Moby Grape—flew to Nashville for an intense three days of recording. When the band arrived, producer Bob Johnston told them he wouldn't tolerate any misbehavior. As Peter Lewis explained to David Fricke in 1992, 'Johnston said to us, "I've heard about you guys. If this record isn't going to be done in three days, then you can go home now."'

The band got down to work. On May 27, they cut no fewer than five tracks: 'Looper,' 'Changes, Circles Spinning,' 'Truly Fine Citizen,' 'Open Up Your Heart,' and 'Now I Know High.' The following day, they recorded another five songs, 'Beautiful Is Beautiful,' 'Love Song, Part 1,' 'Love Song, Part 2,' 'Right Before My Eyes,' and 'Treat Me Right.' Then, on Thursday, May 29, the band recorded a song Jerry had penned with Skip the year before, 'Tongue-Tied.'

Looking back, Don sums up this period of the band's career as 'a struggle':

> Peter wanted to leave, but I think we were contractually obligated to make [another] album. We were so paranoid that we put all the songs, all the publishing, to Tim Dellara. We thought, if we got any publishing, we might make some money, but nobody bought the album. I don't blame them. Even in that, though, there were some nice things. 'Looper' was a cool song. 'Changes, Circles Spinning' was nice. Peter's songs were good. There was the one about Kamoo, 'Truly Fine Citizen.' I

love 'Treat Me Bad.' That's a great song: '*Treat me bad / That's the way it's always been / I love you way too much / ever since I can remember when.*' And 'Tongue-Tied': '*I get tongue-tied and I can't talk*'—that's a great song.

Tennessee was a really good experience. We were down there probably for a week, maybe ten days. I think we had Jonny Cash's bass player. He was really nice. He'd done a lot of session work. It was kind cool. It was a very relaxed atmosphere … it was biscuits and gravy every morning, and fireflies in the evening, and drive-in movies and a bottle of Jameson's. Jerry and I had a good time there. We went to a lot of different clubs and listened to a lot of music, and the recording sessions went well. We got everything laid down quickly. Bob Johnston did the producing, [but] he really didn't do anything much. He just sat there and turned the dial.

Speaking with Harvey Kubernik in 2017, in a piece for cohencentric.com, Peter Lewis shared an interesting memory of the band's time with Johnson. 'When the record was finished he asked me if I wanted to stay after the others went home. He said he liked my voice and wanted to introduce me to Johnny Cash, Dylan, Leonard Cohen etc. Why did I go home with the others and not take my shot at the time? It may have been some crazy idea that Moby Grape wasn't finished yet.'

•

Like the Grape's first and third albums, *Truly Fine Citizen* runs to approximately thirty minutes. In a stark contrast to the artwork for those two records, this time around the band decided to use a photograph of a security guard on the cover. 'He was a cool guy,' Don says, 'and we thought it would be funny to put him on the album cover. There was so much resentment against the police and authority at the time, we thought that album cover would make people angry.'

Advertisements for the album first appeared in September, but on its release the album garnered little fanfare and limited sales. In a pattern of diminishing returns, it would climb only to #157 during its short stay on the *Billboard* 200.

While *Truly Fine Citizen* drew scant attention in the press—a mere handful of reviews appearing in the months following its release—the critical response was mixed. James N. Gillespie's assessment in the Minneapolis *Star Tribune* was mostly favorable. 'Although this set isn't quite as good as their last one—bassist and lead vocalist Bob Mosley quit in the interim—it still offers a fine selection of country-rock songs done in the Grape's easy rolling infectious manner.' Less favorable was Jim Knippenberg's review for the *Cincinnati Enquirer*, in which he wrote, 'The whole album is like a microcosm of their career, containing some fantastic ups, and some of the most terrific downs you've ever heard. … Unless you're a super hung up Moby Grape freak, forget about their *Truly Fine Citizen*.'

In a positive review for *The Philadelphia Inquirer*, Jack Lloyd wrote, 'While the group doesn't knock you over with freshness, or even originality, it does demonstrate a high degree of musical know-how and versatility that keeps the listener interested at all times.' Finally, Robb Baker, one of the band's steadfast proponents, pointed out various highlights of the album in his *Chicago Tribune* review, yet avoided any conclusions about the album's overall quality in what was an ambiguous assessment.

Surveying the rock world of 1969 in the January 15 1970 issue of the *Village Voice*, Grape fan Robert Christgau gave the album at a C+ grade, noting that it was the record 'in which what should have been America's greatest rock group gasps its last. Quite mediocre, despite a couple of lovely Peter Lewis songs.'

With so few reviews in print, and the band inactive, it's unsurprising that *Truly Fine Citizen* became Moby Grape's poorest seller to date. Looking back on it decades later for allmusic.com, Mark Dunning offers the following conclusions:

> There are a few good songs on board, including 'Looper' (which had been in the Grape's repertoire since their earliest days), the

> sunny 'Changes, Circles Spinning,' and the title cut, a tribute to a mystic healer the band had met on the road. But *Truly Fine Citizen* was basically a rush job recorded to finish out Moby Grape's contract with Columbia, and too much of the time that's just what it sounds like, despite the obvious talent of the musicians, and the jazzy 'Love Song, Part 2' and 'Now I Know High,' which at 6:14 meanders twice as long as the album's second longest tune, are clear filler on an album that's barely over a half-hour long. Moby Grape were still capable of making a good album when they cut *Truly Fine Citizen*, but they scarcely had the opportunity to demonstrate that.

•

In June 1968, Moby Grape were reduced to four. In March 1969, the band shrunk to three. By the end of May, there wasn't anyone left. A lonely two-sentence blurb in Diane Morgan's 'The Disc Seen' column in the July 14 1969 issue of the *Press Democrat* offered a tiny ray of hope: 'Most of the original Moby Grape is alive and living in the Santa Cruz Mountains. The group will reportedly hit the concert trail again as soon as a new bassist is found.'

While some of the details are off, Morgan's prophecy was essentially correct. In under two years, the original Grape lineup would once again band together in the redwood covered hills of California, augmented by the addition of Gordon Stevens. Reluctant and hopeful, this reformed iteration of the Grape would be granted a second chance. In an old home on Granite Creek Road, they would once again make music, recapturing some of the magic they once had and once lost. They would even get to return to the hallowed grounds of the Fillmores East and West, weeks before the final eclipses of those musical temples.

Granite Creek marked the second rise and fall of Moby Grape. It's their denouement. But I've already told you that story.

POSTFACE

Moby Grape journeyed great distances, crisscrossing the continent, crossing the Atlantic, treading through the fabric of the times as that very fabric was being woven together. Like a band of tragic heroes, they reached and overreached, as they circumvented the shifting landscape of the 60s, a time that blended possibility with impossibility. The band navigated communal houses, ballrooms, benefits, biker bars, festivals, LSD, mafia-run venues, late-night sessions, jam sessions, redwood-covered mountains—the list goes on. Like Icarus, Moby Grape soared great distances, and, in the end, flew too close to the sun.

Jerry, Don, Peter, Bob, and Skip succeeded beyond their wildest imaginations—and they failed, too. When they were capturing the hearts and minds of audiences, critics, and record label executives, there was a time when the Grape could do no wrong. Yet so much slipped through their fingers. Some of this was their own doing, some was the work of others, and some was the cruelty of misfortune.

When Jerry and I talk about the Grape's hectic touring schedule, he sighs, 'Back in those days we just crisscrossed the country back and forth. You know, you play in Chapel one day and then you play in Augusta. Then you play in San Diego, then you play up in Seattle. It just didn't make any sense.'

He pauses. 'We learned a lot, but it's too bad we didn't know enough to be a little bit more aware. We should've just said, Hey, that's no good! If I go out [on tour] again I'm going to go out like Willie [Nelson]—have a little rig and have every gig about a couple hundred miles from the last one.'

No matter how things turned out, Moby Grape tapped into a unique blend of alchemy and exuberance that no one else had. It's something that Don reflects on during one of our conversations, running through each member's attributes in turn:

> Well, Peter's a fabulous fingerpicker. One of the things Peter did, when he did the beginning of '8:05,' it took him forever to get it. He had to practice it and practice it and practice it. He wouldn't let it go until it was perfect, and he even got better as time went by.
>
> Peter's a poet, you know. He writes beautiful songs. With 'Goin' Down To Texas' he has this great visual in the lyrics. About squeezing some of that mud in between your toes. It had a bit of a country feel to it. We had a country feel in a lot of our music.
>
> Jerry and I are both like neighborhood kids. We're like the guys standing around the barrel singing doo-wop songs. It brings this other reality that's very different from Peter's background to the music. Peter's from Hollywood and he's very poetic, and Jerry and I are more grounded. You know, we're into the two minute and fifty-six second song.
>
> Mosley was just thumping. He would kick your ass. He would take the butt end of his bass and knock your head in! Musically, I mean. He was a tough guy and he played like it. Whenever I hear Mosley singing on our early albums, I can't believe him. His singing was like Albert King or Albert Collins or B.B. King. He had this tenor in his voice that tells you about the blues. And there's no way that you can't believe what he says because … he is the blues. He's got it.
>
> And Skippy … he was from a whole other world.

Another time, Jerry pins down a special element of the Grape when describing 'Chinese Song,' chuckling as he casts his mind back:

> Skip's playing a koto on that one. He got that koto somewhere in New York, I believe. And he was such a genius musician that he could play that dang thing right away! Like anything else he got a hold of. A lot of people don't know it, but Skippy could play—he could play the old Doc Watson stuff. He could play a lot of them old folk tunes. He could fingerpick those old tunes. I didn't even know that, until probably the middle of the second album!
>
> See, what we had with the Grape, the whole idea—I never had the idea of playing with three guitars before Moby Grape. And then, if you've got three *blues* guitars, it doesn't work. But we had Peter, who played the nice fingerpicking beautiful stuff. And Skippy would lay down this awesome rhythm. He put the palm of his right hand on the strings back by the bridge, and when he'd play it would give kind of a popping sound. They used to do that a lot in Texas. It gives a good percussion effect.
>
> Bob and Don were tight with the drums and bass. Then Skippy would build the next rhythm level. Then Pete would play some pretty fingerpicking stuff, and I'd figure out how to glue them all together. With some little hot licks, some blues licks, and a few little jazz licks. You couldn't put three blues guitar players together and make it that easy. But it was easy, because nobody stepped on each other's toes.

Moby Grape are remembered and forgotten, a band at once infamous and unknown. The members of the Grape achieved artistic greatness, and yet they were capable of so much more. In the blink of an eye, and over the years, they've produced exceptional music that will endure. Behind the songs is a story of talent, hard work, excess, waste, persistence, and so many other things. It's an engaging story, a happy-sad story, and a tragic story. Yet it isn't *one story*. Moby Grape is many stories, all fragmented, blurred, and intersecting, threading in and out of one other. Some of these stories are told in this book, although to be honest, I haven't *really* captured the Moby Grape story. Such a thing doesn't exist. It never will.

Moby Grape are real and mythical. As time passes, the events of the 60s become blurrier as they recede into the distance. So it is with the Grape. In finding people in and around the band, in poring over so many things that have been written about the band over the years, I've tried to find as many puzzle pieces as I could, and figure out how they fit together, yet so many pieces are missing. I've chiseled out this narrative, trying to sketch the lives of Jerry, Don, Peter, Bob, and Skip, but it remains a partly finished mosaic. What can we learn from the rise and fall of Moby Grape? What does it tell us about creativity, and the relationship between business and art? What does it show us about luck, loss, and resilience? The answers to these questions are open to interpretation.

•

I pen these final lines in a café in Windsor, Ontario—the city where, over seven decades ago, Skip Spence was born into the world. While his music left an indelible mark, he passed away far too soon, one spring day in 1999. As I write, I wonder what the members of Moby Grape are doing at this moment. Perhaps Don is preparing for a show in Toronto. Jerry may be teaching jazz guitar to one of his students in Tacoma. Perhaps Peter's rehearsing for an upcoming gig with his daughter, Arwen. Bob may be spending time with his family.

Like the ethereal songs of *Oar*, the spirit of Skip lives on in the collective memories of those who knew him, as well as those who know his music. Scattered across different corners of North America, it's unlikely the remaining members of the Grape will ever make music together again—unlikely, but not impossible. With Moby Grape, anything is possible. After all, they recorded an album only a few years ago, but it remains unreleased.

•

One day, Don and I speak about Bob Mosley's debut album, and it leads him to consider the Grape's entire narrative.

> Mosley could've been huge. It's funny. It's like: you could have a thousand students. Let's say half of them grade out at 80 percent. And the other half grade out at, say, 60 percent. So you can take a test, and the ones getting 60 percent suddenly get 85 percent. And the ones who were getting 80 percent now get 60 percent. There's a mean and a spread. Well, Mosley—and all of us, I think—have a performance mean and a performance spread. We have a place where we could be 85 percent or 90 percent. And we have a place where we could be 60 percent. It just depends.
>
> What all of that depends upon is luck. I mean, Moby Grape is not very famous when you look at it from the point of view of fame and fortune. But we were so lucky to get to where we were. How come I'm in San Francisco, you know? Or in Sausalito, playing at the Ark? How did all of this come together? How did we manage to get into this situation, where all these people were coming to hear us? Simultaneous to that, to us playing at the Ark, there are these guys just three hours away sitting in some bar, and they're just as good as we are. Why did that happen? And why did all the shitty stuff happen?
>
> Here we are, we're 80 percenters, and suddenly we're playing at 95 percent at the Ark, playing our asses off having a great time. So much comes down to luck. Suddenly, things stop working out, our management, the five singles; so many things stopped working. How the hell did that happen? Why didn't we do a second album of all our favorite rock'n'roll songs from the 50s? That could've kicked ass, and we could've taken a deep breath before writing new material. I don't know. But I'm grateful and fortunate that—for the history that we have. So I don't know. With Moby Grape, it could've been more, and it could've been less. A lot has to do with luck.

ACKNOWLEDGMENTS

This book was created with the love, kindness, and support of many people.

I must begin with my immediate family—the poor souls who put up with me on a day-to-day basis. My wife and daughters are selfless, thoughtful, and seem to have a bottomless reservoir of patience. Thank you, Sophia, Katie, and Stella from the bottom of my heart. You have walked with me along this path, every step of the way. Without you—well, I can't express how important you are to me.

Of course, my extended family has also been a great pillar of strength, and I appreciate my parents, stepparents, siblings, nieces and nephews, and in-laws. A special thank you to Laurene and Moe Allan and Marilyn Basil, Jen and Colin, Nat, Matthew, Christina, and John … and your all your kin.

As this book has taken form, friends new and old have tirelessly chatted with me, reading excerpts, and offering astute feedback along the way. Thank you, Roberto LiVolsi, Chris Greig, Michael Potter, Rob McCubbin, Ernest Agbuya, Mark Alexander, Rupauk Sircar, Manu Sharma, and Cheryl Wells.

To my editor, Tom Seabrook, thank you for believing in me and in this project. You've been a compass. Along with the folks at Jawbone, you have provided cartloads of astute guidance and caring support day in and day out.

At various stages of this project, I've had the great fortunate of crossing paths with many talented artists, musicians, and music aficionados. Thank you, Larry Bruner, Bruce Edwards, Doug Hawes, Helen Hersh, Steve Katz, Melissa Martini, Joseph Miller, Jim Phillips, Michan Rhodes, Omar Spence, and Wes Wilson. A very special thank you to Mark Alexander, Tim Dellara, Jim Mazzeo, Lorne Saifer, and Burton Cummings. Your participation has been informative, and a tremendous source of energy and encouragement.

I am grateful to Bob and Connie Mosley for chatting with me and providing support. Like Jerry and Don, Bob was ever-patient when I asked him to repeat stories he'd already told me. Bob, you are a Titan!

What can I say about Don Stevenson and Jerry Miller? Somehow, you placed your trust in me, generously giving your time and thoughtfully sharing your perspectives. You approach music today with the same talent and verve that you did over half a century ago—and that's inspiring. Your energy is boundless as is your patience. Even when I'd approach you with yet another Columbo-like inquiry, starting off with 'just one more thing ...' Thank you Don and Jerry.

And, finally, thank you, Moby Grape, for writing such exceptional songs and producing such great albums over the years.

CAM COBB, WINDSOR, ONTARIO, CANADA, JANUARY 2018

SELECTED BIBLIOGRAPHY

BOOKS

Blecha, Peter, *Sonic Boom: The History Of Northwest Rock, From 'Louie Louie' To 'Smells Like Teen Spirit'* (Backbeat, 2009)

Camus, Albert, *The Stranger* (Vintage, 1942)

Carringer, Robert L., *The Magnificent Ambersons: A Reconstruction* (University Of California Press, 1993)

Christgau, Robert, *Rock Albums Of The 1970s: A Critical Guide* (Ticknor & Fields, 1981)

de Ville, Nick, *Album: Classic Sleeve Design* (Mitchell Beazley, 2005)

Edelglass, William, and Jay Garfield (eds.), *Buddhist Philosophy: Essential Readings* (Oxford University Press, 2009)

Emerick, Geoff, and Howard Massey, *Here, There, And Everywhere: My Life Recording The Music Of The Beatles* (Gotham, 2006)

Farren, Mick, and Dennis Loren, *Classic Rock Posters: Sixty Years Of Posters & Flyers, 1952 To Today* (Sterling, 2013)

Fellini, Federico, and Damien Pettigrew, *I'm A Born Liar: A Fellini Lexicon* (Harry N. Abrams, 2003)

Fenton, Craig (ed.), *Take Me To A Circus Tent: The Jefferson Airplane Flight Manual* (Infinity, 2007)

Fitzgerald, F. Scott, *My Lost City: Personal Essays, 1920–1940* (Cambridge University Press, 2005)

Greenfield, Robert, *Bear: The Life And Times Of Augustus Owsley Stanley III* (Thomas Dunne, 2016)

Grushkin, Paul, *The Art Of Rock: Posters From Presley To Punk* (Abbeville Press, 1987)

Heylin, Clinton, *Despite The System: Orson Welles Versus The Hollywood Studios* (Chicago Review Press, 2005)

Hill, Sarah, *San Francisco & The Long 60s* (Bloomsbury Academic, 2016)

Jones, Martin, *Lovers, Buggers & Thieves: Garage Rock, Monster Rock, Psychedelic Rock, Progressive Rock, Folk Rock* (Headpress/Critical Vision, 2005)

Katz, Steve, *Blood, Sweat, And My Rock 'n' Roll Tears: Is Steve Katz A Rock Star?* (Lyons Press, 2015)

Kezich, Tullio, *Federico Fellini: His Life And Work* (Faber, 2002)

Kostelanetz, Richard, *The Fillmore East: Recollections Of Rock Theater* (Summer Books, 1995)

Kubernik, Harvey, *1967: A Complete Rock Music History Of The Summer Of Love* (Sterling, 2017)

Kumar, Ravindra, *Kundalini For Beginners*, (Llewellyn, 2000)

Leary, Timothy, and Ralph Metzner, *The Psychedelic Experience: A Manual Based On The Tibetan Book Of The Dead* (Citidal, 1965)

Lee, Martin A., and Bruce Shlain, *Acid Dreams: The Complete Social History Of LSD: The CIA, The Sixties, And Beyond* (Grove, 1985)

Lemke, Gayle, *The Art Of The Fillmore: The Poster Series 1966–1971* (Thunder's Mouth, 1999)

Lewisohn, Mark, *The Beatles Recording Sessions* (Harmony, 1988)

Lundborg, Patrick, *Psychedelia: An Ancient Culture, A Modern Way Of Life* (Lysergia, 2012).

MacDonald, Ian, *Revolution In The Head: The Beatles' Records And The Sixties* (Chicago Review Press, 1994)

Marks, John D., *The Search For The Manchurian Candidate: The CIA And Mind Control* (W.W. Norton & Company, 1979)

Marsh, Dave, with John Swenson, *The Rolling Stone Record Guide: Reviews Of Almost 10,000 Currently Available Rock, Pop, Soul, Country, Blues, Jazz, And Gospel Albums* (Random House/Rolling Stone, 1979)
Martin, George, with William Pearson, *Summer Of Love: The Making Of Sgt. Pepper* (Macmillan, 1994)
McBride, Joseph, *What Ever Happened To Orson Welles? A Portrait Of An Independent Career* (University Of Kentucky Press, 2006)
Morton Jack, Richard, *Psychedelia: 101 Iconic Underground Rock Albums 1966–1970* (Sterling, 2017)
Owen, Ted, and Denise Dickson, *High Art: A History Of The Psychedelic Poster* (Sanctuary, 1999)
Perkins, V.F., *The Magnificent Ambersons* (British Film Institute, 1999)
Pirsig, Robert M., *Zen & The Art Of Motorcycle Maintenance: An Inquiry Into Values* (HarperCollins, 1974)
Rogan, Johnny, *Byrds: Requiem For The Timeless, Volume 1* (Rogan House, 2011)
Rogan, Johnny, *Byrds: Requiem For The Timeless, Volume 2* (Rogan House, 2017)
Sartre, Jean-Paul, *Existentialism And Human Emotion* (Citadel, 1957)
Sculatti, Gene, and Davin Seay, *San Francisco Nights: The Psychedelic Music Trip 1965–1969* (St. Martin's, 1985)
Selvin, Joel, *Monterey Pop* (Chronicle, 1992)
Selvin, Joel, *Summer Of Love: The Inside Story Of LSD, Rock & Roll, Free Love, And High Times In The Wild West* (Dutton, 1994)
Selvin, Joel, *San Francisco: The Musical History Tour: A Guide To Over 200 Of The Bay Area's Most Memorable Music Sites* (Chronicle, 1996)
Sillitoe, Alan, *The Loneliness Of The Long-Distance Runner* (Vintage, 1959)
Simons, David, *Studio Stories: How The Great New York Records Were Made* (Backbeat, 2004)
Springsteen, Bruce, *Born To Run* (Simon & Schuster, 2016)
Tahsler, Bryce, *The San Francisco East Bay 60s Scene Then And Now: Garage Bands And More (Third Edition)* (Teens N Twenties, 2013)
Tamarkin, Jeff, *Got A Revolution! The Turbulent Flight Of Jefferson Airplane* (Atria, 2003)
Thompson, Hunter S., *Fear and Loathing in Las Vegas: A Savage Journey To The Heart Of The American Dream* (Vintage, 1998)
Thorgerson, Storm, and Aubrey Powell, *The Stories Behind The Sleeves: 100 Best Album Covers* (DK, 1999)
Tomlinson, Sally, and Walter Medeiros, *High Societies: Psychedelic Rock Posters Of Haight-Ashbury* (San Diego Museum Of Art, 2001)
Unterberger, Richie, *Unknown Legends Of Rock 'n' Roll: Psychedelic Unknowns, Mad Geniuses, Punk Pioneers, Lo-Fi Mavericks And More* (Backbeat, 1998)
Unterberger, Richie, *Jingle Jangle Morning: Folk Rock In The 1960s* (Richie Unterberger, 2014)
Welles, Orson, and Peter Bogdanovich, *This Is Orson Welles* (Da Capo, 1992)
Williams, Paul (ed.), *The Crawdaddy! Book: Writings (and Images) From the Magazine Of Rock* (Hal Leonard, 2002)

ARTICLES AND ESSAYS

Alterman, Loraine, 'The Pop/i: The Cowsills, A Clean-Cut Group,' *Detroit Free Press*, October 13 1967
Alterman, Loraine, 'From The Music Capitals Of The World: Detroit,' *Billboard*, July 8 1967
Angel, Johnny, 'Sour Grapes: An Interview With Skip Spence,' *Relix*, August 1994
Associated Press (AP), 'Rock Group In Court Over Drug Charges,' *Los Angeles Times*, February 1 1969
Associated Press (AP), 'Group Therapy Pay Drug Fine,' *Florida Today*, February 6 1969
Baker, Robb, 'The Sound: Music And Radio For Young Listeners,' *Chicago Tribune*, April 30 1968 / November 1 1968 / November 5 1968 / January 17 1969 / February 20 1969 / November 16 1969
Bell, Barbara, 'You Don't Have To Be High,' *New York Times*, December 28 1969
Bluhm, Erik, and Paul Gammage, 'West Coast Branch,' westcoastfog.com, July 28, 2013

Brink, Susan, 'Grape Regroups In *Granite Creek*,' *Miami News*, September 21 1971

Brown, James, 'Pop Album Briefs: *20 Granite Creek*,' *Los Angeles Times*, October 17 1971

Burgess, Neil, Eleanor Maguire, John O'Keefe, 'The Human Hippocampus And Spatial And Episodic Memory,' *Neuron* 35 (2002)

Burke, Ted, 'A Moby Grape Survivor,' *San Diego Reader*, January 29 1976

Campbell, Scott G., 'The Underground Sound: Grape Jam Goes Better than Wow,' *Arizona Republic*, June 16 1968

Christgau, Robert, 'Columns—June 1968,' *Esquire*, June 1968

Christgau, Robert, *'Consumer Guide,' Village Voice, January 15 1970*

Cost, Jud, 'Peter Lewis: The Rebel Hangs Ten In Hollywood,' *Ptolemaic Terrascope*, February 1996

Cost, Jud, 'Moby Grape: The Byrds With The Blues,' *Ptolemaic Terrascope*, May 1996

Cost, Jud, 'Call Him Ishmael,' *Ptolemaic Terrascope*, September 1996

Cost, Jud, liner notes to *Surf Fever!* by The Cornells (Sundazed, 1995)

Delehent, Jim, 'Moby Grape Emerges,' *Hit Parader*, September 1967

Deming, Mark, '*Moby Grape '69*,' allmusic.com

Deming, Mark, '*Truly Fine Citizen*,' allmusic.com

Diehl, Digby, 'Moby Grape Debuts At Hippy Happening,' *Los Angeles Times*, July 14 1967

Donnelly, Dave, 'Interesting Sounds In 10 New Albums,' *Honolulu Star-Bulletin*, February 8 1969

Donnelly, Dave, 'The Teen Beat,' *Honolulu-Star-Bulletin*, April 13 1968 / April 24 1968

Dorworth, Dick, 'Beyond The Mountain: San Francisco Shows Heart, Lays Out Carpet For Skiers,' *Reno Gazette-Journal*, March 22 1968

Douvanis, Dennis, 'Dennis: It's Ringo's Turn,' *Morning Call*, February 14 1970

Finnie, Peter S.B., and Karim Nader, 'The Role Of Metaplasticity Mechanisms In Regulating Memory Destabilization And Reconsolidation,' *Neuroscience And Biobehavioral Reviews* 36 (2012)

Fornatale, Mike, 'What's Purple And Lives At The Bottom Of The Sea?' *Shindig! Annual: Number 2* (Volcano Publishing, 2009)

Freeman, Paul, 'Doobie Brothers: 'We're Still Listening To The Music,' popcultureclassic.com

Fricke, David, liner notes to *Vintage: The Very Best Of Moby Grape* (Sony, 1993)

Gaghan, Jerry, 'Dagmar The Writer Gains $s, Pounds,' *Philadelphia Daily News*, June 16 1967

Gammage, Paul, 'West Coast Branch,' *West Coast Fog: Musical Exhumations From California's Hazy Age*, westcoastfog.com

Gillespie, James N., 'Critic Offers Rock Album Consumer Guide,' *Star Tribune*, September 28 1969

Glaub, Rick, 'Teen Scene: Moby Grape Not Heard,' *Idaho Free Press*, August 7 1967

Gleason, Ralph, 'The Rhythm Section,' *Honolulu Star-Advertiser*, September 29 1968

Goldstein, Richard, 'Pop Eye: San Francisco: The Flourishing Underground,' *Village Voice*, March 2 1967

Gormley, Mike, 'Record Reviews,' *Detroit Free Press*, March 14 1969

Greenwald, Matthew, '*20 Granite Creek*,' allmusic.com

Hall, Claude, 'Vox Jox,' *Billboard*, September 30 1967

Hannon, Ross, and Corry Arnold, 'Moby Grape Performance History 1966,' rockprosopography101.blogspot.ca

Hansen, Terry, 'Grape Juice—A Conversation with Jerry Miller,' *Goldmine*, 1993

Harada, Wayne, 'On The Record: The Swingers,' *Honolulu Star-Bulletin*, April 25 1968 / February 13 1969

Harada, Wayne, 'Wayne's Weekend—Leisure,' *Honolulu Advertiser*, September 24 1971

Harada, Wayne, 'Show Biz,' *Honolulu Advertiser*, September 30 1971

Harris, Lew, 'Sob … Gasp … and Fie On T.R.C.,' *Chicago Tribune*, September 19 1971

Harris, Shirley Lewis, 'From The Music Capitals Of The World: San Francisco,' *Billboard*, August 7 1971

Harris, Scott, and Myrna Oliver, 'Bill Gazzarri, "Godfather" Of Rock In LA, Dies,' *Los Angeles Times*, March 16 1991

Harrison, Jeanne, '"Go Away Little Girl" Still Leading Single,' *Greenville News*, September 19 1971
Hathaway, Bruce, 'How Are Hits Made?' *San Antonio Express*, October 14 1967
Hernandes, Raoul, 'SXSW Music Interview: Peter and Arwen Lewis: Moby Grape Dad and Daughter Make New Music Together,' *Austin Chronicle*, March 17 2017
Hughes, Rob, 'The Story Of Moby Grape: Chaos And Courtrooms, Acid And White Witches,' *Classic Rock*, September 2016
Hume, Bill, 'Record Roundup,' *Albuquerque Journal*, March 12 1969
Hunter, Mathis, 'Long Doobie Running: A Q&A With Patrick Simmons: The Doobie Brothers Singer And Guitarist Talks History, Michael McDonald, And Motorcycles,' *Creative Loafing*, 2014
Jobson, Gary, 'Shaping By Havens,' *Ashbury Park Press*, March 15 1969
Johnson, Pete, 'First Pop Music Festival Draws Large Crowds,' *Los Angeles Times*, June 19 1967
Johnson, Pete, 'Santa Monica Concert Features the Yardbirds,' *Los Angeles Times*, June 25 1967
Johnson, Pete, 'Pop Duet Issues Delayed Record,' *Los Angeles Times*, April 1 1968
Johnson, Pete, 'The Grape Appears in Rock Club,' *Los Angeles Times*, May 20 1968
Johnson, Pete, 'Bob Dylan To Release Album—San Francisco Problems,' *Los Angeles Times*, June 10 1968
Johnson, Pete, 'The Grateful Dead Appear At Shrine,' *Los Angeles Times*, August 26 1968
Johnson, Pete, 'Popular Records,' *Los Angeles Times*, March 16 1969
Keliehor, Jon, 'The Frantics Years—Penultimate Formation—1963–1965.' pnwbands.com
Knemeyer, George, 'Moby Grape And B.B. King,' *Billboard*, June 19 1971
Knippenberg, Jim, 'Soundings: New Albums Stir A Frenzied Beat,' *Cincinnati Enquirer*, March 22 1969
Knippenberg, Jim, 'Lonnie Mack's Back On Comeback Trail,' *Cincinnati Enquirer*, October 19 1969
Kubernik, Harvey, 'How Peter Lewis Of Moby Grape Discovered Leonard Cohen,' Cohencentric.com, May 24, 2017
Lau, Andrew, '*Oar* After Forty Years: Brilliant Or Mere Ramblings?' *Crawdaddy*, November 24, 2009
Leary, Timothy, 'The Religious Experience: Its Production And Interpretation,' *The Psychedelic Reader: The Revolutionary 1960s Forum Of Psychopharmacological Substances* (Kensington Publishing, 1964)
Levins, Hoag, 'Festival "Rocks" Staid Quaker City,' *Courier-Post*, October 21 1968
Linde, Charlotte, 'The Transformation Of Narrative Syntax Into Institutional Memory,' *Narrative Inquiry* 9:1 (1999)
Lloyd, Jack, 'Those Old Bluesmen Jam On In "Memphis Swamp"—Moby Grape: *Truly Fine Citizen*,' *Philadelphia Inquirer*, November 2 1969
Lloyd, Jack, 'Jefferson Airplane Back On Discs, But Best Players Bailed Out,' *Philadelphia Inquirer*, September 19 1971
Loftus, Elizabeth F., 'When A Lie Becomes Memory's Truth: Memory Distortion After Exposure To Misinformation,' *Current Directions In Psychological Science* 1:4 (1992)
Loftus, Elizabeth F., 'When A Lie Becomes The Truth: The Effects Of Self-Generated Misinformation On Eyewitness Memory,' *Memory* 12:1 (2010)
Mastropolo, Frank, 'Doobie Brothers' Tom Johnston Reflects On *Listen To The Music* At 40,' ultimateclassicrock.com, November 29 2012
Mayford, Mark, Steven A. Siegelbaum, and Eric R. Kandel, 'Synapses And Memory Storage,' *Cold Spring Harbor Perspectives In Biology* 4:6 (2012)
Meltzer, Robert, '*20 Granite Creek*,' *Rolling Stone*, October 14 1971
Miletich, Steve, 'Frank Colacurcio Sr., Seattle's Legendary Organized-Crime Figure, Dies At 93,' *Seattle Times*, July 2 2010
Miller, Jim, '*Wow/Grape Jam*,' *Rolling Stone*, May 25 1968
Morgan, Diane, 'The Disk Seen,' *Press Democrat*, May 6 1968 / December 23 1968 / July 14 1969

Morrison, Craig, 'Moby Grape,' craigmorrison.com, 1996

Orloff, Kathy, 'Record World News: Let's Start At The Very Beginning, And This Does,' *Indianapolis News*, March 12 1969

Prado, Mark, 'Historic Ferry Boat The Charles Van Damme On The Move Again In Sausalito,' *Marin Independent Journal*, September 30 2013

Robinson, Richard, 'News from the POP SCENE,' *Fond Du Lac Commonwealth Reporter*, July 24 1968

Roeser, Steve, audio interview with Bob Mosley, 1999 (via rocksbackpages.com)

Rosene, Ken, 'Headlines,' *Honolulu Advertiser*, October 11 1971 / March 6 1972

Santosuosso, Ernie, 'Sight In The Round: Sgt. Pepper's Hot LP,' *Boston Globe*, June 18 1967

Sargent, Jon, 'Valley Vibrations,' *Arizona Republic*, April 21 1968

Schechtman, Marya, 'The Truth About Memory,' *Philosophical Psychology* 7:1 (1994)

Scoppa, Bud, '*Wow* Revisited: The Return Of Moby Grape,' *Rock Magazine*, August 17 1971

Scoppa, Bud, 'Moby Grape,' *The New Rolling Stone Album Guide: Completely Revised And Updated Fourth Edition* (Simon & Schuster, 2004)

Sculatti, Gene, liner notes to *Moby Grape* (Sundazed Music, 2007)

Shelton, Robert, 'Moby Grape Rocks With Procol Harum In Pair Of Concerts,' *New York Times*, February 12 1968

Soocher, Stan, 'Moby Grape Saga: The Lengthy Battle For A Band Name,' *meiea eZine: The Official eZine For Music & Entertainment Industry Educators*, May 2007

Spence, Holly, 'Disc-O-Talk: Improvement With Some Age,' *Lincoln Journal Star*, May 25 1968

Stephens, Dave, 'Moby Grape,' toppermost.co.uk, August 29 2016

Tamarkin, Jeff, 'The Jefferson Airplane Chronicles: Marty Balin,' *Relix*, April 1993

Tiegel, Eliot, 'San Francisco Revisited: Pop Music "Revolutionaries" Create Creative Community,' *Billboard*, October 26 1968

Turner, Mary, 'From The Musical Capitals Of The World: San Francisco,' *Billboard*, May 8 1971

United Press International, 'London Gang Attacks US Pop Musicians,' *St Louis Post-Dispatch*, January 27 1969

United Press International, 'Pop Group Attacked,' *Pittsburgh Press*, January 27 1969

United Press International, 'American Pop Group Attacked in London,' *Pensacola News Journal*, January 28 1969

United Press International, 'London Episode: Pop Singers Attacked,' *Philadelphia Inquirer*, January 28 1969

United Press International, 'US Singers Accused Of Possessing Drugs,' *Cincinnati Enquirer*, January 30 1969

Wagner, Dave, 'Who Is This John Fogerty Fellow?' *Green Bay Press-Gazette*, March 30 1969

Wagner, Dave, 'Simon & Garfunkel Attain Distinction,' *Green Bay Press-Gazette*, May 19 1968

Walker, Peter 'Tab,' 'Listen, My Friends!' annecarlini.com

Wheelock, Benjamin, 'You Must Hear This! The New Tweedy Brothers,' *Salon*, July 17 2015

Wilkinson, Scott D., 'Moby Grape—Live At Stonybrook University, NY, October 22 1968,' *The Attic*, February 17, 2015

Williams, Paul, 'The Golden Road: A Report On San Francisco,' *Crawdaddy*, June 1967

Wilson, Earl, 'It Happened Last Night,' *Courier-Post*, November 23 1967

Yackley, Sal, 'The Sound: Music And Radio For Young Listeners,' *Chicago Tribune*, February 23 1968

Yaryan, Bill, 'Getting Better All The Time: Mystic's Mantra Maddens Beatles,' *Independent Star-News*, May 25 1968

Yorke, Ritchie, 'Pop Scene,' *Globe & Mail*, August 16 1968 / August 28 1968

—, 'Buckinghams, Grape Stage Off-Stage Tiff At Concert,' *Billboard*, July 8 1967

—, 'Columbia Gives Moby Grape A Whale Of A Buildup,' *Billboard*, June 17 1967

—, 'They're Good,' *Cincinnati Enquirer*, June 24 1967

—, 'Grape, Pie Tasty Rock Recipe,' *Billboard*, October 26 1968

—, 'Moby Grape Trio Posts Bail On Marin Charges,' *Daily Independent-Journal*, June 8 1967

—, 'Rock'n'roller Pleads Innocent On Marijuana,' *Daily Independent-Journal*, June 16 1967

—, 'Rock Group Trial Is Reset,' *Daily Independent-Journal*, August 4 1967

—, 'The Grape—Whale Of An Act,' *Detroit Free Press*, June 23 1967

—, 'On The Way Up: The Grape Are Really Great,' *Detroit Free Press*, June 30 1967

—, 'Liner Notes,' *Honolulu Star-Advertiser*, February 18 1968

—, 'Concert, Light Show Offered At The Bank,' *Los Angeles Times*, September 6 1968

—, 'Tonight Moby Grape,' *Nashua Telegraph*, June 25 1968

—, 'New Rock Group In Movie Debut,' *Philadelphia Daily News*, September 1 1967

—, 'Fugs Due At Trauma, *Philadelphia Daily News*, October 5 1967

—, 'Friday And Saturday—Moby Grape,' *Philadelphia Daily News*, October 4 1968

—, 'Gimbels—New Columbia Releases,' *Philadelphia Inquirer*, September 7 1969

—, '3 Moby Grapes Plead Not Guilty,' *Press Democrat*, June 16 1967

—, 'Top Ten—Courtesy Of KPLS,' *Press Democrat*, August 13 1967

—, 'Teens Today: Mcnear Happening,' *Press Democrat*, October 16 1967

—, 'Moby Grape, Nitty Gritty On The Way,' *Press Democrat*, April 22 1968

—, 'The Moby Grape Turn Up Sour,' *Press Democrat*, April 28 1968

—, 'The Cellar,' *Roselle Register*, January 15 1969

—, 'Announcement From Velvet Plastic Productions—Re: Moby Grape,' *St. Louis Post-Dispatch*, June 2 1968

—, 'For Senator Kennedy: Community Memorial Service,' *St. Louis Post-Dispatch*, June 8 1968

INDEX

PHOTO CREDITS

The photographs in this book came from the following sources, and we are grateful for their help. If you feel there has been a mistaken attribution, please contact the publisher. *1967 portrait* Michael Ochs Archives/Getty Images; *The Frantics* courtesy of Don Stevenson; *the Scene* (x3) Michael Ochs Archives/Getty Images; *Don at the Scene* courtesy of Don Stevenson; *Village Theater* (x2), *Skip at Monterey*, *New York recording sessions* (x3) Michael Ochs Archives/Getty Images; *'reflective and inquisitive' portrait* Gems/Redferns; *Skip and Peter* Michael Ochs Archives/Getty Images; *Checker Cab* courtesy of Don Stevenson; *Skip at Fillmore East* Jon Sievert/Getty Images; *Snake Leg* courtesy of Don Stevenson; *reunion* (x2) courtesy of Melissa Marteny; all posters from 1966–67 courtesy of Psychedelic Art Exchange/ConcertPosterGallery.com.